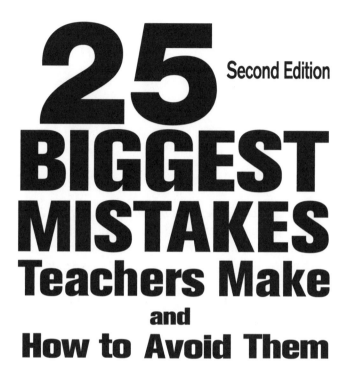

25

Second Edition

BIGGEST
MISTAKES
Teachers Make
and
How to Avoid Them

*A tender rosebud on the verge of blooming, basking in the light
of new loves and life promises was snipped and crushed in a dark moment of despair.
Surely those are her sweet petals being carried away gently and lovingly by a
winged messenger of the kingdom. Goodbye Robertta, you were and always will be loved.*

*This book is dedicated to my Goddaughter, the late Robertta O'Neal
Washington, August 4, 1984, to September 21, 2007.*

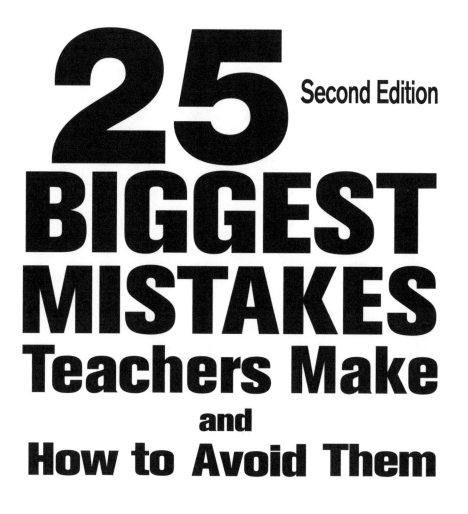

25

Second Edition

BIGGEST
MISTAKES
Teachers Make
and
How to Avoid Them

Carolyn Orange

CORWIN PRESS
A SAGE Company
Thousand Oaks, CA 91320

For information:

Corwin Press
A SAGE Company
2455 Teller Road
Thousand Oaks, California 91320
www.corwinpress.com

SAGE India Pvt. Ltd.
B 1/I 1 Mohan Cooperative
    Industrial Area
Far East Square
Mathura Road, New Delhi 110 044
India

SAGE Ltd.
1 Oliver's Yard
55 City Road
London EC1Y 1SP
United Kingdom

SAGE Asia-Pacific Pte. Ltd.
33 Pekin Street #02-01
Singapore 048763

Printed in the United States of America

Library of Congress Cataloging-in-Publication Data

Orange, Carolyn.
25 biggest mistakes teachers make and how to avoid them/Carolyn Orange. — 2nd ed.
    p. cm.
Includes bibliographical references and index.
ISBN 978-1-4129-3787-0 (cloth)
ISBN 978-1-4129-3788-7 (pbk.)
    1. Teacher-student relationships—United States—Case studies. 2. Effective teaching—United States—Case studies. 3. Interaction analysis in education—Case studies. I. Title.
II. Title: Twenty-five biggest mistakes teachers make and how to avoid them.

LB1033.O73 2008
371.102'3—dc22   2008011275

This book is printed on acid-free paper.

08   09   10   11   12   10 9 8 7 6 5 4 3 2 1

Acquisitions Editor:	Carol Chambers Collins
Editorial Assistant:	Brett Ory
Production Editor:	Cassandra Margaret Seibel
Copy Editor:	Rebecca Keever
Typesetter:	C&M Digitals (P) Ltd.
Proofreader:	Penny Sippel
Indexer:	Judy Hunt
Cover Designer:	Karine Hovsepian

Contents

———————

7. TEACHER CONFESSIONS OF WORST TREATMENT OF A CHILD: THEIR MOTIVES AND FEELINGS 189

Foreword

Anita Woolfolk Hoy

The Ohio State University

———————

What struck me when I read the first edition of *25 Biggest Mistakes Teachers Make and How to Avoid Them* were the students. For a few sentences, I was in their lives—feeling the embarrassment, fear, anxiety, or humiliation that they must have felt. It is difficult for adults, especially teachers who often were good students themselves, to empathize with students who are not so well-behaved or cooperative. "Why would a child act that way?" "What will the class think if I let them get away with that?" "Are they trying to drive me crazy!" All these are very understandable reactions to students' troubling words and actions. But in Carolyn Orange's book, we get to walk briefly in the students' shoes. Of course she does not leave us there, but has solid suggestions for how to avoid and repair the possible mistakes that teachers make.

The teacher has power to do great good as well as great harm. I am struck by how lasting this harm can be when I listen to adult's memories of their difficult experiences in school.What is even sadder is that sometimes students decide that the teacher really dislikes them even though that is far from the truth. But children are not always sophisticated in their reading of meaning or intention. We are learning more and more about the importance of teachers. Results from classroom studies describe the effects of teacher–student relationships in general, but the pages of this book describe the effects in their particulars.

I always have appreciated the way Carolyn Orange connects results of research to her suggestions for addressing the mistakes teachers make, but now in this new edition, she also adds the teachers' voices—some of the thinking behind the actions. Here too are additional strategies for preventing and repairing mistakes—good ideas for new and veteran teachers alike.

Preface to the
Second Edition

The first edition of *25 Biggest Mistakes Teachers Make and How to Avoid Them* has been a bestseller for a number of years and has been translated into three languages, Thai, Chinese, and Slovenian. It has been reviewed in India, used in a school of midwifery in Ireland and in numerous other contexts in many states in the United States and several countries such as Ireland, Romania, India, France, China, United Kingdom, Japan, and others.

When I wrote the book, I thought it had an important message that teachers could avoid making mistakes by being aware of the mistakes of others. However, I was surprised by the global appeal of the book. As I reflected on why the global appeal, I recalled a picture I received. Rachel Livsey, my editor at the time, sent the picture and a message that said, "I thought you might get a kick out of this." My first reaction was why? The picture looked like it was taken in San Antonio, Texas. The children were lined up in straight rows and a male teacher with a stick was directing them to get on a bus. I understood why when I saw that it was a picture in a newspaper that accompanied a book review of the *25 Biggest Mistakes Teachers Make and How to Avoid Them*. After more careful examination and further reading, I realized that it was a scene from a school day in Bangalore, India. Somehow, this scene unlocked the mystery of why the book appealed to educators in different countries.

The answer was that the need for discipline and control in classrooms is universal. How teachers respond to that need, apparently, is also universal. Teachers all over the world realize that in spite of research advocating best practices and teachers having best intentions, teachers make mistakes when trying to control student behavior. Why, because teachers have power, power that can be used constructively or that can be abused. They have the power to determine success or failure, to empower or destroy, to elevate or diminish, to enrich or deprive. Their power is embodied in what they say and don't say, what they do and don't do, what they teach and don't teach. Like any other power, if it's not controlled, it can be dangerous. Unfettered power can prey upon an unsuspecting classroom and wreak havoc on young minds and bodies. Knowledge is also power; knowledge of the difference between words that hurt and words that heal, between actions that praise and actions that diminish, between instruction that enlightens and instruction that confuses, is power. The power of teaching is inherent in the job. The power of knowledge is acquired. Knowledge can balance the power of teaching if it is expanded and used appropriately. This book proposes to expand the knowledge of appropriate discipline, student–teacher relations, instruction, assessment, policy, and teacher behavior.

This second edition has added value in that it seeks to examine what happens when teacher power runs rampant and anger and frustration reign; and why it happens. When 44 teachers were asked about their worst treatment of a student, they answered with incredible candor. Most of them cited anger and frustration as the primary motive for their move to bad actions and subsequent maltreatment of students. This second edition also examines the consequent effects of the teachers' mistreatment that could result in academic trauma. I define academic trauma as a result of a significant emotional event that is caused by an aversive academic experience usually involving a teacher. In such a case, the teacher has overstepped the boundaries of reasonable discipline and used her power to demean, disparage, ridicule, or unduly punish a student. Academic trauma is most likely to occur in early years of schooling. It is usually an unpleasant event that may generate a measure of stress when recalled. The recipients of this trauma are usually psychologically scarred, that is they never seem to forget. Years later, they could still be hurt, disturbed, or otherwise affected by the event. Academic trauma also may affect a person's thoughts, emotions, and behaviors later in life and can cause an adverse reaction to stimuli similar to the original traumatic experience. The second edition probes the motives of teachers, who admitted to mistreating students, to find out why they did what they did. The new knowledge gained from examining why teachers mistreat students and ways to avoid those acts can restore the equilibrium and psychological balance in classroom management that is so necessary to protect the young minds that are our charge.

ACKNOWLEDGMENTS

The debts I owe to those who made the development of this book possible are many. These debts assume many forms, from belief in my ideas, to encouraging words, to research and editing, and to final critiques. I am indebted first, to my students who shared their experiences so candidly; then, to my editor, Jay Whitney, who believed in my idea; next, to my graduate assistants, fondly referred to as "Excellent" Emily Gaston for her typing and editing assistance and Rita "The Sleuth" Brewer for her tireless research efforts.

I also must thank my daughter, Traci "eagle-eye" Hodges, who loves to edit and proof mom's papers. Thank you Claudia Brown for your editing efforts; a friend in need is a friend indeed. A special thank-you for the teachers who critiqued this work and offered their suggestions: Susan Dudley, Janet Haskins, Terry Hildebrand, and Doris Stowers. I'd like to thank my Director, Christopher Borman and my Dean, Dwight Henderson for their support. I must take sole responsibility for any errors in content. Finally, I'd like to thank my husband and colleague, Dr. John H. Orange, for his editing assistance, encouragement, and support.

I am especially grateful to the following teachers who reviewed this second edition and offered their suggestions: Nicole D. Anderson, Jennifer J. Brooks, Larue D. Lang and counselor, Anissa Pennick.

Publisher's Acknowledgments

The contributions of the following reviewers are gratefully acknowledged:

Dr. George Pawlas
Professor of Educational Leadership
University of Central Florida
Orlando, Florida

Mary Johnstone
Principal
Rabbit Creek Elementary School
Anchorage, Alaska

Diane Mierzwik
Seventh- and Eighth-Grade English Teacher, Parkview Middle School
Yucaipa-Calimesa Joint Unified School District in California
Yucaipa, California

Dr. Susan Kessler
School Administrator
Metropolitan Nashville Public Schools
Greensboro, North Carolina

About the Author

**Carolyn Orange**, PhD, is Professor of Educational Psychology at the University of Texas at San Antonio. She has a PhD and Master of Arts degree in Educational Psychology from Washington University and a Bachelor of Arts degree from Harris State University. She began her teaching career in the St. Louis Public Schools where she taught for a number of years. Her work as an educator has spanned about 25 years and includes some time spent working for two corporations. She has worked as a teacher, substitute teacher, consultant, researcher, and professor in a variety of educational settings: elementary, secondary, English as a second language, Montessori, special education, adult education, art, and college. Carolyn Orange also is the author of *Quick Reference Guide to Educational Innovations: Practices, Programs, Policies and Philosophies* (2002) and *44 Smart Strategies for Avoiding Classroom Mistakes* (2005). The first edition of *25 Biggest Mistakes Teachers Make and How to Avoid Them* is a bestseller and has gained international popularity. It has been reviewed in India and translated into 3 languages: Thai, Chinese, and Slovenian. She produced a video on self-regulation and has developed a Self-Regulation Inventory that has been used in the United States, Italy, and Canada. She has published articles in numerous journals. Dr. Carolyn Orange was included in Who's Who Among American Teachers for 1996–2006; Who's Who in America 2001–2006; Who's Who Among American Women 2006–2007; Who's Who in the World 2005–2007. She was inducted into the San Antonio Women's Hall of Fame in 2004. She received the Constance Allen Heritage Guild for Lifetime Learning education Award in 2006.

Introduction

———————

Alas, words and deeds that cut deep to the tender core of the inner self leave scars on the soul that can last a lifetime.

—Carolyn Orange

This bit of prose capsulizes a problem that occurs all too often in class-rooms across the country. Some teachers do and say things that trau-matize students, leaving them psychologically scarred from childhood on into adulthood. I use traumatize in the academic context of psychological or physiological effects that an aversive situation has on a person that results in devastating, long-term effects or lasting negative impressions.

When we reflect on our academic past, most of us can remember one or two teachers that we will never forget for a variety of reasons. For some of us it was the super-strict, no-nonsense teacher that didn't smile until Christmas, or maybe it was the kindly teacher that made each child feel special. Perhaps it was the teacher with the smile in her eyes that believed in us when we did not believe in ourselves. Or, lurking in the shadows of our reflection there is the specter of the teacher who left a lasting negative impression on us through unfair treatment, physical injury, mental cruelty, incompetence, or poor instruction.

Teachers in the latter group have left those of us unfortunate enough to cross their paths diminished in some way. Their overt and covert acts have had lasting effects that have spanned decades for some people. Many adults can remember with incredible clarity humiliating or devastating events that hap-pened to them in second or third grade, as evidenced in the following quotes:

" . . . This happened 33 years ago and I still remember the embarrassment."

" . . . To this day I remember how traumatized I was and how ashamed I felt."

1

" . . . The worst was that when she would yell at me, everyone laughed at me. It still hurts to remember."

" . . . To this day, I'm still apprehensive about math."

" . . . This was her idea of an audition for the play. It was very traumatic."

" . . . I still bear the scars. I haven't sung in public since that time. . . ."

These quotes are excerpts from the student reflections that are the basis of this book.

The reflections are scenarios of students' worst experiences with a teacher in elementary school, high school, and college that I have collected from preservice teachers since 1992. I have collected about 333 scenarios from preservice teachers in St. Louis, Los Angeles, and San Antonio. I became interested in this topic when I taught a teaching laboratory. As a part of the professional development component, I asked students to recall both the best teachers they could remember, and their worst experiences with teachers. Their oral recollections were so powerful that I decided to ask for written accounts. They wrote fondly of good experiences with teachers and they showed some emotion when talking about these teachers. However, when asked to recount their worst experiences with teachers, they did so with such fervor and intense reactions that I felt this aspect of their academic experience should not be ignored. I realized that teacher mistakes are not usually discussed or explored in teacher preparation programs.

Most education classes offer some discussion of positive classroom behaviors that enhance or create a positive physical environment, but little attention has been paid to the negative behaviors that taint the intangible, psychological environment. Teacher mistakes can wreak havoc on the intangible dimensions of classroom interactions that affect the feelings, emotions, and self-esteem of students. If one teaches, mistakes are inevitable.

All teachers make mistakes. By its very nature, a mistake is not intentional. A mistake is an uninformed strategy, an impulsive act, an unconventional discipline tactic, an inadvertent slight, a remark in jest, and the list goes on. Why do teachers make these mistakes and continue to make them year after year? They make them for many reasons. They make them because they are unaware of the impact and long-term effects of their words and actions. Teachers make mistakes because they are unaware of more appropriate strategies and techniques. Teachers make mistakes because they need to feel that they can control their classrooms. In time of crisis, they don't have a repertoire of skills to draw from, so they do what comes naturally with no thought given to long-term consequences.

I agree with Weimer (1996) that teachers learn important lessons about teaching from hands-on experience or by doing. Surely that includes making mistakes. Conceivably, teachers can learn valuable lessons from their mistakes, but if those mistakes are potentially damaging to a student either physically or psychologically, then those lessons are too costly in terms of human capital to learn by doing. Canfield (1990) reminds us that we must create classrooms that are physically and psychologically safe for all students. Therefore, it behooves us to minimize the number and type of mistakes made in teaching. As a preventive measure, it seems plausible that the scenarios in this book could provide an important teaching tool for teacher preparation classes. I think a book that addresses these mistakes will provide a useful tool of prevention and intervention for preservice teachers, practicing teachers, and others concerned with effective teaching. There are many books on positive teaching, discipline, and management, but I have yet to encounter a book that seeks to teach from the proposed "undesirable teaching" perspective offered by the scenarios.

I am writing about mistakes, not because I have never made any, but because I have learned from them. I also believe that we can learn a lot from the mistakes of others. The tone of this book is not to criticize teachers for making mistakes; instead, the purpose is to offer a way for teachers to learn lessons about teaching by learning from the mistakes of other teachers.

Bandura (1986) would call this vicarious or observational learning. Using mistakes as a teaching strategy is much like simulation—to learn important lessons a teacher does not have to actually engage in a mistake to learn from it. I recall making my share of mistakes when I started teaching elementary school. I can remember one mistake in particular where my intentions were good, but my judgment was poor. I volunteered to teach a dance class after school for my fifth graders. We were invited to perform at a neighboring high school and everyone joined in the preparations. I designed their costumes. They wore imitation leopard-skin cloth over black leotards. I added a long, wispy, thin scarf of similar material for effect. The night of the performance, I thought it would be dramatic to have the girls hold candles as they danced. It looked beautiful . . . at first. When I saw some of those scarves come dangerously close to the flames my heart skipped a beat and almost stopped. I suddenly realized that I had put my girls in danger. It was too late to stop the performance because it was almost over. I just prayed that nothing terrible would happen. Fortunately, my prayers were answered; my poor judgment did not result in physical injury to my students. I'll always remember that my students could have been seriously injured and it would have been my fault. I am sure that some of the teachers in these scenarios have similar thoughts and regrets.

This book is designed to present each reflective scenario as it was written. Each scenario is analyzed to identify the key issues and seminal problems. The Rx used in this book is an alteration of the symbol used in prescriptions; in this academic context, it means a solution for a disorder or problem (*American Heritage Dictionary*, 1992). This Rx symbol is used throughout the book to signal the analyses and solutions for the problems in the scenarios.

I acknowledge that my solutions are presented with a personal bias that reflects my years of teaching, my research, my personal experiences, my readings of relevant literature, and my interactions with my students and colleagues. I concede that there are possibly other solutions to the problems presented. However, I have made every effort to present solutions that I believe are based on sound principles and appropriate practice and in most cases are supported by theory and empirical research.

As I read the reflections, patterns of mistakes seemed to emerge from the collection of scenarios. Twenty-five categories of mistakes were identified and organized into the first six chapters. Chapter 7 explores teachers' self-report of their worst treatment of a student. Commentary on the teachers' actions and behaviors is included.

- Chapter 1, Discipline, focuses on the unacceptable or inappropriate methods that some teachers resorted to when trying to control their students. There were different variations of physical aggression, alienation, and ridicule.

- Chapter 2, Teacher—Student Relations, examines interpersonal relations that involved favoritism, discrimination, personal attacks, mistreatment, humiliation, and inappropriate relations.

- Chapter 3, Classroom Policies and Practices, looks at classroom policies and toileting practices.

- Chapter 4, Classroom Management and Instruction, details the employment of a variety of inappropriate educational strategies and assessments.

- Chapter 5, Personality and Professionalism, explores personal areas such as teacher insensitivity and academic shortcomings. It also includes professional areas such as poor organization and administration, reputation, and other blatant errors.

- Chapter 6, Teaching Style and Behavior, investigates teacher bias, unethical behavior, false accusations, sexual harassment, and other inappropriate reactions.

- Chapter 7, Teacher Confessions of Worst Treatment of a Child, offers a rationale and explanation of teachers' mistreatment of students. Including the teachers' self-report of their actions, perceptions, and motives gives credence to the students' self-reporting of their worst experience with a teacher in the previous sections of this book. A motive probe in the form of questions and answers is included for each of the 44 worst treatment scenarios. Some critical commentary is offered for each scenario. The benefit of this chapter is that it offers some illumination and understanding of why certain teacher behaviors occurred in the scenarios in previous sections. This chapter concludes with some suggested ways to avoid making the 25 biggest mistakes teachers make.

- The Epilogue introduces the idea of academic trauma being similar to post-traumatic stress reaction and the implications of that possibility.

Reflective scenarios of students' worst experiences with a teacher and teachers' worst treatment of students, when used as a teaching strategy, can be effective in a variety of educational contexts. They may be particularly useful in professional development seminars, staff development workshops, and education courses. In professional development seminars, they provide real-life examples of undesirable teaching techniques, strategies, and their effects. Working through the scenarios informs students of the psychological minefields present in the intangible environment of the classroom. The solutions and recommendations literally provide them with a map to help them successfully navigate the academic terrain. A sample staff development workshop would involve discussion, interpretation, expanding and building on scenarios, an exchange of personal experiences, and using these scenarios as an intervention or a preventive measure. A sampling of courses that could effectively incorporate reflective scenarios are: Educational Psychology, Classroom Organization and Management, Curriculum and Instruction, Academic Behavior Management, Instructional Strategies, Learning Theory and Classroom Practices, Social Foundations of Education, Sociology of Education, and Teaching Labs. In my Educational Psychology classes, students used the reflective scenarios and the accompanying analyses to identify good behaviors and strategies to use in the classroom, and behaviors and techniques that they should avoid.

The book is intended for practicing teachers, preservice teachers, professors of education, resource teachers, educational administrators, school psychologists, and counselors. I think it would be of interest to practicing teachers to make them cognizant of their overt and covert negative teaching comments and actions that could possibly have a negative impact on their students. Administrators and other teacher evaluators could benefit from this book because it would help them to recognize dysfunctional teaching practices or the potential for them, and help them give teachers some feedback in this area. The book provides an essential tool for inservice or staff development training. It would also be useful as a prevention strategy.

My wish is that readers will view this book in the same positive spirit that it was written. My desire is that, in using this book, readers will learn from the mistakes of others and acquire some positive strategies and approaches. My hope is that this book will help more teachers become better teachers and subsequently will help more students become better adjusted, successful learners. My aspiration is to enlighten teachers who feel the urge to mistreat a student, with knowledge of more acceptable, positive alternatives. If I can spare one child the hurt, pain, and scars that can last a lifetime, then writing this book was not in vain.

1

DISCIPLINE

"Class, who can tell me what I have preserved in this jar?
No, it's not a pig or a baby cow...it's the last student
who got caught cheating on one of my tests!"

Mistake

1

Inappropriate Discipline Strategies

The worst experience I had with a teacher was in the sixth grade. She wasn't a bad teacher but all the kids hated her. I don't recall her being that mean except when the kids were tormenting her. I guess that's why we didn't like her. She would get so upset that her face turned red. She would either yell at the top of her lungs or just sit there and ignore us for the entire day. Her name was Mrs. B. and now that I think back she was probably a really nice lady.

Well, the worst day was right before Christmas day. We asked her if we could sing her a song. She said yes. The song went:

Joy to the world, Mrs. B. is dead,
We barbecued her head.
Don't worry 'bout the body,
We flushed it down the potty,
And round and round it went,
Round and round it went.

The look on her face just killed me.

℞ The two extreme discipline strategies used by this teacher invited the tormenting that she received. She either yelled at the top of her lungs or ignored the students for the entire day. Both behaviors signaled that the students' misbehaviors were having a profound effect on her. These extreme measures reinforced the students' behavior. After a while, they realized that no serious consequences would be forthcoming, so they continued to test the waters with this teacher.

Experienced teachers never raise their voices because they know that once you become a screamer, you will forever a screamer be. Experienced teachers would never ignore students for an entire day, under any circumstances. Ignoring them for a short period of time could be effective in some situations, but not in this case.

I have found that silence is much more effective for getting students' attention than screaming, especially if this is done at the beginning of the year. I would refuse to start teaching until I had their attention and then I would say politely, "Whenever you're ready." That was a very effective strategy for me. Gagne (1977) emphasized the importance of getting students' attention before teaching.

I have found that keeping students engaged and moving smoothly from one assignment to the next leaves little time for them to misbehave. If students are working on meaningful assignments in an environment of mutual respect, there is little need for the acting out that is apparent in this scenario. Wise teachers would work to establish warm feelings and mutual respect. In this scenario the rapport in the classroom had deteriorated to a level bordering on total disrespect. At this point the teacher had nothing to lose. She could have laughed at the cruel little ditty, thereby dispelling any effect it was supposed to have on her. Her nonverbal behavior indicated that she was mortified, which would encourage more ditties in the future. Charles Galloway (1977) found that the nonverbal behavior of the teacher has a significant impact on the classroom atmosphere.

SCENARIO 1.2
Clean in Thought, Word, and "Backtalk"

My twin sister and I were in first grade. We spoke little English and we were both in the same class. One day the teacher asked my sister a question that she was not able to understand. The teacher called her "dummy." I answered the teacher back by telling her that my sister did not understand her. The teacher felt I was talking back and she took me to the bathroom to wash my mouth with soap. I did not question her again, but I remember feeling hurt. I could not understand why she would not try to understand. We were also seated in the back of the classroom.

R̲x̲ This worst-experience scenario is like a porcupine; it has many sticky points. One point was asking a child who spoke little English a question in English and demanding that she understand. To add insult to that linguistic injury, the teacher ridiculed the child and called her "dummy." Another point was punishing the twin who was trying to explain her sister's predicament. A particularly sticky point was using an unconventional punishment for a perceived insubordination. The most damaging points were the deeply hurt feelings and the bewilderment felt by the child. This teacher's reaction and behavior suggests a bias toward non-English-speaking children. Finally, placing these children in the back of the room was, if not intentionally malicious, at the very least, thoughtless and insensitive.

Competent, mindful teachers would anticipate that non-English-speaking children in an English-only classroom might have special needs and would try to accommodate those needs. These teachers would have thanked the twin who offered an explanation rather than perceiving it as "backtalk." The notion of "backtalk" suggests that the teacher thought of herself as the ultimate authority whose words and actions should not be questioned. "Backtalk" is a throwback to turn-of-the-century education in which children were not supposed to speak unless they were spoken to. Washing out the mouth is an obsolete, old-fashioned practice of showing disapproval when a child says something that is considered improper. In this case, the child was appropriately defending her sibling and did not deserve any type of punishment. These children were apparently innocent of any wrongdoing and the pain and humiliation that they had to endure was inexcusable. Seating the children in the back of the room may not have been intentionally malicious, but the discerning professional would quickly recognize that this seating arrangement would be problematic for non-English-speaking children.

SCENARIO 1.3
Nose, Toes, Anything Goes

My worst experience was in the fifth grade. My teacher, Mr. A., could not keep order in the class, so he used very extreme types of punishment. I would have to stand on my tiptoes with my nose in a circle on the blackboard for talking, or I would have to write 500 times, "I will not talk in class." I was a good student and very tenderhearted.

R_x Mr. A. subscribed to unconventional methods of discipline. It seems that he wanted to create a truly effective deterrent to decrease the likelihood that undesirable behaviors would be repeated. His creative punishment combined physical discomfort, a difficult task, shame, and public ridicule, hoping that this combination would be effective. Mr. A. took an "anything goes" approach to discipline in which any form of punishment was acceptable if it seemed to stop behavior. The psychological consequences of this approach are apparent in the student's perception of himself as a tenderhearted person who was the recipient of extreme punishment. The student is correct. A good student should not be subjected to such treatment for the minor offense of talking. The teacher could have warned the student and given the student another chance. He could have offered free time for conversations, telling the students to hold their talk until that time. A more conventional, positive approach was desirable here.

SCENARIO 1.4
Sticky Business

In the fourth grade my teacher, who was fresh out of college, put tape on my mouth because I was talking. She had asked us to stop all talking while working on our worksheets. I did not understand something and asked another student what the teacher had said. She called me up to her desk and put a huge, wide piece of tape on my mouth. I have never been more humiliated in my entire life. I hated her. All the students made fun of me after school.

℞ New teachers who are recent graduates may become very frustrated when faced with the realities of classroom discipline. Sometimes they resort to whatever comes to mind to solve a discipline problem. This is a dangerous practice. Putting tape over a student's mouth sounds relatively harmless, but such an act could incur a number of risks. The student may be allergic to the adhesive or the teacher may risk injuring the student's skin when she pulls the tape off. The most obvious risk is to the child's self-esteem. In this case, the student was humiliated to the point that it evoked a very strong emotional reaction . . . hatred. The instructional strategy is flawed because the teacher demanded that students stop all talking while working on worksheets.

Experienced teachers would recognize a more collaborative approach that encourages talking and interaction to be more effective. These teachers would not put tape over a student's mouth for talking. They would know the importance of students' private speech for organizing their thoughts and ideas (Vygotsky, 1993).

SCENARIO 1.5
Nosing Around in the Corner

The worst experience of my entire life was with my first-grade teacher Mrs. S. The woman hit me on the arm or slapped me across the face at least twice a week. I received six "licks" that year as well. I was never allowed to go to recess and play. My nose was completely raw because the teacher would make me stand against a wall. She was removed from service after my mother and a few other moms went to school and complained loudly. The lady did not belong in the teaching profession.

℞ This teacher was very physical. Her tactics exemplified the cycle that the more one uses physical punishment, the more one will need to use physical punishment. In addition, she appeared to be one of those female teachers who had difficulty understanding the nature of the development of young males and their typical behaviors. This is evident in the constant, repetitive punishment of this child on a daily basis. This type of physical abuse is what made it necessary for some school districts to abolish corporal punishment. If this teacher had to make a child stand against a wall every day and miss recess, she was obviously an ineffective disciplinarian. She did not decrease the undesirable behavior.

The constancy of this child's inappropriate behavior suggests that it was behavior typical of a first grader. Experienced teachers would take a developmental approach to the child's behavior to ascertain which behaviors are typical and which ones are intentional misbehaviors. Effective teachers would help the child focus on appropriate behaviors as they work together to temper natural behaviors that are not compatible with classroom activities.

SCENARIO 1.6
Sneaking a Peek

The worst experience during my school years happened when I was in first grade. I was an innocent child back then. One day, this girl was looking at my paper during a spelling test. The teacher said I had let the girl look. I ended up locked up in the coatroom. The teacher turned off the lights and left me there. That was the worst experience.

℞ Almost daily, some teacher somewhere falsely accuses a student of some action. The pain of false accusation is compounded when the teacher acts on his or her false assumption. In this scenario, the punishment was extreme and probably traumatic for a very young child. A first-grade child is very imaginative and can conjure up all sorts of terrors lurking in the dark. Leaving the child in the dark room was unconscionable.

In a situation like this, wise teachers would try to be fair and give the student the benefit of the doubt. They would instinctively know that the student may have let the other student look on her paper or the student may not have had any control over who looked on her paper. In such a case, no one should be punished if fault cannot be established. It would have been better to move the student who was looking on the other student's paper and find out if that student had some questions about the assignment.

The teacher could offer the student who was "cheating" more assistance with the assignment and thereby reduce the need to "cheat." Good teachers often circulate among students as they are working. The teacher's presence is usually an effective deterrent for would-be cheaters.

SCENARIO 1.7
Water Sprites Strike

In first grade, a friend of mine taught me how to take the top part of the faucet off of the sink in the bathroom. So every bathroom break we would perform our plumbing techniques and watch the water shoot up from the top. Well, eventually, one of our cohorts told on us, and of course we were sent to the office. The principal scared us to death. He threatened and yelled, and even showed us his paddle. By the end of the event he had two terrified girls on his hands. But to make matters worse, I never told my parents about it and we had open house the very next week; therefore, it wasn't long before I was in much more trouble. Needless to say, since that first-grade experience, I have never once been sent back to the office.

℞ The students in this scenario were threatened because they were taking the tops off faucets to see the gush of water. Erik Erikson (1963) would say that these children were showing "initiative," which is a natural part of the psychosocial development. At this stage of a child's development, educators and parents are challenged to encourage initiative and to help the child understand that he or she cannot always act on their natural inclinations or tendencies. Knowledgeable professionals are aware of child development and will see that the children are showing initiative. These professionals will try to find ways in which children can still show initiative, but will explain to them about water damage and why they should not continue to dismantle working faucets. Resourceful teachers may find a way to rig up a faucet and let the children play with it.

Erikson (1963) warns that unhealthy resolution of a developmental crisis can affect a person later in life. Punishing children for showing initiative would be an unhealthy resolution for the initiative-versus-guilt crisis. There is a grain of truth in this because the adult student that wrote this scenario has never forgotten it and was never sent to the office again.

SCENARIO 1.8
Give a Hand, Get a Hand

I was in private school from kindergarten to first grade. For second grade, my parents decided I should go to public school, so off I went. The first day, I met lots of friends, but I had a problem with the teacher. I was sitting across from a girl who brought nothing with her (no paper, Big Chief, box, nothing!). So, my parents being who they were, I almost had two of everything.

The teacher left the room and told us to sit quietly. When she left, I started to divide my things and push them across my desk to the girl's. As I pushed, I got on my knees in my chair and raised up to get the things across. The teacher saw me and came up behind me and said, "Do what you just did!" I didn't understand, so she grabbed the back of my skirt, pulled me up and spanked me (more like a swat) in front of everyone.

My parents never spanked me, not even once. So I was pretty shocked and embarrassed. I told my mother that I was *bad, very bad.*

℞ This caring child was trying to help another student and inadvertently disobeyed the teacher. Although she was quiet and semi-sitting, the teacher saw this as a blatant disregard for her instructions. The teacher assumed she knew what the student was "doing" and her expectations led her to believe that punishment was in order.

Discerning teachers try to dig deeper and go below the surface of a problem, recognizing that things are not always as they appear. In this case, the teacher should have asked the child what she was doing before she decided to punish her. Instead, she said, "Do what you just did!" and obviously her mind was already made up. Good teachers ask questions first and take action later. Having the child ask for permission to share her supplies with the less-fortunate child could have been humiliating for the child with no supplies. In this case, the teacher could have thanked the child for her expression of kindness and let the incident pass. Correction of every misbehavior is not necessary (Irving & Martin, 1982).

SCENARIOS 1.9, 1.10, and 1.11
Knuckle Whackers

I remember having to sit in the dunce chair and getting my knuckles whacked by Sister A. for talking. I thought I was going to die.

We had gotten our first homework assignment and we needed to return it the next day. I went home, did it, and my mother and I put it on my desk so I wouldn't forget it. I forgot it. When it came time to turn the homework in, I pretended like I turned it in. The teacher went through the papers and marked each child that brought one in. At the end, a little boy and I were left with no mark next our name. When she asked where my homework was I told her I did it but forgot it at home. She told me she didn't like me telling lies and to go over to her desk. She slapped my hand with a wooden ruler; it left paint on my hand. My friend tried to comfort me as I cried and told me not to worry because all those teachers were mean. For the first time I realized that the teacher was African American.

Sister M. was my first-grade teacher in Catholic school. She was very strict and mean and I was so scared of her. She used to discipline her students by hitting their knuckles with a ruler. I was one of those students.

℞ Hitting students on their knuckles is a destructive practice that fosters anger, hatred, fear, and resentment. It may also be illegal. Corporal punishment in any form is banned in 21 states. Whacking knuckles can be very painful for young children. Curiously, all of these young students were in first grade. In addition to the pain, the damage to students' dignity and self-esteem may be great. This form of discipline may change the student's perception of the teacher, causing them to see her as mean or scary. In one scenario, race became an issue; it was not an issue prior to the punishment. Exemplary teachers know how to discipline and keep the student's dignity and self-esteem intact. Dunce chairs and knuckle whacking are turn-of-the-century discipline tactics that should be abandoned.

SCENARIO 1.12
The Lineup

In first grade, the class had a few students who were being silly (giggling, talking, etc.). Mrs. G. (I'll never forget her name) made the entire class line up in front of the blackboard and she paddled every one of us. I was totally embarrassed and furious that I was treated so unfairly by someone I trusted.

℞ This teacher paddled her students, which is now illegal in some school districts. A more significant sin was her global use of punishment where she punished the guilty and the innocent. I also question the nature of the punishment in light of the "crimes." Giggling and talking do not merit paddling.

Wise professionals would never punish the innocent, even at the risk of letting some of the guilty ones get away with the offense. If the teacher cannot easily discern the culprits, justice is better served either by dropping the matter or by offering a stern warning. If the behavior continues, they try rewarding the students who are not misbehaving, which avoids giving attention to the offending students. If punishment is needed, it should be appropriate for talking and giggling. Sometimes, giving the students five to ten minutes to giggle and talk might eliminate the need for punishment.

SCENARIO 1.13
Attila the Nun

I had a nun in third grade who was very old, very impatient, and probably should not have had much to do with children. I got in trouble for talking. First she called me to the front of the class and hit my hands, then she put duct tape over my mouth, and cut off some of my hair.

℞ This form of punishment is so unconventional that it borders on pathological. What kind of behavior change would cutting a child's hair effect? The extreme, bizarre nature of the punishment suggests a very authoritarian climate. Sprinthall, Sprinthall, and Oja (1994) point out that an authoritarian approach to discipline does not permit any deviation from a strict discipline policy. This is a very antiquated approach to discipline that is very reminiscent of the "hickory stick" era.

The informed teacher would have a repertoire of procedures and consequences that are appropriate for the offense and that consider the age of the child. This teacher had a repertoire of consequences but they were all inappropriate and unconventional. A more contemporary approach would be to recognize the child's need and right to talk sometimes and to accept that talking can be a good thing.

SCENARIO 1.14
Injustice and Punishment for All

I was in the fourth grade. Several students had to stay after school because we had gotten in trouble during the day for various reasons. (What the reasons were, I don't remember.) We had to write "I will not . . ." sentences. Some girls were whispering and the teacher added more sentences, then someone rolled their eyes and she added more, then someone groaned and she added more. I remember thinking what a mean and uncaring person she was. As far as I can remember, none of the students liked her; she was my worst teacher.

R̽ This scenario is a classic example of the disadvantages of group consequences. In this scenario, a number of students were detained after school to write repetitive sentences. They were punished as a group for the misbehavior of various members of the group. They had no control over these students' actions so they should not have received any punishment for acts they did not commit.

The insightful, caring professional would recognize the pitfalls of group consequences and use them sparingly, if at all. Groups should not endure punishment because of an individual or individuals over whom they have no control (Epanchin, Townsend, & Stoddard, 1994). The teacher should only have assigned extra writing to those students who were causing problems. I have known teachers who have assigned extra tasks to the group not because they were mean and uncaring but more because of impulse and a desire to "control" the group. Assigning group consequences requires a serious, thoughtful approach. The risk involved in using this approach is being perceived as mean and uncaring and of being unfair to some students.

SCENARIOS 1.15 and 1.16
Dubious Misdeeds

When I was in fifth grade, I don't remember what I was doing wrong, probably talking, and the teacher made me move my desk away from the rest of the class. After I moved my desk, I put my head down and cried and cried. I remember my classmates trying to console me.

The worst experience I ever had with a teacher was in the sixth grade. Her name was Mrs. H. She was very big and scary. I do not even remember what I did. I was probably talking. She took me outside and yelled at me. It was right before Thanksgiving. I remember telling everyone she wanted to eat me as her Thanksgiving turkey. I do not think I had ever been so scared.

℞ In both of these scenarios, the students seemed unaware of their offenses and assumed that the punishments were for talking. The problem here is that neither teacher made either student aware of their offense and did not connect the offense to an appropriate consequence. Both teachers reacted in an impulsive, hostile manner, which is ineffective.

Effective teachers would like to decrease the likelihood that unacceptable behaviors will continue and increase the likelihood that acceptable behaviors will continue. The ABCs (antecedents → behaviors → consequences) of Behavioral Learning Theory (Skinner, 1950) suggest that behaviors should be connected to consequences to determine if that behavior will occur again. If the consequences are good, the behavior is likely to occur again. If the consequences are not good, the behavior is not likely to occur again.

Lee and Marlene Canter (1992) would probably agree that the problem in both of these scenarios is a teacher-owned problem. They suggest using assertive discipline to deal with these types of problems. If assertive discipline were viewed through a lens of Behavioral Learning Theory, the "ABCs" of assertive discipline would be as follows: (A = antecedents) Teachers establish rules, give clear explanations of the rules, and teach students how to behave appropriately; (B = behavior) students make choices about following the rules; and, if they don't follow the rules, (C = consequences) assertive teachers follow through with appropriate consequences. They warn against passive or hostile consequences. If children choose to break the rules, they should be reminded of the rules and asked what they would do differently next time. This question forces children to think about what they have done, what they should have done, and what they will do next time. Assertive discipline would have been very appropriate for both of these scenarios.

SCENARIO 1.17
Pay Attention!!!

In third grade, I had a teacher who yelled at me. We were having some type of quiz and we were only supposed to have one sheet of paper. I don't remember if I didn't have any or if I just decided not to listen. I used a pad of paper. When she saw that, she squatted down right in front of my desk and yelled right in front of my face. I was so humiliated. I still remember I just put my face real close to my paper and cried.

R̩x The student in this scenario was obviously distracted or not paying attention. The "crime" was not following directions. Bending down and yelling in front of the student's face was an authoritarian tactic that meant "do as I say." This teacher seems to have had a need to be in control and took the child's inattentiveness personally.

Knowledgeable teachers would know that it is not unusual for students, and adults, to become distracted in a group setting where they are forced to pay attention. Armed with that knowledge, the teacher can be patient and understanding and repeat the instructions in a civil tone. Some students need to hear the directions for an assignment more than once. If the students still do not understand after one or two repetitions, the teacher could demonstrate or have class members explain the assignment in their own words until everyone understands. Before giving instructions, it is always advisable for a teacher to wait until she has everyone's attention.

She should model the instructions as much as possible using the actual materials. If not paying attention had been a habit with this student, the teacher could have let the student know, before the instructions were given, that the student would be expected to help by repeating the instructions to the class.

SCENARIO 1.18
Cheating Exposé

I was in middle school and I was caught cheating. The teacher took up my paper and asked, in front of the class, if I thought that it [cheating] was worth it.

R̩x The teacher exposed a cheater in class. On the surface, this seems reasonable. The teacher's intent seemed to be to embarrass the child enough that this cheating behavior would cease.

Insightful, experienced teachers know that students cheat when they do not know the material or they are afraid that they do not know enough of the material. Sometimes, students feel pressure from parents and high-achieving siblings or peers to do well in school. Thus, the motive for cheating becomes an important issue. If teachers are aware of the cheating motive, they can help students with the problem, effectively eliminating the need to cheat. A public exposé could cut off any means of communication. A soft reprimand in private would be more effective (O'Leary, Kaufman, Kass, & Drabman, 1970). In private, the teacher is more likely to get an explanation. Issuing a referral for cheating should be a last resort.

SCENARIO 1.19
Biting in Self-Defense

My fifth-grade teacher made me apologize to another student for biting her. The other girl was trying to take my shoes away and I had no other resort. We were in the restroom, and she was much bigger than I was. She ran to tell the teacher, and I was forced to apologize. What I did wrong was that I did not give my side of the story because she had no reason to take my shoes.

℞ Conflicts among students often escalate into violence. Studies have shown that most conflicts among students are usually not effectively resolved (DeCecco & Richards, 1974). In this scenario, the teacher did not manage student conflict appropriately. She listened to one child and in a perfunctory manner, she made the wrong child apologize. She did not bother to find out what happened.

Resourceful practitioners would ask both children what had happened. If both students insisted that the other was wrong and the conflict could not be resolved, they could use peer mediators to help the students settle their dispute (Johnson, Johnson, Dudley, Ward, & Magnuson, 1995). They would not arbitrarily decide that one student was right and the other was wrong.

SCENARIO 1.20
No Apology Needed

My second-grade teacher was Mrs. M. I remember that the girl behind me was not behaving correctly. She was talking when the teacher was teaching. So the teacher got mad. She got up and went toward the girl, but before she got to her she hit my shoulder, then she grabbed the girl and shook her. I was surprised but scared. Every time we saw Mrs. M. we were quiet. I remember telling my mom. My mother went to talk to the teacher, but the teacher denied everything.

℞ Anger is a breeding ground for inappropriate actions. In an irate attempt to discipline a student, the teacher accidentally hit the wrong student, an innocent bystander. The teacher failed to acknowledge her mistake and she later denied it ever happened, which only added insult to the child's injury. There are a variety of reasons that the teacher failed to acknowledge her mistake. She was

oblivious because of her rage. Sometimes angry people want to hold on to their anger, and stopping to apologize would diffuse the anger. Another reason could be that the teacher did not feel it was necessary to apologize because she was the teacher and the student was just a student. Perhaps there are more reasons, but whatever they are, they do not justify the teacher's actions.

Any reasonable human being would stop to apologize and say "excuse me." If a teacher is too angry to do that, she may be putting too much of herself into controlling student behavior. Such anger can push a teacher across that reasonable, litigious line separating appropriate and inappropriate discipline. The professional teacher with integrity would admit her mistake, and thereby eliminate any need to lie to parents to cover it up.

SCENARIOS 1.21 and 1.22
No Explanations, Please

In the second grade I received a paddling for pinching a classmate. The classmate and I had made a bet to see who could pinch each other the hardest. I took my pinch. When I pinched her, she started crying and I got in trouble. I thought we both should have gotten in trouble because she pinched me too, but I didn't cry.

It was kindergarten, my first day, and boy was I in trouble. I was all tomboy and very used to being in charge. I punched a boy who was continuously picking on me and my friends. Well, I hit him so hard he fell over and began screaming. Here comes Mrs. M. "Who did this?" "I did, but he . . ." "That's enough. We are going to have to call your mother." So I sat in a chair in the corner scared to death until my mom came. From that day forward I remembered the "look" that my teacher had given me. Did I do it again? Well not in kindergarten—not until first grade. Even now twenty years later when I see her, she still gives me that "look."

℞ In both of these worst experience scenarios, the teachers did not bother to ask for explanations or to hear both sides of the story. In these cases, justice was blinded by a lack of explanation and no consideration of circumstances. Such an authoritarian approach to discipline leaves no room for clarification, explanation, or illumination.

Diplomatic professionals, who exercise sensitivity in dealing with all children, would listen to both sides of each story without hesitation. If they still felt that punishment was necessary, they would make sure that it was meted out fairly. This may mean that both children will be disciplined, rather than just one.

SCENARIO 1.23
Whodunit?

In kindergarten, the teacher paddled me for sitting at a table where one of the girls called the other girl fatso. However, the teacher didn't even ask if we had, she just took the girl's word and paddled all of us because we were at the table.

℞ The teacher was not monitoring the students' behavior as they sat at the table. She could not possibly know who actually committed the "offense." Additionally, calling names is not acceptable but scarcely warrants paddling.

It was inappropriate for the teacher to take one student's word over that of another, considering that she did not know who was guilty. Resourceful practitioners would use this situation to discuss the hurtful effects of name-calling and would suggest that the students show some empathy for the victim. Punishment is out of the question because the teacher does not know who to punish. The teacher could begin by offering the students an apology and by admonishing the act in general. She could model a more prosocial approach by making a positive comment about the student. Empathy facilitates prosocial behaviors (Ormrod, 1998).

SCENARIOS 1.24 and 1.25
Sitting Ducks

My math teacher in elementary school was calling on me. I didn't hear him. To wake me up, he threw a piece of chalk at me.

Ms. G. would throw erasers in class, hit students, and call students stupid and ignorant. She was very old and very crabby. She grabbed my arm once and it turned black and blue. My mom went to the school and complained to the principal.

℞ Throwing objects at students can be a very dangerous practice. The projectile can miss its mark and cause serious injury. Although the teacher may choose something soft like a chalkboard eraser, as the object gains momentum, the impact may sting a little. Whatever the object, the teacher runs the risk of damaging a sensitive area like a student's eye. When I was teaching fifth grade, a colleague often used rulers to make angry gestures at her students to try and get them to sit down or to stop talking. In one tragic incident, the ruler slipped out of her hand and accidentally hit a student in the eye. One of my elementary school teachers would throw erasers at students in the classroom. He prided himself on the element of surprise. I lived in fear of being the target of one of his erasers. It was a very ineffective technique. The unruly students thrived off the attention and the orderly students withdrew in apprehension.

In the current classroom environment, astute teachers have to learn to navigate the choppy waters of classroom discipline and avoid lawsuits. Most school districts have a "hands-off students" policy that without question includes hitting students with objects. In this scenario, the teacher should have let the sleeping student continue to sleep until the teacher had a chance to investigate the circumstances of the child's need to sleep in class. If there are no significant problems at home such as abuse or having to help support the family, the teacher should use conventional ways of waking a sleeping student. If the sleeping continues, a referral to the guidance counselor may be appropriate.

SCENARIO 1.26
Boys Will Be Boys

When I was in the third grade, a boy raised my dress and I screamed. My teacher got mad and made me go stand in the hall. The boy did not get in trouble, but I sure did. This was, believe it or not, the first time I remember getting in trouble in school.

℞ A supposedly harmless prank such as a male student raising this little female student's dress is no longer as widely accepted as it once was. For years, little boys did little naughty things of a slightly sexual nature to girls with few, if any, consequences. As a matter of fact it was widely accepted and often joked about. When I was in grade school, girls had to be careful that boys did not try to put mirrors on the floor to look under their skirts or they had to fight off young boys who tried to touch them on private parts of their bodies. Girls can be very humiliated, hurt, and shamed by such acts. During my senior year in high school, we all autographed each other's sweatshirts. I was mortified when a boy came up to me and drew two circles with dots in the center around my breasts. He laughed and everybody thought it was funny. I did not think it was funny because I had to walk around like that all day. When teachers dismiss these acts, they are part of the problem. The teacher in this scenario added insult to injury when she punished the young woman for screaming and did not punish the young man.

Today's savvy teachers would never punish the victim and ignore the perpetrator. Informed professionals know that sexual harassment is a real issue that is not to be ignored. They also know that there is a delicate balance between child behaviors that are innocent and those that actually fall into the category of sexual harassment. The astute teacher has to be very careful not to compare minor child behavior with mature behavior that has sexual overtones. The explicit sexual content of some TV programs may encourage children to model some of the adult behaviors they see in these programs. The teacher should recognize that a first-grade boy kissing a little girl on the cheek cannot compare to a much older boy looking under a girl's dress. Some states are taking a very hard stand on children sexually harassing other children. Good teachers would make the class aware that such behaviors cannot be tolerated and that there are serious consequences should they occur. The teacher should make sure that parents are aware of any laws pertaining to sexual harassment that could affect their child. In this scenario, the teacher should have admonished the boy's behavior and given him some consequences. State laws would determine if she would have to report the incident to someone else. Prevention is best for sexual harassment. The competent teacher will make students aware of consequences and will monitor student behavior as a deterrent.

SCENARIO 1.27
Copious Copying

In fourth grade, Ms. T. made me copy several pages from the dictionary as punishment for misbehaving. I think it was the time my friends and I were in the bathroom looking at glow-in-the-dark rubber balls with the lights off.

℞ If a student is forced to copy the dictionary as punishment for misbehaving, Behavioral Learning Theory (Skinner, 1950) suggests that the child may learn to associate using the dictionary with punishment. This would be unfortunate if the teacher wanted to assign useful dictionary work. Copious copying might also make them hate writing. If the teacher were trying to punish students by giving a boring, tedious assignment, it would be better to create a passage with a positive message and have the students copy that instead of the dictionary. Informed teachers would be very cautious about using reading, writing, researching, copying, and so forth as forms of punishment. The risk of turning students off on these educational activities is too great.

SCENARIO 1.28
Assault With a Deadly Playground

The worst experience with a teacher was when I was in second grade. I was outside on the playground and a kid somehow fell or got hurt on the barrels. It was raining. I somehow got wrangled into being at fault (and maybe I was). I got dragged into the school and had to go to detention which was absolutely awful.

As an education major, I can see that the teacher didn't see it and so had to just do what she thought she heard. Maybe I was to blame.

℞ The legal term "assumption of risk" usually applies to adults who knowingly enter a dangerous situation where they might get hurt. If they get hurt, it is their fault. A second-grade child cannot be expected to assume the risk of playing on the playground. Playground safety is an adult responsibility. The playground should be as childproof as possible. If a child gets hurt on the playground, there may be something wrong with the playground setup. The teacher assumed the child was at fault and physically dragged the child into detention.

Experienced teachers know that the school is responsible for playground safety and that a child engaged in reasonable play should not get hurt. The student in this scenario seemed to be engaged in reasonable play and may have caused an accident. The teacher should have tried to comfort the child while examining the child to determine the extent of the child's injury.

Punishment should not have been on the agenda.

Resourceful teachers would have the nurse tend to the injured child and would have seized the moment as an opportunity to review playground safety rules with the class. The other students could learn from what happened to this student. This could be a very effective learning experience because the other students in the class can also learn vicariously from the injured student's consequences (Bandura, 1986).

SCENARIO 1.29
Punishment Befitting the Crime

During my senior year, I was kicked out of a physics class for excessive talking and laughing and was threatened with expulsion.

℞ This is obviously a case where the punishment does not fit the crime. To expel someone for talking and laughing is excessive. In many cases, it is not so much the offense that is important, but it is the underlying need for control and the power struggle that has polluted the classroom climate. When teachers have a "do as I say or else" approach, students can experience some bizarre punishments. Wanting to curb a student's talking is very prevalent in classrooms. For some students, school may be their primary source of socialization. They risk the wrath of the teacher because they have to steal class time to interact with their peers. This is especially true in high school where there is no recess. Extreme punishment of this nature only serves to contribute to the drop-out population and it is entirely inappropriate.

When my son was either a freshman or a sophomore in high school, he was suspended for ten days because he and some other young males were caught throwing paper off the roof of the school. He was in advanced math and science courses. A ten-day suspension would have put him so far behind in his course work that he would risk failing some classes and jeopardize his graduating on time. This snowball effect could have been so discouraging that he might have even considered dropping out. Luckily, I was able to intervene and reduce the time. A more fitting consequence for throwing paper off the roof might have been to have the young men clean up all the paper around the school on a Saturday. I see little to be gained by suspension. Students often see it as a vacation and this attitude could make suspension a negative reinforcer, increasing the likelihood that undesirable behavior will continue to occur.

The knowing teacher has the foresight to make the punishment fit the crime. In education, the purpose of consequences is to minimize student problems, not to create problems of greater magnitude.

SCENARIO 1.30
Old Betsy and What's Her Name

My second-grade teacher never remembered my name and called me by my older sister's name the whole year! She hit students with a ruler she called "Old Betsy."

℞ I find it ironic that a teacher could place enough importance on names to call her tool of punishment, "Old Betsy," but didn't think it important to remember to call a child by her given name. Many teachers might confuse siblings initially or occasionally, but to not use the correct name for the entire year is dehumanizing. It is a refusal to recognize the child's individuality.

During a session when my undergraduate students were orally relating their worst-experience scenarios, one student recalled a teacher who gave each student a number and called them by that number all year. This made her interaction with her students less humantistic and more mechanistic and routine. Not using a child's name is degrading. It undermines the teacher–pupil relationship that is necessary for good classroom rapport.

I learned in teachers' college that the sweetest sound to a student is the sound of his or her name. Teachers who learn their students' names early in the school year have an advantage. They can minimize discipline problems, can engage students more easily, and can start to build good classroom relationships early. Competent teachers usually know all of their students' names by the first week of class if not sooner. Of course, teachers with multiple classes may take longer.

Mistake

2

Physical Aggression

SCENARIO 2.1
Punishment or Perversion?

My worst experience in school was the beating I received from my fourth-grade teacher for not completing a homework assignment. This teacher seemed to enjoy paddling students because she did it a lot. The beating I received was four swats with a walnut paddle with holes drilled in it. I was so hurt that I was unable to return to school for three days. Damn Mrs. M. wherever she may be.

℞ A nonsexual connotation of sadism is a delight in extreme cruelty. There are several bits of evidence that suggest that this teacher may have had some sadistic tendencies. For example, the frequency of the beatings, the extreme nature of the pain and suffering inflicted, the perception that some delight was derived from the paddlings, and the use of a specialized instrument of pain. The most incredulous part of this problem is that such a person could get away with injuring a young child to the extent that the child would miss school for several days. This abnormal behavior has no place in the classroom.

Most teachers are caring but firm disciplinarians. A teacher that would engage in the deviant behavior described in this scenario is certainly not the norm. Good teachers know that missing homework is a minor offense that does not warrant flogging. They are aware of a variety of appropriate consequences if they find that consequences are necessary. Suggestions can be found in most classroom management textbooks (Charles, 1983).

SCENARIO 2.2
Pit Bully

I was in first grade. I can't remember my teacher's name, but I do remember her jerking me up by one arm from my desk after I had spilled some glue. She then pulled me toward the corner of the room. I tripped and my head hit the corner of a wooden table, then she jerked me up and put me in the corner. I remember great pain and a wicked woman. I heard years later that she had been in trouble for breaking a child's arm.

℞ The madness displayed in this scenario is nothing short of child abuse. In her rage, this woman risked serious injury to a small child, first by jerking the child up by the arm and then by causing the child to trip and sustain a head injury. The head injury is especially troublesome. To add insult to the child's injury, she jerked her up again with no words of apology or concern. To call this woman wicked is much too kind. Her temperament and abusive behavior make a plea for professional help. The young age of her victim suggests that there might be some bullying behavior involved in this situation. She might be reluctant to pull such antics on an older student.

If this teacher had been a competent, informed teacher, she would have expected a first grader to have accidents such as spilling glue. At that age, a child's fine-motor skills have not fully developed. Grasping and manipulating objects is more difficult for a younger child than it is for an older child.

Knowledgeable teachers anticipate and plan for accidents. They use drop cloths or newspaper, and they have cleaning supplies handy. Good teachers are usually patient and understanding. They rarely exhibit the short-fused behavior described in the scenario. Effective teachers help their students learn and have fun in spite of the students' developmental limitations.

SCENARIO 2.3
Putting the Squeeze On

My teacher in fourth grade was very sensitive to noise. She didn't like it when students talked without being asked. During that year, we had three children in the class whom she had problems managing. Usually screaming, jerking them to the principal, and sending them to sit in the corner were the usual punishments. Her "favorite" way of dealing with "problem" cases was squeezing the neck to make them obey. Pain, humiliation, and usually obedience followed this act.

One time we had home economics and we were working on some projects. I missed her demand of silence and continued talking to a friend of mine.

She didn't give me any warning, but immediately grabbed my neck. This had been the only time I've ever had some sort of experience like this. I still remember it because I screamed, turned bright red, and tried to get away, which made her grip harder. The other students started laughing.

℞ Squeezing a child's neck is a form of physical aggression that could result in serious permanent damage. Spanking is against the law in many states, so some teachers use squeezing a body part to inflict pain as a way around the law. Technically, they are not spanking. This teacher seemed to do all of the wrong things. Her default reactions of jerking and screaming and squeezing are ineffective. She needed to learn more acceptable methods of dealing with discipline problems.

Effective teachers use a variety of acceptable discipline strategies, such as eye contact, warnings, proximity, gentle reminders, nonverbal cues, and gestures, to quiet their students and to get the students to focus on their work. Novice teachers can acquire these types of teaching techniques by observing master teachers and asking for suggestions. Levin and Nolan (1996) stress reminding students of what they are expected to do. They offer several useful strategies for quick compliance.

SCENARIO 2.4
The Hair-Raiser

The teacher would not allow grooming in the classroom. One day I forgot and started to brush my hair. She came up from behind me and pulled my brush the opposite way I was brushing, to pull my hair. I saw her pull out hair from several students. Also, if your locker was not clean, she would throw everything to the floor, and she did not care what broke.

℞ A person's personal boundaries should be observed at all times, in the school, at work, everywhere. Parts of a person's body and personal belongings are protected by personal boundaries. This teacher consistently violated students' boundaries. Pulling out students' hair can be considered assault—an offense that should never happen. Breaking students' belongings is an illegal act in that it involves the destruction of property.

In our litigious society, "let the teacher beware." Informed teachers are fully aware of the legal consequences of certain acts committed under the guise of discipline. They limit their discipline to effective methods that have been tested and that are backed by research. In this case, the teacher could have confiscated the hairbrush until after class if the child had been using it inappropriately; however, it is imperative that the teacher return it after class. Wise teachers keep their hands off of their students' bodies.

SCENARIOS 2.5 and 2.6
Perils of Paddling

Reflecting back, my worst experience was really not that bad. I was in seventh grade back in the 1960s and I was in the middle of an outdoor riot at M. Junior High. I was just walking by when I was attacked by three or four black kids. They thought I was white. E. was a black friend of mine and stopped the fight. He told the other kids that I was Mexican and they all apologized to me. It was the first time I realized what racism was all about. But I wasn't upset. I remember understanding. We all became friends. This took place before school started that cold morning. In first period I was talking about it to a student during the saluting of the flag. Mr. N. became so angry that he took me into the hallway and paddled me six times. But then he, too, apologized after class and told me I should not talk during flag salutation. I believe now that back then he knew he was wrong to paddle me six times.

I had a geography class in sixth grade. The teacher had us read aloud from the text-book. He called on the student he wanted to read next. If he called on you and you did-n't know what to read next, you got paddled. The class was so boring that, almost everyday, someone got a spanking. A few years ago, this teacher was in the news. He was being accused of child abuse/molestation.

℞ For some teachers, paddling can become a knee-jerk reaction to anger over infractions, no matter how minor they are. One of the perils of paddling is that everything becomes punishable by paddling. Teachers that paddle do not have to think of effective alternatives. The teacher's mood rather than the nature of the offense may dictate the number of swats that a child receives. Consequently, a child can receive excessive punishment for minor offenses, such as talking during saluting. Another peril of paddling is that boys are more often subjected to physical punishment than are girls.

A danger of excessive paddling, such as in the second scenario, is that the teacher may have derived some sexual or perverted satisfaction. This is not usually the case, but the possibility exists.

Reasonable teachers manage their anger to avoid making hasty judgments and performing impulsive disciplinary acts. It is prudent to isolate the student from the activity before any disciplinary action. This allows the teacher time to regroup if he or she is angry. With a reasonable time lapse between the behavior and the action, teachers are less likely to make bad decisions.

SCENARIO 2.7
Go for It

I was to be the one in front of the line to go into lunch for second grade. I stood in front of the door waiting because I didn't know if my teacher said to go on in. The teacher was coming out of the classroom and it seemed to me that she was waving me to go into the lunchroom. I hesitated and couldn't tell if she was telling me to go or wait. The other kids were telling me to go, so I went. Then I heard her say stop. She was mad and she yanked me like a rag doll and told me, "I told you to wait." She kept yanking me in front of the whole class and then I had to go to the end of the line.

℞ Miscommunication is not equivalent to misconduct. The child in this scenario misunderstood the teacher's commands and was punished too severely for the mistake. Excessive shaking can be dangerous for young children. Having the child go to the end of the line was adding insult to injury. Finally, the teacher was placing the burden of the miscommunication on the second grader. She did not take any ownership of the problem.

Experienced teachers know that if they give a very young child an important responsibility, the child might make a mistake. They know that if the task is that important, they should not make the child responsible. Good teachers are tolerant of students' mistakes and encourage them to try again and to try to do it better next time. Effective teachers know the right questions to ask to help students determine what they need to do differently to be successful.

SCENARIO 2.8
Handle With Care

I pretty much had good experiences with my teachers, most of who were nuns. The worst though must have been Mrs. M., the kindergarten teacher. She would grip our arms hard enough to leave bruises. She would not let children go to the bathroom, so many had accidents. I don't remember a particular incident with me, but I do remember others being afraid and crying.

℞ Parents entrust their precious packages, their children, to teachers with the expectations that their children will be handled with care. Teachers have an obligation to send the children home at the end of the day in the same condition as they found them in the morning. Sending a child home with bruises is unprofessional, inexcusable, and potentially litigious.

Prudent teachers have a hands-off policy that is always in effect unless the teacher has to touch children to help them. Teachers, particularly male teachers, may underestimate their strength and inadvertently bruise or otherwise damage children if they grab them. Clever teachers find innovative ways, such as hug coupons, to communicate to their students that they care about them. Young students want to be touched and hugged by their teachers but the risks associated with making physical contact with students is more than most teachers want to assume. Touch if you must, but handle with care.

SCENARIO 2.9
Pupil Plucking

I knew this teacher did not like me. Even as a child, I felt the bad vibes. I sat in the back and I started stretching from one side to another in an effort to see the board. She finally asked, "What is the matter?" I answered, "I can't see." She came over to me and plucked a few strands of hair from my temple and as she pulled she said, "Well, get over here!"

℞ This teacher preferred to use physical aggression and hostility rather than professionalism to address a student's problem. Plucking hair from the student's head is a bodily trespass that reeks of disrespect and dislike. The student was probably right about the teacher disliking her. Good teachers would seek a simple solution that would preserve the momentum of the lesson. They would simply try to accommodate students that need assistance seeing the board.

Scenario 2.10
Sweet Smile of Sorrow

My second-grade teacher, Ms. J. will forever live in my memory. In 1965–1966 spankings were not only allowed but, in retrospect, must have been encouraged. Ms. J. was an expert. Everyday she lined children up in the front of the classroom for every possible infraction there may have been. Perhaps a student's eyes did not follow her as she paced the floor or the student did more homework than necessary (obviously not paying attention when she said "odd" only). I lived in fear because I did not want to be like my friend D., who received at least one spanking a day and sometimes three or more. D. always smiled as we saw and heard the paddle hit his buttocks. I knew I'd never smile, but would cry from humiliation. To prevent the situation of possible humiliation, I was sick regularly. My stomach hurt, my head hurt, I had a fever (at least the bulb did), and anything else that would give me a day off. I missed the maximum number of days allowed before my mother guessed there was a problem. After talking to the principal, she was told the teacher had personal problems.

℞ This is a sorrowful example of how a teacher's pathology contaminated her classroom. No matter how well a school district tries to screen applicants, privacy laws and the confidentiality of medical conditions increase the odds that some teachers with mental disorders will be hired. Unfortunately, monitoring what goes on in a classroom may be viewed as spying on the teacher. This perception should not be a deterrent. Administrators should be on the alert for excessive physical discipline; it usually precedes physical abuse. In fact, it would be prudent to establish a policy similar to the one at Robert Wood Johnson Medical School (RWJ

Medical School, 2007) that maintains a commitment to preventing student abuse through education, by setting standards of mistreatment that will not be tolerated, by giving examples of inappropriate, unacceptable behavior, and by supporting victims by responding with corrective action. Effective administrators visit classrooms often and listen to students' complaints. The teacher in this scenario could not get away with spanking large numbers of children for ridiculous "infractions," such as letting your eyes wander, if an administrator visited the class frequently.

It would seem that in the absence of an administrator, neighboring teachers should be aware of the teacher's misconduct and alert the administration. Teachers must be advocates for children; they have a moral and legal obligation to report suspected abuse, even if a coworker is the perpetrator.

Mistake

3

Purposeful Alienation

I was supposed to bring markers to class for a group project and I forgot them. When my teacher asked me where they were, I told her I had forgotten them at home. She immediately went to the front of the class and got everyone's attention and said, "OK, class, S. forgot something so little as markers, therefore, since she forgot the markers, we can't do our fun project—Now we know we can't depend on S. anymore to remember anything of importance!" The whole class was mad at me for forgetting the markers, and the teacher seemed to encourage them to alienate me.

℞ To expect a child to provide the materials necessary for a lesson is a heavy burden of responsibility to place on a child. Children have a shorter attention span than adults and may, understandably, forget something important. The teacher bears the ultimate responsibility for the smooth execution of a lesson. An important part of teacher preparation is to anticipate the unexpected and have alternate plans and necessary materials included in the lesson planning. The teacher further exacerbated the problem with a public reprimand, which usually invites hostility or encourages withdrawal. Effective teachers know that soft, private reprimands are usually more effective. The teacher could have minimized the child's agony by privately suggesting a second chance and by providing some helpful hints on how to remember to bring the markers next time. Sensitive teachers would have produced the needed markers and told the class that S. accidentally forgot the markers but has promised to bring them the next time.

Mistake

4

Public Ridicule

SCENARIO 4.1
Confession ≠ Contrition

When I was in junior high, I received a progress report with negative comments and a failing grade. I was asked to have my mother sign the form and return it. I did not want to get in trouble so I signed my mother's name. I thought I was in the clear until about a week later, the report came in the mail. I was grounded for two months and had to get up in class and tell them why what I had done was so wrong. The two months would have been nothing but I had to live with the torment of my classmates teasing me. They all constantly asked me if I had forged my report cards, absentee notes, tardy notes, whatever needed to be signed.

℞ Forced public confession sows the seeds of hypocrisy in very fertile ground. By forcing the student to stand up and tell the class what she did and why it was wrong, the teacher was encouraging hypocrisy. It was a false act. Obviously, the student did not think it was very wrong; she did it. The public confession also damaged the student's credibility with her classmates. The torment she reaped far exceeded her crime.

There was no obvious benefit to having the student confess to the class; certainly there was no genuine contrition or any rectification of the problem. The astute teacher would instinctively know that the forgery is a private matter that should be settled with the child and her parents. McFee (1918) was a historical voice of reason, as evidenced by the following quote from her book, "Many a bad boy or girl has been reformed by a kind talk from the teacher in private, for such talks are rarely forgotten" (p. 26). A private talk would have been more effective in this case and may have sparked sincere repentance.

SCENARIO 4.2
Don't Bother to Raise Your Hand

When I would raise my hand to answer, my teachers would never call on me. When I would get in trouble for talking, Mr. F. would make me sit in a desk right in front of the class. I felt so dumb. I hated the fact that the teachers always would put the smart students on everything. They forgot about the rest of us.

℞ I had a professor who said, "The best way to extinguish good behavior is to fail to recognize it." This bit of advice is rooted in Behavioral Learning Theory (Skinner, 1950), which suggests that failure to reinforce a behavior decreases the likelihood that it will occur again. The teacher's failure to call on a student who raises her hand to answer almost guarantees that the child will eventually stop raising her hand. Failing to recognize a child could lead to alienation and hostility or rebellion. The child may decide that she will never answer a question in this class as an expression of her frustration.

Competent teachers are well aware of the power of recognition and praise. They would make every effort to acknowledge every student who wanted to contribute to the class discussion and offer acceptance of the answer, praise when appropriate, or assistance when needed. They try to create a supportive environment that encourages participation. Resourceful teachers would develop some systematic technique for making sure that each student is called on at some point in time (Weinstein, 1996).

The purpose of questioning is to ascertain a student's level of understanding. This includes all students, not just the popular students or the smart students. Wise teachers would never assume that the lower achieving students would probably have wrong or "silly" answers and avoid calling on them. On the contrary, they realize that such assumptions and behavior might cause the student to become a nonparticipating member of the class (Harvard University, 1988). Caring teachers know that it is humiliating and hurtful for children to raise their hands again and again and never be recognized.

SCENARIO 4.3
Adding Insult to an Unjust Injury

In sixth grade, my teacher embarrassed me in front of the class because he thought I was talking and he made me stand in the corner! He then asked me to apologize in front of everyone. I refused and walked out of the class. I was in an honors program and I had to get out because if I stayed in, I would have had to take his class. He then had the nerve to deny to the principal that this incident ever happened. Of course, they believed him.

℞ This scenario is a classic case of adding insult to injury. After erroneously punishing the student very publicly, the teacher baited the student into insubordination and misconduct by demanding a public apology. The indirect consequence of the student dropping out of the honors program was an unforeseeable injustice. The denial of his actions makes this teacher's motives suspect.

Most teachers are honorable and their intentions are good but they sometimes make mistakes. Sagacious educators know that they are not infallible and that there are times when they might be mistaken. These teachers would never draw so much attention to such a minor offense as talking. The disruptive effects of conflict and confrontation far outweigh any positive benefits that may be gained from public censure. This unfortunate event could have been avoided with private reprimand or what MacDonald (1991) referred to as the use of I-messages in a private one-on-one conference. In the conference, the teacher would have found out that the child had not been talking. It would have been easier for the teacher to apologize, in private.

SCENARIO 4.4
Saving a Red Face

The worst experience I had in school was when my sixth-grade teacher ridiculed me and made fun of my answer. Then I made a comment to her that was rude and she made me stay after school and write dialogue out of a book verbatim. I was literally punished for trying.

℞ It takes courage for a student to raise her hand to answer a question and risk the embarrassment of giving the wrong answer. Students' worst fears are realized when a teacher publicly ridicules their answers. In this scenario, the teacher's cavalier disparagement of the student goaded the child into some discourteous face-saving behavior. The subsequent punishment deflated the student's attempts to save face and salvage her self-esteem. The injustice of it all was mentally tucked away to be nurtured for years and years.

Truly professional educators would never ridicule a child's answer. They know their job is to help children come up with the correct answer. They employ a variety of techniques to achieve this outcome. An effective approach to handling student responses is to offer students cues or prompts, to accept part of the answer, or to look for something positive about the response to move the student closer to the correct response.

SCENARIO 4.5
Old School—1899 or New School—1999?

My family moved so I had to start second grade as a new student. I was scared. I didn't know anyone at my new school. Everything was fine until PE class that first day of school. In PE, the coach asked the class to line up and the lines were supposed to start on designated little circles. Needless to say, I wasn't accustomed to their style of lining up, so I formed my own individual line that wasn't on a circle. Unfortunately, the coach noticed I was out of line, so he yelled at me and rudely asked me to follow his directions, not knowing that this was my first day of class. My self-esteem dropped at that moment. He didn't realize that I was trying to meet his request but misinterpreted his directions.

℞ Outdated, antiquated, passé, or archaic, by *any* name the practice of having students line up on specific circles and follow specific directions is a relic of a bygone era. Turn-of-the-century teaching (1890s–1930s) featured a similar technique where students had to literally toe the line and recite their lessons. During this period, teachers told students how and where to sit or stand, if and when to talk, and so on. Students often waited for the teacher to give the signal to start and the student "body" was expected to move in lock-step fashion as one (Cuban, 1984). The coach publicly ridiculed the unsuspecting student who was unaware of the practice. Perhaps the coach would have been a little more lenient if he had been aware that the student was new, but given his strong need for control and his tendency toward loud reprimand, I doubt it.

"There is an objection to reproving the pupil publicly. . . . Ridicule is another weapon that should never be used. . . . It is the modest, conscientious child that is most affected," (McFee, 1918). These quotes are evidence that perceptive, sensible teachers were around at the turn of the century. This old-fashioned advice is timeless and timely. Effective teachers are aware of the effects of public ridicule and shaming on a student's self-esteem and usually avoid it in favor of soft, private reprimands. In addition, they would have rules or practices posted or they would offer a new student orientation.

SCENARIO 4.6
If You Muse, You Lose

In fourth grade, I was not paying close attention when the teacher was reading a story to the class. At the end of the story, another boy and I were asked to come to the front of the room and repeat as much of the story as possible. I had to go first and needless to say, did not recall much of the story. The boy did very well. I remember how embarrassed I was.

℞ There are two apparent problems in this scenario. One, the student was inattentive, and two, the teacher's response to the student's lack of attention was to make him embarrass himself in front of the class. I think the teacher's objective was to encourage students to pay attention so she set this student up as an example. Sprinthall et al. (1994) view such public shaming as an inappropriate, miseducative experience.

The effective teacher would not begin her lesson until she had everyone's attention. Gagne (1977) points out that gaining attention is the foremost activity in the events of learning.

Informed practitioners are well aware that some fourth graders are easily distracted. They would have a variety of methods to bring their strays back into the academic fold. They could ask distracted students if they are on the same page. They could direct everyone's attention to a picture in the book. If the students did not have a book, the teacher could warn them, saying that they need to pay close attention because they will be called on later. If they cannot get the children to pay attention, a private, soft reprimand, known only to the individual student, could be effective (O'Leary & O'Leary, 1972).

SCENARIO 4.7
To Laugh or Not to Laugh, That Is the Question

In third grade, the teacher was talking about Pearl Harbor. She talked about the bombing and the deaths. I was totally involved, paying total attention. When she finished, she had summarized a very important day in U.S. history. Then she asked for questions. I raised my hand and asked, "Did she die?" She asked, "Did who die?" I said, "Pearl Harbor." She and the entire class laughed; it seemed like forever. I didn't ask a question again for a long time and I am still afraid the question I have may be stupid and I'll be laughed at. Now I know better and try to teach my students that your question can't be stupid if you don't know the answer.

℞ Human ignorance is exceptional fodder for comedy and entertainment. A talk show host recently increased his comedy offerings to include interviews with people in a mall, asking them questions such as, "Where is Pearl Harbor?" and "Where did we drop the atomic bomb?" Their less-than-knowledgeable responses bring guffaws, hoots, and peals of laughter, much like the student and teacher responses in this scenario. This behavior humiliates the person who gave the ridiculous answer. Although teachers cannot stop their students from laughing, they can set the tone and duration of the laughing response. In this case, the teacher joined in with the students, thereby prolonging and condoning the laughter.

Consummate professionals know that no matter how funny, hilarious, or ridiculous a student's answer might be, as professionals, they must make every effort to stifle their laughter. They also must make it clear to the class that outbursts of laughter will not be tolerated. To take the wind out of the sails of laughter, the teacher can gently correct the student with a smile and affirm the student by acknowledging that all of us make mistakes sometimes. The skillful teacher will get back on track and regain the momentum of the lesson.

2

TEACHER–STUDENT RELATIONS

"Everyone in my biology class voted against dissecting a frog.
But we almost had enough votes to dissect the teacher."

Mistake

5

Favoritism

SCENARIO 5.1
Snob Appeal

I never really think about this being the worst experience. I was always, and still am, a talker. I was, however, a good student so somehow I guess it balanced out. My parents never really got on me for talking/conduct because I had good grades. Anyway, I guess the teacher I disliked or felt uncomfortable around the most was Ms. W. in third grade. In elementary school I had lots of friends, but never the cute "girlie" types. Ms. W. was always so obvious about who her favorites were; the girls were always rich, white, and dressed right out of Talbot Kids. She was a snob and always made me feel quite small.

℞ Snobs are people who admire and seek to associate with other people they regard as their superiors and may ignore people they feel are inferior (*American Heritage Dictionary*, 1992). The student seemed to think the teacher in this scenario was a snob. Several factors support that notion. The little girls the teacher preferred had snob appeal: They were upper class, very well-dressed, and members of the dominant culture. Most teachers are not rich; they're usually considered middle class. The teacher could have possibly regarded the favored children and their families as superiors. The student was obviously not rich, not well-dressed, and probably not white. The teacher reportedly ignored the student. It seems the teacher does fit the perception of a snob. I say perception because there might be another, less apparent reason for the teacher's perceived favoritism.

Where there are rich, well-dressed kids, there are probably rich, influential parents somewhere in the picture. Perhaps the teacher catered to this favored group of children out of fear of their rich and powerful parents. The teacher's motives are not as important as the negative effects her behavior had on the less-favored children. The student said the teacher made her feel quite small.

Astute teachers are aware that inequity within gender groups invites resentments. They know that in peer groups, students invariably compare themselves to each other. If teachers favor and esteem certain members of a peer group, the remaining children will understandably have a diminished sense of self-worth. Insightful teachers appreciate the need to take a personal inventory periodically to examine their thoughts and motives. Such an inventory can serve to fetter out both social class and gender bias. If good teachers suspect that they have a bias, they try to become more aware of their snobbish behavior and its effect on students, and they try to take steps to curtail the behavior. They might start with making efforts to find positives in children they possibly regard as inferior.

SCENARIO 5.2
Sugar, Spice, and Very Smart

My high school junior English teacher was constantly on my case about talking (maybe because I'm a guy), but she would let the class valedictorian and salutatorian (both girls) talk away right next to me. I really disliked that teacher. That was the first time I ever got a C in any class.

℞ Expectations, sexual stereotypes, and tolerance are major factors in gender bias, a dimension of favoritism. The old adage descriptors of "snakes and snails and puppy dog tails" for males and "sugar and spice and everything nice" for females epitomize sexual stereotypes. Initially, it was thought that teachers favored females who were nicer, less aggressive, and easier to teach. A study by Good and Brophy (1991) indicated that teachers favored girls. Brophy and Evertson (1981) found that young males received more disapproval and blame than did young females. A study by the American Association of University Women (AAUW; 1992) provided contrary evidence that schools shortchanged females in a variety of ways. These studies leave no doubt that males and females are often treated differently. Sometimes males are favored; sometimes females are favored. Which ones are favored depends on the teacher, the situation, how the teacher exhibits gender bias, the student's socialization in sex roles, society's conventions of what is appropriate for each sex, and what is expected of each sex.

In this scenario, gender bias is combined with achievement bias, a provocative combination that favors young females. The teacher gave the top-achieving females more liberties than were given to a young male who was not rated as a high achiever. It is possible that he was a high achiever in other classes because he said he received his first C from this particular teacher. His low grade may have been influenced by the teacher's bias. A different perspective of the problem in this scenario is that the teacher expects females to talk more and her tolerance level for males talking was much lower.

Fair-minded teachers know the importance of treating males and females equally. To teach without bias is to discard sexual stereotypes, socialization processes, and educational practices that focus on treating males and females differently. The key to eliminating favoritism is consistency.

Teachers must be consistent in their treatment of all students. Before they can do that, they must be cognizant of how much gender affects their expectations of their students. Once they are aware of their preferences, biases, and expectations, they can change both their behavior and their thinking, and try to balance their treatment of both sexes. For example, teachers can give boys more interaction privileges and can take girls more seriously as they encourage both groups to be independent. The bottom line is that it is unfair to treat either group better than the other.

SCENARIO 5.3
Teacher's Pet

In fifth grade my teacher made me her "pet." I was new in the school so all the kids hated me for it. Then I had to go to middle school and later high school with these same students. This same teacher also used to come and ask my opinion about her cat that had to be put to sleep. That was devastating to even think about, even though it was best for the cat. She would even cry about her cat, and what was I, at 10 years old, going to tell her?

℞ "Teacher's pet," is a label dreaded by any self-respecting preadolescent. Students resist roles that cast them outside of their peer group, especially if it is an adult role. The teacher in this scenario probably sensed an unusual measure of maturity or responsibility in this ten-year-old and made the child her classroom companion. Sometimes teachers of young children are very isolated and devoid of adult interaction. Inadvertently, some teachers strike up a friendship with a student. Unfortunately for these teachers, the line that is drawn between what is shared with adult friends and what is shared with students becomes fuzzier and fuzzier. Inevitably, these teachers cross that line and start treating students like adults. The role and the burden of an adultlike friendship are often cast upon an unsuspecting, unwilling child.

Wise teachers know that they have no right to put their students in a position to be an object of ridicule and scorn to satisfy the teachers' needs. That's exactly what happens when teachers favor a particular child. Other classmates laugh at and make fun of the child, and many will dislike the child. It's a terrible predicament for a young child who wants to belong and be cared for.

Ten-year-olds are still very dependent on parents and teachers and find it difficult and unnerving when the roles are reversed. If students have to be there for their teachers, surely they wonder or worry about who is there for them. Teachers have an obligation not to cross the line with student friendships. They should actively seek to establish collegial and personal relationships with their adult peers.

Mistake

6

Physiological Discrimination

SCENARIO 6.1
The Antifat Motive

When I was in ninth grade, I tried out for the cheerleading/pom-pom squad. I made it. I was thrilled. I was excited because even though I was a little overweight, I had been chosen. I went to practices, games, followed the routines, and tried to have fun. It was difficult sometimes because the others girls would make fun of me or call me names. Now during this time, I didn't really lose or gain any weight. So here was the issue. My coach called me into her office and said that one of the main reasons I was on the team was so that I could get more physically fit. Boy was I taken aback. I was so hurt and disappointed in her and myself. I still love being a "stand cheerleader," but I never tried out again.

℞ The coach obviously had a hidden motive for selecting the overweight student for the cheerleading squad: to make the student lose weight. When the student did not lose weight, the coach felt compelled to reveal a personal "antifat" motive. This candid revelation clearly communicated to the student that she was not okay, that she was fat and she needed "fixing." Perhaps the coach's intent was to shame her into losing weight by telling her that she was chosen because of her weight problem and not her merit, skill, or value. The coach's motive was self-serving. If the student lost weight once she was a member of the team, the coach could claim credit for healing the student's "fat affliction." The cost of this "benevolent" act to the student's self-esteem was immeasurable. Although the teacher may have felt her intentions were good, her behavior was indefensible and needlessly painful for the student.

Caring teachers realize that fat children are often targets of ridicule. Children of normal weight frequently discriminate against overweight children. Society seems to condone the practice of making disparaging remarks to overweight people. Sensitive teachers, who are aware of potential damage to an overweight student's self-esteem, have zero tolerance for the disparaging remarks that schoolchildren make about these children. Unfortunately, many teachers have some bias toward overweight students and often communicate that directly or indirectly. A first step toward changing their discriminatory behavior would be to acknowledge their feelings and work to change their image or impression of overweight children. A second step would be to showcase the positive features, behaviors, and accomplishments of overweight children for the class and the school. Teaching children tactful, empathic ways of interacting with overweight children is a priority.

SCENARIO 6.2
Writing Well at Any Cost

My worst experience in school was when I was in first grade and was learning to write. I attended school in Spain at the time. The teacher at school was so mad at me because I could not write well that she made me stay after school every day to practice. I missed my bus to go home each time, and had to wait for the bus to go to my house at 3:30. This ride was for the high school so I had to endure ridicule from much older kids. There wasn't an escort to the correct bus, so I often got on the wrong one and had no ride home. On those occasions I was left at school with no one around until my mother came looking for me.

℞ Some teachers erroneously believe that responsibility for their students ends once the children leave school property. This may not be a conscious thought, but it is reflected in some teachers' actions, such as making a very young student miss the bus. In this scenario, the teacher placed an academic task above the well-being of the child. There was little or no concern for what could happen to the child if she missed the bus. The primary concern was that the child learn to write well. The obsession with making sure that children are writing well appears to be an egotrip or a way for this teacher to appear competent. I wonder if the teacher ever asked the question: What good would it do children to learn to write well if they didn't live to write? This teacher's actions endangered a child's life and, at minimum, placed the child at risk.

Sensible teachers would not put their students at risk under any circumstances. They realize that they are liable if their actions endanger a child. This little first grader was at risk from older students and undesirable characters that may hang around schools. Astute teachers know the possible dangers and they make sure that all of their very young children are escorted to their bus and are accounted for. They are aware of the fears and anxieties a child experiences when they are lost or alone in a situation and they would not subject their children to such an experience.

SCENARIO 6.3
Blurred-Eye View

My worst experience in school was not being able to see the chalkboard because I needed glasses. I was called on to read and explain a lesson we previously did, but I couldn't see. Everything was a blur. The teacher got upset with me and embarrassed me in front of the class. She said that I needed to stop squinting my eyes and making faces at her and just read and get involved with the rest of the class. I was trying. She sent a note home, telling my mother that maybe I needed my eyes checked. Well, I got cat eye-glasses and hated to wear them, but I did. Mrs. J. had everybody turn to look at me.

℞ Students with visual impairment exhibit obvious signs such as squinting, holding their book far away from or close to their face, and leaning forward trying to see the board. These students may complain of headaches, of blurred vision, or of irritated eyes. Some students may stop paying attention to assignments that are difficult to see. Students with this type of physical challenge need help, not shame.

Well-trained educators "red flag" behaviors such as squinting and neck craning. They monitor the student's behavior to confirm that the student is having a visual problem. If their suspicions are confirmed, caring teachers tactfully ask the student if he or she is experiencing difficulty seeing the board or assignments. Once teachers have established that there is indeed a visual problem, the next step is to notify parents and/or appropriate school professionals (DeMott, 1982).

SCENARIO 6.4
Discrimination by Isolated Exits

My worst experience was in high school when the school wanted me to leave class later than everyone else because they said it was dangerous to have a wheelchair in the halls with all the students. I had a real problem with this because I wanted to see my friends and be a part of the crowd. To me, they really made me feel different than everyone else. This is something I've always tried not to do.

℞ This student's predicament is at the core of the hotly debated issue of inclusion. The movement toward full inclusion involves the education of all students in the regular classroom regardless of the severity of their handicaps or disabilities.

The Education of All Handicapped Children Act, Public Law 94-142 (1975), was amended in 1990 to require states to embrace the concept of doing whatever is necessary to provide the least restrictive environment. This amendment requires states to integrate all students into the regular classroom even if it means employing special services or facilities. The law defines the least restrictive environment as one that approximates as closely as possible the regular academic environment of their nondisabled peers. The law requires that students with disabilities enjoy the same opportunities for achievement and socialization as their nondisabled peers. The school was in possible violation of the law by denying this disabled student an opportunity for social interaction.

Resourceful professionals would find a way to regulate the flow of student traffic to accommodate students in wheelchairs. A common practice is putting in wide ramps that would allow for a wheelchair and companions. This would allow the student to interact with other students and minimize the danger to classmates. Knowledgeable professionals would avoid any practices that clearly violate the law and that would make the school vulnerable to a lawsuit. The value of inclusion is questioned by many, but I agree with some of the studies that maintain that all students can benefit from a diverse classroom that opens its doors to all students (Gearheart, Weishahn, & Gearheart, 1992). I also recognize and appreciate that inclusion presents some difficult challenges for regular classroom teachers. In many cases, it seems the benefits for teachers and students outweigh the challenges.

SCENARIO 6.5
Baby and the Beast

In the fourth grade of my school experience, I endured a painful experience, which unfortunately I can still remember. This was the first male teacher that I ever had. He assigned seat numbers according to the grades that each student had. For example, the highest grade sat first chair, and the lowest grade sat in the last chair in the back. One day we were talking about health and foods. Being that I was very thin and he (the teacher) was very robust, he grabbed my arm and encircled it with his hand in front of the whole class. He proceeded to tell them how I did not eat, that I was a weakling, a skinny fellow, etc. To this day, all I can envision are his huge fingers around my wrist and the humiliating laughter of the class.

℞ There are two very blatant mistakes that are apparent in this scenario. The first mistake is a flawed attempt at ability grouping, namely having the highest grade occupy first chair and the lowest grade last chair. This practice seems punitive and illogical. The second mistake conjures up an image of a helpless small person seized upon by a beastly character. The author's indelible memory of huge hands encircling his wrist illuminates that image. The teacher violated the student's personal boundaries when he touched him without permission.

When I was a kid, I can remember an advertisement in comic books about the "skinny 90 lb weakling" that was bullied by a big muscular guy on the beach. The weakling was humiliated in front of his girlfriend. The ad was for an arm exerciser that a person would pull and stretch to develop his muscles. Of course, in the end, the "90 lb weakling" was transformed into a very muscular hunk that returned and beat up the bully and got the girl. Unfortunately, the child in this scenario did not have a magical exerciser that could zap him with muscles that would enable him to get some payback from the teacher bully. Instead, he turned the teacher's sarcasm and the humiliating laughter of the class inward and internalized it.

There are two possible explanations for this teacher's boorish behavior. It appears that he was unprepared for his class and lacked interesting, engaging material that was supported with visual artifacts or appropriate media. This teacher's actions speak volumes about his ineptitude as a teacher and his lack of preparation for this lesson. He was teaching a lesson on foods. A knowledgeable teacher would have instructional objectives (Gronlund, 2000); humiliating a student would certainly not be one of those objectives. This mistake could have been avoided if the teacher had planned properly and if he had a personal policy of respecting students' boundaries. No teacher should make a hostile assault on a child's person no matter how minor that assault may be perceived by the teacher.

SCENARIOS 6.6 and 6.7
Stuff and Nonsense

I went to Catholic school. My teacher was a nun named Sister M. J. The experience was if you wrote with your left hand you were the devil's child. Well, guess which hand I wrote with? You are correct; I wrote with my left hand. She came from behind me and surprised me with a swift slap with a ruler she held fast in her hands. Not only did she physically hurt me, but Sister M. J. verbally lashed out that I was damned for "conspiring with the devil." A second student recounts, "I've been left-handed since birth, but when I entered third grade, my teacher Ms. G. wanted to make me right-handed by hitting my left hand. She also would say the left hand was the devil's hand.

I remember being in kindergarten. My teacher asked the class to put the hand you write with on the paper in front of you. The teacher then walked around nodding "yes . . . yes . . . yes" and then stopped when she got to me. I had my left hand on the paper. She said, "No, we write with our right hand." She gently corrected me and placed my other hand on the paper, uniformly like all the other children. At this time, I guess teachers were allowed to do things like this to make their life a little easier when teaching how to write.

℞ The uninformed often resort to superstition to explain and justify that which mystifies. The term *sinistral* or sinister, which dates back to Middle English, sometimes means left, or left hand. For years, some folklore has equated left or the left hand with something sinister or evil.

Two of the teachers in these scenarios were probably taught to believe that the left hand was the devil's hand or that left-handedness was unlucky or evil. This folklore of "conspiring with the devil" is not only ludicrous, it defies logic and, like much folklore, it is unfounded. Such a glaring accusation is sure to focus all of the shame, hellfire, and damnation lights on the students and practically ignores the teachers' inability to effectively teach left-handed students to write.

In our society, right-handed teachers and students are dominant and, understandably, instructional techniques and materials are geared toward them. Wenze and Wenze (2004) note that life for left-handed students is full of challenges, equating it to living life as if you are always looking in a mirror, where everything you do is backwards. Their powerful metaphor underscores the need for teacher understanding and empathy to ensure the successful adaptation of left-handed students. Teachers who are unprepared and lacking in the knowledge of ways to teach left-handed students view left-handedness as a deviation from the norm and subsequently a problem. Left-handedness, like some other human differences, is shrouded in myth and cloaked in superstition. It would be interesting to see to what nonsense such educators would attribute ambidexterity or the armless using their feet as hands.

Teachers well-versed in the knowledge of human development know that students are not responsible for handedness. Knowledgeable, flexible teachers recognize that there is no single magical way to teach all students. The prepared teacher will be aware of student differences and will seek ways to address those differences. In today's educational environment, left-handed students are a minor challenge.

Many teacher resource books offer techniques to facilitate teaching left-handed students. For example, most writing texts illustrate the correct way to hold a pencil for left-handed and right-handed students. In the absence of appropriate materials, ask an expert. Teaching left-handed students should not be a problem and certainly does not require an exorcism as two of the scenarios suggest.

Mistake

7

Personal Attacks

My worst experience was during my senior year of high school. I was taking two English classes with two different teachers. (I was pregnant the previous year.) The teacher for my sophomore English class is who I am about to talk about. My sophomore English class was with a bunch of lower levels and troublemakers. The teacher told us that none of us would ever go to college. I could not believe this teacher was telling us that. She's a teacher!

℞ The "psychic" teacher in this scenario has predicted that none of her low-achieving students will ever to college. This gloomy prediction is rooted in the teacher's low expectations for low achievers. Her discouraging statement could make her prediction a reality. Sprinthall, Sprinthall, and Oja (1994) acknowledge that teacher approval is a powerful reinforcer that can shape student behavior. I think teacher disapproval is equally powerful in shaping behavior. Disapproval and discouragement can derail a student's intent to pursue the college track.

Appearances suggest that the teacher made the comment because the students were behavior problems and were not achieving. Discouraging remarks, such as the ones made by this teacher, may place students in a cycle of discouragement and misbehavior. Some students who are behavior problems may in fact be discouraged students (Dreikurs, Grunwald, & Pepper, 1982).

Effective teachers prefer encouragement to discouragement. They know their charge is to help all of their students to be all that they can be. This goal is more readily attained when students have the approval, encouragement, and support of their teachers. The student was shocked that a teacher said the students would never go to college because teachers are thought to be the embodiment of student hope and encouragement. Good teachers would not tell students that none of them would ever go to college. They know that these words have the power to destroy confidence, to dispel hope, and to instill doubt. They would rather tell students that the sky is the limit for what they can accomplish, if they are willing to work hard.

SCENARIO 7.2
Risqué Rumor

My sixth-grade teacher, Sister C., pulled me out of class to tell me people were wondering about me; I acted too much like a boy—I should be more ladylike, etc., etc., etc. Why did I have to play kickball with the boys all the time? She made me feel weird.

R̲x̲ Under the guise of being helpful, the teacher projected her biased perceptions of the student's behavior onto the student. She implied that the student was homosexual because she acted too much like a boy. Moreover, she revealed that this student was the subject of malicious gossip. The teacher's need to discuss this matter with the student reeks of homophobia, an aversion to a homosexual lifestyle. Perhaps the teacher was trying to be helpful, but the student's reaction of feeling "weird" suggests otherwise.

Knowledgeable teachers are beyond the gender-specific roles typically assigned to boys and girls. They respect androgynous behavior, where students may exhibit both female and male characteristics. They realize that a student's nonconformist, atypical behavior does not inform their sexual orientation. These knowledgeable teachers would not predict that she would become less feminine because she played ball and participated in typically male activities.

SCENARIO 7.3
Job's Comforter

I struggled during my ninth-grade year. I would miss a lot of school. This one teacher pulled me out into the hall and told me horrible things I still remember to this day. She said that my looks and clothing weren't always going to be there for me. She said I was going to work in McDonald's the rest of my life. Even to this day I can't figure out if it was to help me or not.

℞ The dictionary defines Job's comforter as "one who is discouraging or saddening while seemingly offering sympathy or comfort" (*American Heritage Dictionary*, 1992). Job was a famous man in the Bible whose faith in his God was sorely tested. He lost his children, his property, and finally his health, but he remained steadfast in his faith. Job's friends pretended to comfort him but they were insincere and were actually trying to find fault with him. The term Job's comforter is based on the friends' actions.

The teacher in this scenario falls into the category of Job's comforter. She makes discouraging, disparaging remarks about the student under the guise of helpful advice. The teacher's focus on the student's looks and clothing suggests some underlying jealousy or displaced anger. The dire predictions made by this teacher sounded like a mean-spirited wish rooted in jealousy. The experience left the student confused and scarred, but obviously undaunted. The student is now a preservice teacher aspiring to be a teacher.

Good teachers seek to be a wellspring of student hope and encouragement. They realize that the way they communicate their expectations can have a profound effect on students. They help students maximize their strengths and minimize their weaknesses in their struggles to reach their goals. Caring teachers are the antithesis of Job's comforter. They are comforters in the truest sense of the word; they usually want what's best for their students.

SCENARIO 7.4
Mirror on the Wall, Who's the Worst Student of All?

My worst experience with a teacher happened during my sophomore year in high school. I was in an honors advanced algebra class with sophomores and juniors. Every other class, my teacher would have us take a homework quiz. We had to neatly tear a sheet of notebook paper into four pieces, and write the answer on a little sheet during the first five minutes of class. I was not that good in math and in this class, since it was honors, my teacher didn't really teach us how to do and understand algebra. One junior named S. and I always had trouble with these quizzes and with the class in general, and when Mrs. S. would pass back quizzes every other day, she would say, "E., you didn't do the worst this time," or "S., someone did worse than you did." Not only did S. and I hear this, but the whole class was aware of her comments and thus of our poor performance in class. It was the only class and teacher that I can honestly say I hated. I struggled for a B-/C in that class. The following year I changed to regular math and I learned in that next class.

℞ Honors students, like most students, may take a course and find that it is a weak area for them. They may have difficulty grasping the course content. The teacher had high expectations for the honors classes and let them take responsibility for their learning. According to the student, the teacher made no effort to teach the class or to help them to understand the course material. However, she made it a point to focus on the students who had the worst performance. This is not a common practice among teachers. They usually focus on the top-scoring students. She made very destructive criticisms and comparisons about these students in front of the class.

Apparently, she thought public disclosure would motivate the two students to improve their performance. Her personal attacks on the students were unprofessional and ineffective; these attacks only served to make the students hate the teacher and the class. She made her low expectations and poor perceptions of these students very evident. Although the student managed to pass the course, she didn't feel that she had learned anything in the class. Perhaps she was misplaced because she felt she actually learned in a regular math class.

A simple remediation strategy for students performing poorly in an advanced class is to offer them retreat privileges without penalty. If students feel that they are not doing well in a course, they can take the class that's a level lower and not lose their honors status. Responsible teachers may opt to offer lagging students more instructional assistance.

They realize that honors students encounter difficulty in certain courses just like any other students. They can reasonably expect a high level of autonomy and responsibility from honors students, but when it seems that someone is drowning alone in their own little pool, it's the teacher's responsibility to jump in and give some assistance and reteach problem concepts when necessary. I took a graduate calculus course that was practically self-taught. The professor gave us copies of his typed manuscript as our text. We were thrown into the choppy waters of calculus and we had to sink or swim to survive. We had to complete so many chapters and take a test before we could move to the next level. By the time we were ready for Integral Calculus, many of us were sinking fast. Finally, in a desperate move to save the class, the professor started having class again and actually started teaching the course material. He made no comments or jokes about our poor performance. His assistance helped us to regain our confidence and pass the course. Effective teachers are alert to student difficulty and assume the role of instructor or facilitator, whichever is most appropriate for the learning situation.

Mistake

8

Inappropriate Teacher–Student Relationships

SCENARIO 8.1
My Teacher, My Friend?

My worst experience with a teacher was my senior year in high school. I was taking AP chemistry, and I needed to write about some research I had done for a scholarship essay for college. My chemistry teacher and I came up with a project for me, developing a lab for students, and I stayed after school one day to go through a stack of lab manuals, looking for ideas. As I sat in the lab looking through the books, my teacher hung about and started telling me the sad story of his life—his past few years of unemployment, his having to go back to teaching in order to work. He had often acted like he considered me a friend or perhaps even a colleague since I was the best student in the class and was planning to teach. He would call me up and explain to me his rationale for the seating chart and suggest that I consider using it someday, and explaining the seating chart involved telling me other students' grades. This teacher had a very unprofessional manner toward me and overstepped the conventional boundaries between teachers and students. I did not respect him as a teacher and therefore did not learn very much from him.

Rx Each age level has its own rules of social interaction and socialization. Henson and Eller (1999) investigated the developmental nature of friendships and found that adolescent reasons for being friends differ remarkably from adult reasons. They found that adolescents wanted someone who would be there for them and not give them a hard time, whereas adults wanted someone that they could talk to and someone who would give honest feedback. The teacher in this scenario is guilty of trying to impose an adult concept of "friendship" on a child. He expected the student to talk to him and give him honest feedback. His actions suggest a lack of social cognition or knowledge of how to reason and act in social situations (Eisenberg & Harris, 1984). He told the student the story of his life and sought honest feedback on a teaching strategy that he was using. Understandably, the student was uncomfortable with the teacher's behavior. Teachers who choose to act like their students' "friend" often undermine their own credibility and lose the respect of their students.

Savvy teachers know that no matter how mature, focused, and "adult-like" children seem, they are not adults and they should not be treated as peers. To treat children as peers puts too much emotional and psychological responsibility on them. Astute teachers are sensitive to the social boundaries separating children and adults and they make every effort not to cross those boundaries.

Students clearly see the delineation of social roles. They understand that teachers are not supposed to be their "friends" or their peers. They do not want or need to know intimate details of their teachers' lives. Adolescents are usually able to sense hidden motives or unspoken intentions. They are not limited by the egocentrism and the inability to see another's point of view often found in young children (Piaget, as cited in Woolfolk, 1998). Children who are imposed upon may feel powerless and reluctant to show their overt resentment of adult social advances. Covertly, they may harbor resentment and harsh feelings that may affect them for years, such as in this scenario. Good teachers are "friendly" and they believe in letting a child be a child. They seek their companionship and feedback from interested adults.

SCENARIO 8.2
A Wolf in Teacher's Clothing

Even though I have had numerous experiences that were "awful" in school, most of them taught me positive lessons. I learned to voice my concerns and let people know what I feel. I also learned that people can abuse others' positions. I suppose the worst experience would be the inappropriate behavior one male teacher exhibited toward the "attractive" girls in school. He was fired a year after I graduated. One girl finally was pushed too far and complained. Since then, I've had other experiences that were worse, but I felt that this experience would have the "biggest" impact.

℞ Pedophiles are adults who are sexually attracted to children. They have no place in the classroom. This sexual deviation would be difficult for such a person to control in the presence of so many children. There are laws to keep pedophiles out of the classroom. The potential risk and possible injury to children justify denying anyone with pedophilic tendencies a job teaching children. In this scenario, the teacher may rationalize that the attractive girls are almost women and that he is not a pedophile. The fact remains that the "attractive girls" were school-age children and his pursuit of these children suggest pedophilia.

Teachers who suspect they have some pedophilic tendencies should get some professional help and change to a profession that does not offer so much temptation. There is no other answer. The "recovered" pedophile may not exist. A confirmed pedophile featured on national television begged to be castrated because he could not control his urges. In all fairness, there may be some of these people who can suppress their urges, but what if they could not in a moment of weakness? They could ruin a child for life. Caring teachers would make the well-being of their children a priority. They would seek different employment.

Mistake

9

Deliberate Mistreatment

In first grade I went to Catholic school. My teacher was Sister A. I hated school. I was afraid to go and cried every morning. My grades were Ds and Fs, and my self-esteem was zero. The main reason for this is because Sister A. would make fun of me every day in front of the whole class. She would have me stand in front of the room and tell me how stupid I was. She would regularly hit students very hard on their legs and hands with rulers. Today this would be called child abuse.

In first grade, I didn't know anything about death or funerals. I had a goldfish that died and that was about it. When the parish priest died, his open coffin was in the church. Sister A. took her class to see him. I was so scared. She wanted each of us to go up to his coffin and say a prayer. I didn't want to go. She forced me to go up to his coffin and then she pushed my head down to look at him. I was screaming and crying. In second grade, my mom and dad put me in public school and I made straight As. I loved school. I wasn't afraid. I could go on and on about the things Sister A. said to me. It's because of her that I said I'd never put my kids in Catholic school.

℞ Evil usually refers to something bad, immoral, malicious, wicked, harmful, ruinous, and the list goes on. Sister A. is a personification of evil; she fits many of the previous characterizations. Her wickedness is obscured by her holy robes, which have long been associated with goodness and purity. Her evil enjoyed a daily feast of physical, emotional, and psychological abuse of children. Her academic status gave her full license to indulge her evil in the classroom. She is a traitor to the cloth and her charge. She is not good and she has betrayed and abused the children entrusted in her care. The evil within her is laid bare in her treatment of the child and the dead priest. The act of forcing the screaming child's head down into the priest's coffin erases any doubt about the nun's malevolent intent.

Child abuse often finds its way into the classrooms via teachers who may have been abused as children. These teachers may find themselves terrorizing and humiliating their students and hating themselves for it, yet they are powerless to stop.

Insightful teachers who realize that their behaviors and words are abusive take ownership of the problem and seek solutions. They explore their own history of abuse and unrealistic expectations of children, their stress and tolerance level, and their need to control their life. Teachers are caregivers and they fall into the same categories as parents. If they are abusive, like some parents, they need the same treatment as abusive parents. Caring professionals will get some help and counseling and will work on their issues.

Good teachers who have addressed their own issues and dysfunction can provide the care and understanding needed to discuss death with small children. Sensitive teachers know that children's feelings run deep. They would not force children to view a dead person against their wishes. Death education is an important part of child development. This type of education is best accomplished through bibliotherapy, social studies of cultural practices, and religious beliefs about death. A caring adult in a warm, supportive environment should handle death education, exercising caution to avoid creating anxiety or stress for the child.

SCENARIO 9.2
It's Snowing Down South

I had an experience of having to go in front of the class to give a book report with my slip hanging out. Even though the teacher knew about my problem, she made me go in front of the class anyway. This happened in third grade.

℞ Speaking in front of an audience can be difficult for most people. If speakers are aware that something is wrong with their appearance, the experience can be traumatic. The teacher in the scenario sacrificed the student's psychological safety for a book report. She forced the child to go to the front of the class to report knowing that the child's slip was hanging down. Teachers who would do such a thing are either mean-spirited or indifferent to children's feelings.

Caring teachers are aware of the fragility of children's self-esteem and seek to keep it intact. Astute teachers can anticipate situations that may cause students distress and will avoid them. Good teachers would have the student give the report from her seat rather than have her embarrass herself in front of the class. Another alternative would be to let the child go to the restroom and either repair or remove the slip.

SCENARIO 9.3
Sins of Big Sister Visited on Little Sister

My ninth-grade year, I was taking geometry with Ms. M. She also taught my eleventh-grade sister trigonometry. My sister and Ms. M. did not get along because my sister would correct her answers. Ms. M. invariably took this out on me. She was very nasty to me.

R̵ The battle rages on. The teacher picked up the gauntlet to continue the fight with a new student who happened to be the sister of an old enemy. Apparently, the teacher was entertaining a great deal of displaced anger and was directing it toward the younger sister. Some teachers project undesirable qualities of former students onto their brothers and sisters. There are some teachers that expect their current students to follow in their brother or sister's footsteps. When they fail to live up to those expectations, these teachers make them feel inferior with comments like "You're nothing like your sister; she was a good student." Some teachers give siblings less credit for assignments and assume they copied the work of their sister or brother.

Discerning teachers know that students are individuals and not extensions of their brothers or sisters. Each student should be allowed to fail or succeed on his or her own merit. Good teachers wipe the slate clean for everyone that leaves. This gives all incoming students a fresh start. If teachers have a bad experience with former students, they should address the problems when they occur or let them go away with the students that caused them. The sins of a big sister should never be visited upon her sibling.

Mistake

10

Racial and Cultural Discrimination

SCENARIO 10.1
Cross-Cultural Confusion

My worst experience was when I was in first grade. My teacher was a racist and I felt she really had it in for us (another Hispanic little boy and me). She made me stay after school every day. I hated going to school. She would yell at me in front of the whole class because I couldn't understand what she was instructing me to do much less read in a language that was so foreign to me. The worst was that when she would yell at me, everyone laughed at me. It still hurts to remember.

℞ Culture may be described as socially transmitted behavioral patterns, knowledge, values, beliefs, attitudes, interactions with others, arts, products, and thoughts. Is there any doubt that different sociocultural groups will understand and perceive the world in different ways? I think not. Members of a culture may effectively transmit implicit information or information that is understood although it is not expressed directly to another member of that culture. However, when the same implicit information is communicated across cultures, there may be some miscommunication or confusion (Delpit, 1988). The children in this scenario seem to be experiencing this type of confusion. They were having difficulty understanding what the teacher wanted them to do. Unfortunately, the teacher appeared oblivious to what was really happening in this exchange. Apparently, she thought that yelling and public ridicule would solve her communication problems. Her less-than-professional tactics, possibly conceived in prejudice, only served to damage the self-esteem of these language minority students and make them hate her and hate school.

Enlightened teachers are aware of the problems of cross-cultural communication. They are very explicit in their communication of directions, rules, answers to questions, and so on. They know that children from different cultures may misinterpret their directions or instructions. Heath (1983) concedes that minority students may misinterpret veiled teacher commands. The students may take such commands literally because they do not understand the implicit meaning. Professional teachers want to be aware of their biases or discriminatory behavior. They want to expose them to the light of truth. They know the potential psychosocial costs to their students and demand the eradication of any biases.

SCENARIO 10.2
Cinderella in the Classroom

My worst experience in elementary school was in the first grade. The first day of class, our teacher told us that girls should not wear shorts to class because it would distract the boys. The following week, my mom decided to send me in shorts; even though I begged her not to put shorts on me, she insisted. I was terrified of what might happen to me that day. When I arrived to class, my first-grade teacher embarrassed me in front of all the class and told me to go home because shorts were not allowed in her classroom. I began to cry as I walked to the office. My mom was called and was very upset because she had embarrassed me in front of the class for wearing shorts. I was placed in another class; however, after that incident, I was afraid of teachers and became very timid.

℞ To assume that all teachers are rational and emotionally stable would be a grievous error. I question the teacher's rationale for banning shorts in her classroom. I seriously doubt that little girls in shorts would distract first-grade boys. I think given the choice, boys this young would be more easily and readily distracted by a toy matchbox car. I think she was overzealous in her efforts to enforce such a rule. It seems her own dark thoughts had clouded her vision. If the children were much older, maybe a little concern would be justified.

Teachers who understand child development realize that first graders have not achieved the level of sexual maturity that would cause them to be "distracted" by the opposite sex. These astute teachers would think it ludicrous to impose a rule that reflected such outmoded, puritanical beliefs. Caring teachers are wise enough not to punish a child for actions that are beyond their control. When I was a graduate student working as a substitute teacher, I encountered a similar situation. I had a second-grade class that was supposed to attend an awards ceremony that was being held at a neighboring church. The church had a rule that no shorts were allowed. Unfortunately, a little girl came to school in shorts.

She appeared to be a neglected child. The teachers were quick to swoop down on her, demanding to know why she wore shorts. The child just cowered and looked down at the floor. Some of the more verbal teachers told her that she would not be attending the ceremony and that she would have to remain at the school.

This was a big annual event that everyone would be attending except a few staff people. The little girl said nothing. I asked if I could call her parents and ask them to bring her something else to wear. Several teachers laughed and said the mother was probably passed out from drinking. When I offered to drive to the little girl's house during the break, several people said it would not do any good. I realized there was only one other alternative: I had to buy her something to wear. I rushed out during lunch and asked the shopkeeper to help me. When I told her what I was trying to do, she pitched in to help me find something, and she gave me a discount. I rushed back and enlisted the help of another teacher. I thought it was better to have someone else present to help her get dressed. The little girl went into the bathroom to change her clothes. We helped her button up; we washed her face, combed her hair and put her new barrettes on her hair. The kids in the class were teasing her when she was wearing shorts. When she came out in her new dress, everyone just looked at her quietly. Everyone in class attended the ceremony, but wonder of wonders, the only person to win an award was the little girl. She won first place in an art competition. It would have been a shame if she had missed that honor through no fault of her own. When she received her award, she turned to look at me and smiled. That smile has warmed me through the years whenever I think about her. The moral of this story is if children must be punished, make sure it is for something that they can change; otherwise it is a wasted act of futility that may extol a heavy emotional price on the child.

SCENARIO 10.3
English-Only Spoken Here

The worst experience that I had with a teacher was as a senior at L.H.S. I was caught speaking Spanish in the restroom by a teacher who reacted by giving me some "licks" with a wooden paddle. He had me grab my ankles in a hall where students were walking to their respective classes. The irony of this experience was that the teacher was a Mexican American just like myself. He told me it was against the law to speak Spanish at school and that he had to make an example of me.

R̽ This Mexican American teacher's notion of "English-only spoken here" adds a new, punitive dimension to the concept of total immersion. Apparently, in the name of immersion in a second language where students hear and speak the second language only, there is zero tolerance for defaulting back to the native language. In addition to the confusion of the cognitive codeswitching that is necessary when speaking two languages, students must also cope with the confusion of being punished for a perfectly natural act (speaking in their native language). The teacher may have been well-meaning in his misguided attempts to make sure that his students become proficient in English, a must if the students are to become part of mainstream America. Unfortunately, the English-only approach focuses a "deficit" lens on speaking Spanish that diminishes students' sense of self-concept and self-worth. Some theorists believe that the consequences or adverse effects of total immersion are short-lived and worth it (Collier, 1992; Lindholm & Fairchild, 1990). However, I believe that if punishment is used to enforce immersion,

the adverse effects live on, such as in this scenario.

Astute teachers who are well-acquainted with issues of diversity know that each child is different and that what works well for one child may not work well for another. There are a variety of approaches to help a child become proficient in a second language. Partial immersion allows students to use their native language about fifty percent of the time. Research has shown that bilingual education, where students receive instruction in their native language as they learn a second language, is more effective and enhances students' self-esteem (Garcia, 1995; Moll & Diaz, 1985). Effective teachers will choose the approach that best suits the learning situation.

SCENARIO 10.4
The Transparent Mask of Prejudice

In second grade, I remember having a female teacher who seemed to be always upset about my presence. She never would tell me what I did wrong but would use a tone of voice that I knew she was upset at me. Once she sent me to the principal's office and I never knew why. The principal was never unkind to me and he sat down and showed me a book and asked questions about the pictures. I was also sent back to the class and I always wondered about that teacher. Even just a week ago, I started to remember that teacher and how cold she really was with me, but now that I'm 38 years old, I know the problem was that she was discriminating against me because I was the only Mexican in her class. This happened during the sixties when prejudice was at a very high rate.

℞ The sting of prejudice is painful for anyone, but it has to be confusing and painful for a child who is trying to understand and trust the world. Although the Mexican child in this scenario could not identify the problem, she knew something was wrong by the

teacher's tone of voice and her reactions. This teacher may not have been aware of her prejudiced feelings or that they could be so easily detected by a child.

Teachers must become global personalities, capable of teaching and caring for every child, regardless of ethnic background, religious orientation, or physical or mental challenge. Effective teachers know that they must possess adequate knowledge of diverse cultures. They must embrace and celebrate their students' differences and reject any notions of deficit concerning a particular culture (Gersten, 1996). All children want and deserve to have their teachers like them. Whenever they have a new teacher, their emotional antennae go up, searching the teacher's face and body gestures for any sign of love and acceptance or of dislike and rejection. Student antennae are sensitive to the subtlest slights. Teachers need to be aware of their feelings about certain groups of children, particularly minority youth or children who are different. They cannot hide them from the children. A candid inventory of prejudiced feelings and childhood teachings about other groups would help teachers take a good look at their feelings and attitudes and make changes where necessary. Prejudice exacts a heavy toll on those who would entertain it and on those who have the misfortune of encountering it. Prejudice has no place in a classroom.

SCENARIO 10.5
Separate and Unequal Treatment

In the first grade, the teacher put my desk in the back of a room and separated me from the rest of the class. Her reason for doing this was because I did not speak English.

℞ How to teach language minority students has been a source of controversy and debate for a long time. Researchers have offered a variety of techniques and approaches for teaching limited-English-proficient (LEP) children, but none advocate singling out LEP students and isolating them by banishing them to the periphery of the classroom where they become out of sight and out of mind. The teacher's actions may be rooted in racism, but her fear of not being able to rise to the challenge presented by LEP children also seems evident.

Teachers who successfully teach LEP children would never employ such a discriminatory practice. They realize that isolating children because they are a teaching challenge violates all the rules of effective pedagogy. The charge of teachers is to teach all children, regardless of the challenge they bring to teaching them. Delgado-Gaitan (1990) contends that language may be a major source of student academic failure.

Torrey (1983) proposes that poor academic performance of children speaking nonstandard English may be attributed more to the school's reaction to the nonstandard English than to the grammar itself. The same may be true of limited-English-proficient children. The teacher's reaction may be more of a factor. The teacher in this scenario had an unacceptable reaction to the student's language. Effective teachers react appropriately to students with language limitations. There are several strategies for teaching LEP children. Macias (1986) offers some strategies that are appropriate for this scenario; give clear directions, describe tasks accurately, demonstrate and explain new information, pace instructions, actively involve the students, and expect that all children will succeed. These basic tenets of effective pedagogy cannot be accomplished if the student is placed in the back of the room and ignored.

SCENARIO 10.6
Lesson in Oppression

My worst experience in education was undoubtedly in the fifth grade. We had just moved (again) to Montgomery, Alabama, and the year was 1962. Today I still have difficulty reminding myself of the horrors people put upon other people.

The school was integrated but that didn't matter because few blacks attended school there. Students or their parents had to purchase their own textbooks and worksheets, which excluded many from attendance.

There was one black student, D., and even though he had no books, no shoes, he still tried to make it work. Many of the students actually helped D. or tried to, but in the end, the teacher failed him miserably. I can still see his face, choking back tears at the indignation heaped upon him by this supposed "teacher."

℞ Overt racism is an insidious contaminant that befouls all that embrace it, encounter it, or just witness it. The author of this scenario witnessed man's inhumanity to man through the teacher's race-based ill treatment of another student. The teacher's intent was to hurt or discriminate against the black student, not realizing that some of the white students would experience that hurt vicariously. A study done by Woolfolk and Brooks (1983) showed that teachers are influenced by a student's physical appearance and, in some cases, may withhold smiles, approval, and eye contact, yet may readily disperse disapproval of students they perceive as less desirable. This teacher's prejudices, biases, and lower expectations for the black student obscured her view of his efforts and struggle and hardened her resolve to fail him. The long-lasting negative effects of her actions are evidenced in this author's inability to forget what happened.

Effective educators realize that they cannot let the way that they feel about children influence the way that they teach them and interact with them. This is a tall order to expect teachers to put aside their bias or prejudice toward members of a group and treat them fairly. Prejudice is a learned behavior that is fostered by stereotypes and fueled by ignorance. The good news is that prejudice can be unlearned if teachers care enough to find out more about a particular culture, to embrace diversity, and to celebrate differences. Fortunately, some changes have been made for black students since 1962.

Today, over 40 years later, teachers are beginning to accept multicultural education as an integral part of the curriculum. Today we are approximating educational opportunity for all students. We have not totally eradicated racism from the classroom, but thanks to diversity training and to advocates of multicultural education, we have chased it into a dark corner so that it is not as blatant as it once was. When enlightened educators see children struggling to overcome the effects of poverty, the barbs of racism, the barriers of class, and the shackles of ignorance, they lift those children with their words of praise and support, their high expectations, and their beliefs in their students' ability to make it. Sprinthall et al. (1994) caution that teachers must be aware of their own attitudes because those attitudes can seriously impact what is conveyed to students. Banks and Banks (1993) offer a variety of approaches to multicultural education that can help today's teachers avoid intentional or unintentional discrimination against students.

SCENARIO 10.7
Culture Clash

My worst experience that I understand now but didn't then was the teachers' lack of understanding of students' cultural background, specifically for those students who were learning English as a second language.

℞ The changing face of our nation's schools presents a host of challenges for teachers. A major challenge is the culture clash that frequently evolves from a predominantly white, female teacher workforce and an increasingly diverse student body. The U. S. workforce is 87% white and 72% of that number are women (Smith, 1995). By the year 2020, there will be 61% more Hispanic children between the ages of 14 and 17 and 47% more between the ages of 5 and 13 in the U.S. schools. The number of limited-English-proficient children increased from 1.25 million in 1979 to 2.44 million in 1995 (Smith, Young, Bae, Choy, & Alsalam, 1997). This culture clash is rooted in the differences in the cultural knowledge and economic background of teachers and students. White teachers are more likely to be middle class and minority children are more likely to be urban with low socioeconomic status. The problem as articulated by Cushner, McCelland, and Safford (1992) is that white, middle-class teachers may not be very interested in understanding the cultural differences in their more diverse students. "At best, such teachers are predisposed to regard diversity as interesting; at worst, they are likely to regard it as deficit" (p. 8).

Insightful teachers know the importance of being knowledgeable and respectful of cultural diversity. Whether they are black, white, Hispanic, or Native American, these teachers are ready for the future. They have accepted America's charge to educate all children. These teachers incorporate a variety of strategies to bridge the gap between the cultures, such as respecting students, attaching value to their responses, making classroom activities more meaningful by incorporating students' life experiences, values and culture, and by rejecting a cultural deficit model of diversity (Gersten, 1996). Most important, they will seek to understand from the child's point of view.

Mistake

11

Humiliation

While I was in high school, I had a lot of problems understanding geometry and algebra. I remember the first day I was shown higher algebraic problems and was terrified. Mr. B. was also very intimidating to me. He taught very fast and harshly. One day in class, we were doing problems on the board and he called me up to work a problem. Being that I was shy, I was struck with fear. I went up to the board and attempted to work the problem not knowing what I was doing. Mr. B. said harshly, "What are you doing? Don't you know you can't do that? What is this?" He totally humiliated me in front of the class and made me feel like an idiot, and I still have a fear of talking to teachers about things I don't understand because I don't want to feel like an idiot. I fear math to this day.

℞ Some teachers seem to think that calling students to the chalkboard grants them a license to humiliate. Chalkboards have frequently been the settings for exercises in humiliation and degradation. Teachers can call students to the board at will. Students usually don't have a choice; they must go or suffer the consequences of insubordination. Once students are at the board, they're at the mercy of their teachers. The students are psychologically naked, exposed, and at risk of looking stupid in front of the class.

Many teachers erroneously believe that they can shame students into performing well. They readily chastise or berate a student in front of an audience believing that this rather noxious form of humiliation will get better results. In some cases, it may change student behavior. Students may study and pay attention to the lesson to avoid being embarrassed in front of the class.

On the other hand, for shy students like the author, being called to the chalkboard is a terrifying experience. Shy students are afraid of exposure and are hypervigilant in their efforts to ward off shame. When they are faced with a barrage of criticism and scornful, disparaging remarks, like those remarks delivered by the teacher in this scenario, they tend to internalize them into a form of "toxic shame" (Bradshaw, 1988, p. 7) that evokes a sense of worthlessness. Instead of these students becoming better performers, they develop fears and phobias about whatever it is that evokes their shame. The author developed a fear of talking to teachers about things she didn't understand. This type of fear is bound to hinder academic performance, which suggests that shaming may reinforce poor performance.

Reasonable teachers observe a chalkboard etiquette that dictates that students should be treated with respect and understanding whenever they are forced to go to the board. These teachers are patient and helpful to students who are trying to solve problems. Judicious teachers rarely use the chalkboard as a public forum for humiliating students who don't understand the lesson material. They use chalkboards to help students. The board allows them to see the work of several students at once and to readily see who is having problems. They can help the students in trouble or dispatch other students to the board to help. If students work as teams at the board, it takes the pressure off individual students and increases the probability that students will solve the problem as they work together. Such a cooperative effort minimizes the stigma and shame associated with incorrect responses.

SCENARIO 11.2
Be Still and the Shame Will Settle

In second grade, my gym coach brought it to everyone's attention that I could not do the required pull-ups for the skills test. This was in front of a gym full of students, several combined PE classes. It was so embarrassing. There were other coaches around, but they did not say anything to help my pride.

℞ An insensitive gym coach focused a spotlight of shame on an unsuspecting student. The coach sought to humiliate her as a reprimand for not doing the required pull-ups for a skills test. He showed unabashed contempt for the student by bringing her shortcomings to everyone's attention. The poor student, unable to escape the glaring light of shame, felt exposed and caught off guard. She felt an inability to cope with the situation and looked around for adult intervention and assistance. None was forthcoming. She felt an inability to cope with her situation in the presence of so many onlookers. In effect, she was experiencing shame as embarrassment (Bradshaw, 1988). This is probably what the coach intended. He was using shame as a motivator to get the student to do the required number of pull-ups.

Sensitive, knowledgeable teachers know that shame is not a motivator; in fact, shame can be an inhibitor. Children can internalize shame and continue to feel its effects into adulthood. Good teachers would first rule out any physical reasons that the student could not perform the pull-ups. Next, they might use a multiple intelligences approach in teaching the student to do pull-ups (Campbell, Campbell, & Dickinson, 1996). Using this approach, teachers must believe that students have strengths across content areas and must encourage them to pursue those strengths while minimizing their weaknesses. If the student does not have the arm strength to engage in pull-ups, perhaps she can improve her arm strength by lifting weights or by working out on a rowing machine.

SCENARIO 11.3
Shake, Baby, Shake

My worst experience was in second grade. My teacher would grab us by the arms, shake us, and get right in our face and yell at us. I remember being so embarrassed after she did this. She yelled at me because I was crying about having no friends; boy that really helped. NOT!

℞ The same dynamics that underlie shaken baby syndrome (Lancon, Haines, & Parent, 1998) are present in this scenario. In shaken baby syndrome, caregivers become very frustrated in their efforts to console or quiet a crying child. They resort to grabbing the child by the shoulders and shaking her back and forth in such a way that her brain hits the inside of her skull. The child may suffer a serious injury and, in some cases, death.

In this scenario, the teacher's actions were the same but the prognosis is better because the children were older and the shaking was milder. The teacher did grab the child and shake her. The child's crying triggered the teacher's actions. The teacher apparently lost control and started yelling. There was no sympathy for the child's friendless plight, only humiliation.

Effective teachers would try to find out why the child is crying rather than try to suppress the crying through humiliation and physical aggression. If they find that they cannot console a child, they know that it's okay to let the child cry. Perceptive teachers use sociograms (McConnell & Odom, 1986) to ascertain student popularity, student cliques and friendships, and students who are social isolates. Once they are aware of the unpopular or isolated students, they can make efforts to help those students. One strategy might be to pair students to work together to pave the way for friendship. Good teachers might offer one-on-one help sessions on how to make friends. A foolproof strategy for making a friend is for the teacher to volunteer to be the child's first friend.

SCENARIO 11.4
Girls Will Be Girls

My two best friends and I were in music class and while the teacher wasn't looking, we wrote the names of the boys we liked all over the chairs. After music, we returned to our separate classrooms and went on with our business. At the time, they were constructing a new building with classrooms, so the two sixth-grade classes were in a portable building separated by a wall and a door that could open up to both sides. About thirty minutes later, our music teacher opened the door and stood in the middle of the classrooms. She told both our teachers she needed to see me and my two best friends, and the three boys whose names we wrote on the chairs. All of us had to go to the music room, and the boys sat there while we cleaned the chairs off. When we were done, we returned to class and everybody knew what happened. How embarrassing!

Rx Three young female students, under the influence of cupid's sting, felt compelled to express their love by writing the names of their love interests all over the chairs in their music class. Unfortunately, writing all over the chairs is the willful defacing of school property, which can be considered vandalism. The teacher was taking appropriate action by insisting the girls return to the class and clean up the chairs. She overstepped her boundaries when she demanded that the young men named on the chairs come and watch the young women clean up. The teacher's motives were suspect. What was her purpose, to correct undesirable behavior or to evoke shame?

Understanding teachers are aware of the preteen period where young girls develop secret crushes. The crushes are secret because the girls are so immature that they don't quite know what to do with their newly acquired love feelings. Most girls find harmless outlets such as diaries and telephone conversations. Crushes are an important dimension of a young girl's psychosocial development that should be respected. Sensitive teachers would have punished the girls' undesirable behavior while respecting their privacy and keeping their dignity intact. These teachers know that students should be punished for their offensive behavior but not for their feelings. Prudent teachers would not pull the young men from their classes to participate in the shaming of the young women. The young men were unwilling, unknowing players in the young women's little escapade; there was no reason for them to be present. If the girls had written teachers' names all over the chairs, would the music teacher insist that the teachers come and watch the girls clean up? I have my doubts.

SCENARIO 11.5
Tomāto or Tomäto? Pēcan or Pecän?

I just moved to Texas from Georgia. I was in the fifth grade. I was selected to read out loud. I came across the word pecan. I said "pe-can" instead of pecan. My male teacher quickly corrected me and made me feel dumb for saying it wrong even though that's how I was taught to say it.

℞ The teacher publicly corrected a student for using a different pronunciation of the word *pecan*. The student was humiliated because she was made to feel ignorant about something she assumed was correct.

Knowledgeable teachers know that the phonology, or speech sounds, of the English language are varied and in some cases interchangeable.

Words like *pecan* and *tomato* may be pronounced one way in one part of the country and another way in a different part of the country. Either way is correct. These teachers accept the student's version of the word as correct. Privately, they may make the student aware of the alternate pronunciation of the word, but they will not insist that students adopt their pronunciation of the word.

3

CLASSROOM POLICIES AND PRACTICES

"I don't like to give a lot of homework over
the weekend, so just read every other word."

Mistake

12

Inappropriate Classroom Policies

SCENARIO 12.1
New Kid on the School Block

When I moved during the middle of a school year to a new school, the teacher at the new school didn't really make me feel welcome. I was so nervous on school days that I literally "threw up" before school. Why I was scared of this teacher, I really don't know. Eventually, it got to the point where I would refuse to go to school! No one was going to make me go to school! Thereafter, I was placed in a new room and enjoyed my school year. The bad experience was that the teacher was cold and uninviting to new children. I believe she expected me to already know the material that she had been teaching. I had no idea what was going on in her classroom. She really didn't take time to explain things to me.

R The cold reception that the teacher gave this new student suggests that she viewed the new student as an "unwelcome" responsibility or perhaps a burden! The administration may have forced her to take a new student at a time when she felt she already had too many students. She apparently took out her frustrations and hostilities on the unsuspecting child. She was able to act out her displeasure by refusing to explain anything to the child and by refusing to do any extra work to bring the child on board.

Insightful educators would realize that any anger or hostility directed toward a new student is probably displaced. If there is a teacher–pupil ratio problem, the teacher and the administrators own it and not the new student. True professionals will make any efforts that are necessary to bring the child up to date; they will provide tutoring if needed and will try not to make the child feel deficient in the process. Wise teachers give new students warm welcomes, mostly because they want to, but also because they know that today's disaffected, alienated new student can be tomorrow's discipline problem.

SCENARIO 12.2
Banished to the Underworld

I remember being spanked on my hands with a ruler for talking in class in fourth grade. This same teacher didn't like me so she put me in a lower level of reading. Guess what? That only lasted one day because my mother came to the school the following day and things changed. I went back to the higher reading group. To this day, I still don't care for Mrs. C. I'm trying to forgive her but incidents like this stay with you all your life.

℞ Some of the laments that have echoed through educational corridors for decades are: "The teacher didn't like me so she put me in a low group," "she gave me a bad grade," or "she kept me in for recess." These unfortunate perceptions usually emerge from a lack of communication between teachers and students. In some instances, these charges are true. I believe the scenario teacher deliberately put this child into a lower reading group as a punitive measure, particularly because she had to move the child from the higher reading group. She had spanked the child earlier for talking and it seems she exploited the negatives and stigma associated with low-level grouping and used them as a discipline tactic.

Effective, caring teachers would not use low achievement status, grades, or the like as a means of discipline. This strategy is unfair and ineffective. It only serves to alienate the student. If there is a need to place a child in a lower reading group, the teacher should feel assured that the benefits of such a move would outweigh the risk of harm.

The desirable strategy would be to communicate to the student the rationale for moving that student to a lower group. An even better approach would be to get the child's consent and agreement that spending some time in a lower group might be helpful. If the child has some input and ownership in the move, the change may be more palatable and effective. If the child is against the move, she has a right to remain in the group and to try to do better. Moving the child to a lower group should be a last resort.

SCENARIO 12.3
It's Now or Never

The incident I remember most involved my tenth-grade math teacher. I had been sick for a few days and the day I returned, she made me take a test. I asked her if I could take it a couple of days later, as I had been too sick to study while out. We also didn't have syllabi at my school, and I remember being surprised that there was a test. She was very rude to me and with an ugly tone she said she didn't care and I had to take it now, during that class while the rest of the class moved on. Needless to say, I didn't know the material well and did quite poorly on the test.

℞ A common fear among teachers is the fear of being duped and misled by students making excuses for missing a test. The fear is compounded by a fear of looking foolish. To protect themselves from such occurrences, some teachers take a very hard stand and refuse to give anyone make-up assignments. Over the years, they harden as they sacrifice compassion and empathy for rigidity and control. The hostile tone of voice, the lack of caring, and the air of indifference become barricades that say, "don't dare try me."

Insightful teachers know that it is possible to be compassionate, understanding, and empathic and still be a strong teacher. They are secure enough as teachers that being duped by a student, some of the time, is not a major problem. Of course, these teachers may ask questions, require proof, or reserve the right to check into a situation before granting a student's request, but they do it with an open mind. They make every effort to say yes to students' reasonable requests.

Another important point to consider is that tests are merely a means of providing feedback. Forcing the student to take the test only told the teacher what she already knew, that the student was not prepared to take the test. Reasonable teachers would say, "I'm sorry you were ill. I'll schedule a make-up test for you in a few days." Conditionally, they might require that the student furnish a doctor's statement or have a parent verify the illness. A last, not so minor, point was the student's surprise that there was a test. This could be the student's fault or the teacher's fault. If it is the teacher's fault, it could indicate a flawed testing policy. It is true that scheduling tests at variable intervals can be very effective and can encourage persistence (Skinner, 1950), but to keep students on their toes, it is necessary to make them aware that there may be surprise tests or pop quizzes so they can stay prepared.

SCENARIO 12.4
One for You and One for You and None for You

One negative thing happened to me in second grade. I was struggling with my times tables, but the class seemed to be going so fast. The teacher, who I really liked, told us we were going to have a pop times test and it would be timed. She said it should be so easy. So she gave it to us, calling out, "2 × 2," "5 × 5." Everyone around me jotted down the answers. I was lost and so frustrated. At the end of the test, she had us turn it in and while we read, she graded them. She handed them out, congratulating the class. She said, "You all did so great. Mostly 100s!!" There were all but two 100s and I was one. She gave all the 100s a penny and told them to go to the office and get a piece of gum. I felt so left out and cried in front of everyone! I will never forget that.

Rx This teacher has the mistaken impression, shared by many teachers, that group competition is an effective motivator. She announced that the test was going to be "so easy," which implied that everyone should be able to do it. In spite of the teacher's overconfidence, two of the students did not make a perfect score. She seemed happy that there were mostly 100s yet she only rewarded the students that made 100. Her actions suggested that she expected perfection; 100% of the students making 100%.

Skilled professionals recognize that there are very few tasks that are mastered by 100% of the class at any given time. Such expectations are frustrations under construction.

Instead, reasonable teachers recognize student effort when evaluating student performance. This teacher could have established a policy of recognizing self-competition as well as group competition. Self-competition takes effort and improvement into consideration. She should have given everyone in the class a penny and she should have recognized the efforts of the two students that did not make the grade. She could motivate them by saying, "I could see you were trying very hard. I'm going to help you practice your times tables and I'm sure you'll do better next time." Effective teachers know that there is much more mileage to be gained from encouragement than there is from exclusion.

SCENARIO 12.5
Sour Note Switch

When I was a senior in high school, I was first chair flute in the symphonic band and the marching band. I was a soloist, and the only flute player who could play a specific solo in a piece. However, I was always out of tune on the high notes and could never figure out why. What was bad about this was when the band was on a trip to a competition. My teacher waited until an hour before our performance and suddenly informed me I wasn't going to play that solo and gave it to the second chair flutist (who didn't know how to play it but had a nice tone!). I was rather humiliated by the way he did this, and then, afterward, on the bus, he informed me that the band hadn't even been competing! He did this to encourage the second chair to be interested in band for the next year, but then she quit, so it was all for naught. He was brusque, gave me no warning, and then tried to act happy!

If he needed to do that and I can see why, he did it in a very poor manner and offended me, my pride, and should have explained things a bit better. I would hope I would avoid bruising students' pride.

Rx The band teacher hit some sour notes on several counts in this not-so-virtuoso performance. He failed to give the student appropriate feedback on her achievement. He

understandably was not happy with her performance but he chose a very ineffectual method of apprising her of the changes he planned to make. Giving the solo to the second chair at the last minute was less than honest and showed a reckless disregard for this student's feelings. His motive for making the change was questionable. He gambled with his student's pride and he lost.

A true maestro would be up front and honest and provide students with useful feedback and constructive criticism. He would make his students aware of their status in class and help them devise strategies for improvement. The sagacious teacher will always consider students' feelings and pride when making evaluative decisions.

SCENARIO 12.6
Broken Bones: Give the Student a Break

It happened years ago, while attending classes at Tidewater Community College. It was my sophomore year; I was taking twelve credits at the time. One weekend prior to the beginning of the class, my TV antenna fell off. I climbed on the roof, fixed the antenna, and as I was coming down from the roof, my foot slipped and I fell down to the ground. I broke both of my wrists and had a cast put on both of my arms up to my shoulders.

This is not all. I had to drop some of my classes and of course the first one to go was Drawing II. I was also taking physical science. I did not want to drop this class, thinking that with a tutor's help and the understanding of my teacher, I could pass this class. I worked very hard. I took a cassette with me every day. I had one of my classmates take notes for me, but at the end of the course, I received an F. I am not complaining about the grade even though I did not think it was fair. I am complaining about my teacher not communicating with me prior to the cut-off day of the drop–add date.

℞ This student's accident precluded her ability to participate in school as she had previously done. She reasoned that she could succeed with some tutoring and with the teacher's understanding. In spite of her hard work and efforts, she received an F for the course. The teacher obviously did not share the student's optimism and, judging from the student's comments, there was very little if any communication about the status of the student's grade or of the student's progress.

Proficient educators anticipate that students may have emergencies or illnesses that interfere with their education, so they have liberal policies in place to accommodate these students. The scenario teacher could have been more understanding by offering the student some assistance, by being flexible about assignment-due dates, and by keeping the student aware of her progress. In this student's case, it would have been prudent for the teacher to advise the student to drop the course if the student was unable to make suitable progress. Teachers that are very rigid and inflexible about student illnesses are ineffective and are often a barrier to student progress. I had a math professor whose policy was three absences—an automatic F. I had the flu and I missed class for a week. Up to that point, I had a B or better in the course. I could not believe that anyone could be so unfeeling about student illness, so I thought if I stayed in the class and worked really hard that she would give me some consideration. At the end of the course I had a B+ but she gave me an F because of the absences. To this day, the college has factored this F into my grade point average and they refuse to change. I took the course again and they still would not change it. I gave up trying years ago. My math teacher's rigid policy had very far-reaching effects. Rigid teachers are concerned about students taking advantage of them. I think it is better to err on the side of leniency than to err on the apex of inflexibility.

SCENARIO 12.7
The Shaming of the Crew

The worst experience I had with a teacher was when I was in the second grade. I had trouble pronouncing my Rs so the teacher took all of the kids that were having trouble with pronunciation to another class. In the other class, another teachers' aide helped the kids having trouble. I don't know why this bothered me so badly, but it did and it has stuck with me ever since. Now though, I am glad I had extra practice, and the teacher I know had good intentions. I guess I felt like an idiot in front of all the other classmates.

℞ The student in this scenario was feeling the classic effects of the stigma that is often associated with remediation. The scenario teacher's handling of this situation generated unnecessary shame and stress. She very publicly pointed out the students' deficiencies and assigned those students to another class for additional instruction. The problem was that it was a lower level class, and the student was shamed in spite of the teacher's good intentions.

Perceptive educators would anticipate that sending a child to a lower class could cause shame if it was done publicly. Sending a child to a lower class should be a last resort. Considering there was only one skill involved, pronouncing Rs, why didn't the second-grade teacher try to work with the students before sending them to someone else? Perhaps a reason not to try to help them was that there was an obvious speech problem that needed the special attention of a speech therapist. I doubt if that was the case because there were so many students having problems. All of them didn't have speech problems. If the teacher thought it was truly necessary to send the students to another class, she could have done so without the rest of the class knowing why or by doing it under the guise of the students going to help with the students in the lower grade. Of course, as they are "helping," they also would receive additional instruction.

SCENARIO 12.8
Last Picks

My worst experience during my younger years was probably PE. Until the middle of the eighth grade, I was one of the shortest in the class. I was also, to put it nicely, one of the scrawniest kids. In picking teams, the coach would have two of the most athletic kids pick teams for sports. Almost every time, I was the last or the next to the last chosen.

My revenge was during my eighth- and ninth-grade years when I "bloomed." I worked out over the summer breaks and was on the junior high football team. I would pick the smaller kids as well as the athletic ones.

℞ The practice of letting the good players choose their teams has been around for decades. Countless children have been psychologically scarred by this practice for a variety of reasons. They were too fat, too slow, too scrawny, too clumsy, and so forth, and they were usually among the last to be picked. Teachers rarely intervene in this process.

Insightful teachers can usually predict the outcome of this potentially discriminatory practice and prefer to seek alternative methods of team selection. Random methods of selection are more appropriate. These teachers will anticipate that some of the better players may groan or make derogatory remarks about less-able players, but they usually make it clear that there will be zero tolerance for such comments.

SCENARIO 12.9
Speak First, Think Later

My worst experience in school happened in my first semester of college. My sociology professor asked the class if anyone personally knew someone who committed suicide. He then proceeded to go through the class one by one hearing each student's answer. If they had known someone they said how they were associated with the person and how the person died. Needless to say, halfway through class it was my turn. My mother shot and killed herself less than a month before so it was hard for me to answer. I physically shook as I answered. I flatly said that my mother had shot herself a month ago. It was difficult because of the recentness of her death but also because of the others who had spoken before were obviously just speaking of some they had heard of or a mere acquaintance.

℞ Asking sensitive questions that have the potential to psychologically damage a child is an inappropriate educational practice.

The teacher in this scenario was probably a novice or a nitwit. To ask students if they knew someone who committed suicide is akin to lighting the fuse of a potentially explosive charge and standing back to observe the fireworks. If the student knew the suicide victim, therein lies the probability that the student may have had feelings for that person. What objective could possibly be accomplished by probing vulnerable psyches with such sharp, blunt questions?

Insightful practitioners would be astute enough to have a firm policy of avoiding asking inappropriate questions. Experienced professionals anticipate the psychological minefields that surround intrusive questions. If a teacher wants to discuss a sensitive issue, such as suicide, it might be prudent to first ask the students if discussing the subject would be uncomfortable for anyone or if they would prefer to save this topic for a later time. Offering to postpone the discussion would give any student who is uncomfortable, but reluctant to say so, a way out of the discussion. Prepared teachers anticipate changes in topic and prepare the day's lesson accordingly. Caring teachers will think through their questions to avoid saying anything that may cause their students distress or discomfort.

SCENARIO 12.10
The Perils and Pearls of Mandatory Attendance

I grew up with strict academic codes, so it was difficult for me to miss days from school. This was especially true as a young child when my parents dictated everything in my life. While this strict rule helped me out for a great deal of my life, it also backfired a few times when I was forced to go to school even if I was feeling under the weather. I remember one sick day when I was in my seventh-grade English class. We were required to read a play in class while our substitute teacher supervised us. This was one of the worst flu seasons according to the teachers, and a good portion of our class was missing. I was in class even though I had the flu. As I sat in class reading the play, I was so ill and tired from reading, that I unknowingly fell asleep. All of the sudden, the virus decided to show itself via vomiting all over the person sitting in front of me. I was sent home for a week until I got over the flu.

℞ The perils and pearls of strict classroom policies are evident in this scenario. The student acknowledges that a strict attendance policy was beneficial most of the time, but it seemed to backfire in difficult situations such as illness.

Overly strict adherence to rules, with zero flexibility, rapidly approaches pathology. Knowledgeable teachers would hesitate to have an attendance policy where children are forced to attend class whether they are sick or well. Wise teachers would send a sick child home immediately. Experienced teachers usually have a policy to handle illnesses. They ask parents to keep their children at home if the child has a fever. Parents and children are usually motivated to try to keep perfect attendance records and they favor attending school in spite of illness. Teachers can resolve this dilemma by having flexible rules that do not count excused absences against perfect attendance. If attendance is an administrative matter, administrators should consider the approach previously outlined for teachers.

SCENARIO 12.11
Sounding Off

The fifth-grade teacher would say the meanest things about me. She would make me leave the classroom to blow my nose—"nobody wants to hear that." She would give everybody else stickers just because she "liked" them, not because of their academic qualifications. No Band-Aids can ever make it right.

℞ The teacher in this scenario had a natural reaction to an offensive body sound. She reacted so intensely that the child was offended and perceived her comments as mean-spirited.

Practical teachers know that in a classroom situation, potentially offensive body sounds such as blowing the nose, hacking coughs, passing gas, belching, or burping are inevitable. Experienced teachers ignore these sounds if possible. For situations that are impossible to ignore, these teachers set up an effective classroom policy to address these foreseeable events. They might have a "quick pass" that students can pick up at any time that they need to excuse themselves. The "quick pass" alerts the teacher that the student has a personal emergency that requires immediate attention. Teachers should explain the rules of using the "quick pass," such as the shorter length of time, and so forth. The goal is to take care of students' needs without drawing attention to the student or disturbing the class.

SCENARIO 12.12
"Loser of the Week": A Real Loser

In high school, my math teacher would ask each student to tell the class something that had happened to them. This tidbit could be something that was stupid, embarrassing, or silly. Then she would choose what she called "Loser of the Week." This person had to stand in the front of the classroom where the entire class would salute him or her by making a big "r" sign with his or her arms. We had this helmet we had to wear and a special desk in the front of the room. I was the loser many times.

℞ The first two sentences of this scenario raise the question of "What is the point?" The practice of selecting the loser of the week is either a sadistic, malicious act, or a bad joke that has gone too far. Having students taunt and ridicule the student who had the dubious honor of being chosen is reminiscent of the bygone days of Roman persecution of people with different religious beliefs. Forcing the "victim" of this hapless practice to wear a helmet and sit at a special desk conjures up the specter of a jeering audience surrounding a helpless person in the coliseum. The author of the scenario was obviously a naive, trusting child because the child continued to reveal sensitive, embarrassing information. The teacher betrayed that confidentiality each time with shaming behavior. This worthless practice places the child at risk for internalizing this negative labeling and class ridicule. The label "loser" could lower the child's self-esteem and could become a self-fulfilling prophecy (Rosenthal & Jacobson, 1968). It is chilling to think of what a teacher hopes to gain from such pathology.

When teachers ask students to reveal sensitive information, that information should be handled with a priority level of confidentiality. Anything less than this violates the students' trust. Once revealed, this sensitive information must not be used against the student. Parents are paying more attention to the types of questions or inquiries given to their children. Recently in Texas, parents were disturbed by an intrusive psychological questionnaire that was administered to their children. To avoid a lawsuit, the school district banned the questionnaire and agreed to let some of the parents observe them shredding the documents. The best practice is to avoid asking students for sensitive information unless it is absolutely necessary and only if the benefits of such an inquiry clearly outweigh any potential harm to the child.

SCENARIO 12.13
Only "Smart" Questions, Please

The worst experience I ever had with a teacher was when I was in the seventh grade. The teacher would always seem to pick on me as if I was doing something wrong. He was like a sergeant in the army. If you moved, your name went on the board. If you raised your hand to ask a question, he would say, "You'd better not be asking me anything stupid." I couldn't understand him because the whole purpose for raising my hand was to ask questions if I didn't understand. If I had the choice, I wouldn't recommend him to anyone.

℞ Control. The crux of this problem is the teacher's excessive need for control. He could control students' behavior but he found it difficult to deal with the uncertainty of what they might say. To minimize his powerlessness over their questions, he intimidated his students by daring them to ask a "stupid" question. Students that do not understand the instruction may not know if their question is stupid and rather than appear stupid, they will not ask. Shutting his students up is also an insurance policy that will guarantee that he will not be asked anything that he cannot answer.

Rational teachers realize that there are no "stupid" questions if a child does not understand. Different people process information in different ways. They selectively attend to some incoming information and ignore other information. Most important is that they perceive information in different ways. Considering the differences in information processing, it is understandable that a student could misunderstand some instruction or confuse it with information that was learned previously. Experienced teachers try to cultivate a classroom environment that is conducive to learning and asking questions. Truly perceptive teachers can read students' body language and anticipate that they have a question and ask those students if they understand. Teachers should exercise caution using this approach, being careful not to call on any one student too often, lest it suggests that the student is slower or less capable than are other students. The best strategy for teachers is to flirt with uncertainty and invite questions, but be willing to admit it when they do not know the answer. They can always tell the students they will try to find the answer later, or they can find the answer as a class.

SCENARIO 12.14
Help Wanted

I did not understand how to subtract and no one was willing to work with me.

R_x A brief scenario such as this one is deceptively complex because of its simplistic form. This student's unanswered plea for help has profound underpinnings of "academic negligence." The teacher was negligent in that she was responsible for helping her students acquire and understand new concepts and obviously she did not do that. Experienced teachers review prerequisite knowledge before they attempt to teach new concepts. They teach the concept or idea and follow up by trying to ascertain if everyone understands. This probing can be accomplished by questioning students about their understanding of the new material. If there seems to be some confusion or misunderstanding, skilled teachers have a repertoire of instructional techniques to provide alternative ways of imparting knowledge. If some students still do not understand the material after repeated attempts to teach the new material, good teachers will work with them one-on-one to help students learn the new information.

SCENARIO 12.15
Off on a Tangent

My tenth-grade algebra teacher—I never learned anything in that class because all we did was to try to get him talking about other things. Because of this, I feel that I didn't like algebra (hated it) and I didn't think I would ever need it again—until college. College algebra was and still is my worst subject and worst grade I have ever had. It was boring in tenth grade and even more so in college.

℞ This algebra teacher routinely allowed his students to distract him or get him "off on a tangent," as it was called when I was in high school. Apparently, he did not have a lesson plan or syllabus. The consequences of this type of distraction are many: The students are not engaged, little if any learning occurs, and the students become disenfranchised with the course. The scenario teacher failed to make maximum use of class time. He failed to create a sense of responsibility about doing the work because he showed little concern for delivering the instruction.

Competent educators usually prepare for each class. They have goals and objectives to meet and they use a syllabus or lesson plan to guide them and keep them on task. These teachers are flexible enough to allow for some deviation from the topic if the subject is provocative and the students are very excited. However, wise teachers are watchful for deliberate attempts to distract them. Skilled professionals know how to bring the students back to the lesson. They have an obligation to manage class time effectively to maximize the instructional contribution to their students. Good teachers periodically assess their progress with the material they plan to cover and make adjustments as needed. The old adage, "Those who fail to plan, plan to fail," applies here. A lesson plan, or at the very least, an agenda, is necessary to stay focused.

SCENARIO 12.16
Worksheet Workout

In fifth grade I was placed in a different class than all of my friends who were together in one class. The class I was in was much slower, boring, and the teacher seriously didn't like me. We were forced to do silent worksheets and spelling tests all year, which was extremely boring.

℞ A blatant misuse of seatwork is evident in this scenario. To force students to work silently on worksheets all year is counterproductive and boring. Worksheets are usually reserved for follow-up work to reinforce concepts learned in direct instruction. Some teachers occasionally use worksheets as time fillers or busy work. To be effective, worksheets should be interesting and engaging and should not be boring or useless. The latter makes it difficult for students to stay on task (Charles, 1983).

Resourceful educators will employ a variety of instructional strategies and materials to effect behavioral outcomes. Informed teachers are aware of the research that suggests that student learning is enhanced when students are allowed to talk, to work together, and to move about as they engage in learning tasks. Worksheets can be effective if they are used for follow-up, practice, and individualized instruction. They should never be a singular mode of instruction.

SCENARIO 12.17
Let Your Fingers Do the Reading

When I was in sixth grade my teacher divided us into groups in my reading class by the way we pronounced words on a list. I of course went into the slow readers group. I never liked to read after that. It was never fun because she made us follow along with our fingers and to me that was degrading. In my senior year my English teacher got me to read a book and I now enjoy reading this certain author plus other books. All it took was an interesting book and a teacher who had a positive effect on me to change my views of reading in a positive way again.

℞ This ineffective teaching practice of grouping students based on such limited criteria is bound to have some undesirable consequences. Grouping students by the way they pronounce words is a practically useless strategy. This selection process invites error and has the potential to distress a child who has been erroneously assigned to a lower group. Understandably, children in this situation would feel degraded by being forced to follow along with their fingers because this practice reflected the teacher's expectations for the low group. Kerman and Martin (1980) found that teachers have lower expectations for low-achieving groups and give them less feedback. The author of this scenario acknowledges that a lack of feedback and low expectations made her dislike reading for a time. A teacher's belief in her ability to read a book restored her interest.

Effective teachers would explore alternatives to grouping, considering the controversy that surrounds ability grouping. If they elect to use groups, the selection criteria would be explicit, appropriate, and functional enough to allow the teacher to organize students into groups of preferably five or more students to facilitate efficient, effective instruction. This type of grouping can best be accomplished by first determining a child's skill level through appropriate assessment and then matching the task to the skill level. To communicate high expectations for children, encourage them to read alone and offer assistance only when it's needed. Positive feedback plus high expectations fosters a love of reading and facilitates reading achievement.

SCENARIO 12.18
Rigid Mortis

One of my worst experiences at school was during the fall of 1995 while attending college. That semester my father-in-law passed away unexpectedly on Halloween.

I immediately notified my professors that I would not be in class for the remainder of the week. The professors were willing to work with me, with one exception.

Upon returning the following week, I approached my world geography professor about giving me a one-day extension for an exam that was scheduled that Monday at eleven o'clock. This professor indicated that he could only extend the test to another class that same day at two o'clock, but he preferred I take the test when scheduled since I was already there. I was too emotionally drained to even try to plea with him, so I took the test and failed it miserably. As if that weren't enough, my own father suffered a heart attack the week before finals leaving me totally unable to focus. I finished that semester with two Cs and an A. This greatly affected a GPA I had worked hard to build up.

℞ This professor has a severe case of "rigid mortis." He was unyielding and unmoving in his academic policies. He failed to realize that tests are merely tools for feedback. In this case the feedback merely reflected that the student was unprepared. The etiology of his "condition" seems to be rooted in a deep fear of being taken advantage of by his students. His "deaf ear" is symptomatic of a lack of compassion for student problems.

He could remedy his condition by simply judging each student's situation with a positive, open attitude and by showing more flexibility in his academic policy. compassionate professionals would make every effort to say yes to a reasonable student request. These professionals would only test a student under appropriate conditions to ensure the score would more accurately reflect a student's progress. They would also have a great deal of empathy for students with serious problems. Empathy is an important characteristic of the effective educator (Rogers, 1969).

SCENARIO 12.19
Almost Perfect Attendance

My worst experience in school can be shared by two incidents. The first was when I was in the third grade and during lunch time my teacher came into the cafeteria to tell me that my mom, grandma, and two-year-old baby brother had been in a serious car accident. My neighbor had to come and pick me up from school to take me home. The second worst memory was in the second grade. My middle brother had been hit by a car and I had to go to school. It was the worst day of my life wondering whether he was going to be okay or not. All throughout that day (I was only 7) I kept wondering if he was going to die. Such morbid thoughts for a seven-year-old to ponder, I remember crying at school and my teacher telling me my brother would be all right. I kept telling her, "But you didn't see his face." That is the most vivid memory that comes to my mind. I went to school that day because my mom didn't want me to ruin my perfect attendance.

℞ The scenario teacher seemed to be a caring individual who tried to comfort the child. Unfortunately, the teacher was treating the wrong symptom. The attendance policy is an underlying problem in this scenario. It was not very accommodating.

Reasonable teachers have flexible attendance policies where excused absences, such as death or serious crisis, do not count against a student's perfect attendance. In this case the teacher would assure the parents that he child would be excused and the perfect attendance record would remain intact. To maintain a rigid policy with no exceptions to the rule would encourage the anxiety and trauma that this child experienced. If, in spite of assuring the parents that it is okay for the child to miss school, the parents insist on the child staying in school, the prudent teacher would refer the child to the school counselor or social worker for intervention.

Mistake

13

Inappropriate Toileting Practices

> ## SCENARIOS 13.1, 13.2, 13.3, 13.4, 13.5, and 13.6
> ### You're All Wet

Six scenarios are presented to emphasize that inappropriate toileting practices are a frequently occurring problem. Clustering makes their commonalities and emergent patterns more apparent.

My worst memory took place when I was in first grade and I needed to go to the bathroom very bad. I asked for permission, but the teacher humiliated me in front of the class by telling me (almost screaming) that she was going to allow me to go to the bathroom just because I was being silly. I felt so embarrassed when she told me that in front of the other students. I had to walk out of the classroom because I was crying. I really needed to go, but instead of her understanding me, she yelled at me. I was embarrassed to face the rest of the class.

It was in first grade. I was five years old and going to a private school. One day during seatwork time, I raised my hand because I had to go to the bathroom really badly. Mrs. P. was busy working at her desk, and she didn't look up. My hand was up for a long time, and Mrs. P. still didn't notice me. I was too shy to go up to her desk, so there I sat at my desk. In five seconds there was a yellow puddle underneath my desk, and everyone was staring.

My worst experience with a teacher was when I was in first grade. I recall that I had to go to the bathroom and was not allowed to go. I was a quiet child in school. As a result of not being able to go, I wet my clothes and had to stay like that until it was time to go home. I recall there being a bathroom in our classroom but she would not allow us to use it. This teacher was old (60s, at least) and scary to me; she also was not very pleasant.

My first-grade math teacher was as mean as she could be. She never let us speak out of turn or get up from our desks. Worse than that, she would not let us go to the bathroom. We were six years old and had her for two hours in the middle of the morning and we couldn't go to the restroom!

Well, I had a bladder control problem that I had to take medicine for. At this time we didn't know about my problem. This teacher never let me go to the restroom so I would just have to go back to my desk and wet my pants. This happened at least five times and I was so embarrassed. Finally my parents told her she had to let me go. She was still mean though.

My single worst experience in school would take us way back to my kindergarten class in the year of 1981. I remember sitting on the floor in a circle with my classmates. The teacher was having some sort of "show-and-tell" demonstration. Then, I suddenly had to use the restroom, but I could not go unless I received permission from the teacher. I raised my hand and waited. The teacher didn't call on me. A few more minutes passed and nothing. I waved vigorously, moved around a lot, and wiggled tremendously. Well—I could not wait any longer. Yes, I admit I "peed" all over myself. I was so embarrassed. The only good thing was that it happened at the end of the day just before my mom came to pick me up.

The doors of knowledge had been shown to me. My mom held my hand as she led me through the door of my kindergarten classroom. I knew this was the beginning of something I didn't know. But I knew everything was going to be great. Mrs. H. had gotten over all the pushing in line, not sharing with the other students, and the wide-eyed, all-smiles naptime. She had even given me a star for behaving better. I stuck that star, which was the size of a quarter, on my forehead. Naptime came around and I tried to sleep. I really tried but I had to pee. I asked permission: I begged. I was squirming up and down and side to side. It didn't work. I felt it. A warm liquid drenched my pants and ran down my legs into a small puddle around my two little feet that only had their white socks to block out the urine. D. P., which I called her because she was huge and her named was D., sent me to the nurse who told me I need to be clean and asked me to go to the restroom. She gave me old used underwear and shorts. She gave me a note for my mom. It asked her to wash the clothes and send them back the next day. I sucked it up and finished the day. From that day on if I had to go to the restroom and my teacher said no, I would and did walk out. That was later. D. asked me every ten minutes if I had to go use the restroom. I'd go, just to walk around and waste that darn naptime.

℞ In all of the previous scenarios, students were not allowed to go to the restroom and they consequently wet their pants. Some teachers have cruel, sadistic toileting policies that leave lasting scars on innocent children. I was intrigued by the commonalities present in all of these scenarios. All six situations occurred in kindergarten and first grade. The adult authors still remember what happened in first grade, which conveys the gravity of the effect the teachers' toileting practices had on these students. In all six scenarios, the students indicated that they had to get permission of some sort to go to the restroom. They usually raised their hand or had to ask. None of the students were ever allowed to go to the restroom on their own. Three of the six referred to the teacher as mean or scary. Two of the six indicated they were shy or quiet students, the rest did not appear to be very assertive. In five out of six of the cases, there was no follow-up action or apology from the teacher. The one student who did receive some help was admonished as if wetting her pants was her fault. In all six cases, it was clear that the teacher had the power and exercised it freely. Some ignored students raising their hands, they humiliated students who dared to ask, and some just flatly denied permission to go.

One of the biggest mistakes teachers make is to presume to know if and when a child needs to use the restroom. To make such a presumption is a form of arrogance that feeds a teacher's need for power and fosters humiliation and degradation in students. Teachers have no right to deny children an opportunity to satisfy a basic human need (Maslow, 1970). It seems so cruel and inhuman that, after causing a child to have an accident, teachers force children to sit in urine-sodden clothing for long periods of time in a public place. Two patterns emerge from these scenarios. One is that physiologically, the primary grades, particularly first grade, are a critical time period for children making an adjustment to using the restroom at school. Two, psychologically, it seems to be a critical

time because accidents at this age have such lasting negative effects. I was not aware that children that young would be so affected by wetting themselves.

Control is the culprit in these unfortunate situations. Teachers are concerned that students will play, dawdle, or waste time during their trip to the restroom. They try to discourage students who want to go to the restroom by ignoring their raised hands, telling them to try to hold it, telling them to wait until recess or lunch, and some just say no. Some teachers feel that students are lying or faking a need to go to the restroom to get out of class. I say, so what if they play or enjoy getting out of class. I have made my exit from important meetings because I needed a break. Teachers should have liberal restroom policies that allow students to go when they feel the need, as long as they are quiet and orderly. Such a policy would probably let some fakers get out of class, but it would not deny students who had a legitimate need to go to the restroom. Effective teachers have techniques for dealing with students that misuse a liberal policy.

I was given an opportunity to experience what children must go through when they are not allowed to go to the restroom. I participated in Dr. Richard deCharms's famous motivation training workshops. Before one of the activities, the facilitator informed us that we would not be allowed to go to the restroom or do anything until the activity was over. The activity was scheduled to last for a long period of time. As the realization set in, there was audible grumbling and whispers of disapproval. At first, no one said anything.

One or two people decided to test the policy. The facilitator effectively admonished them and, using her best teacher voice, she made them sit down to wait. The power of suggestion is strong. Most of us started to feel a need to go to the restroom, a feeling that became increasingly uncomfortable as we waited and waited. No one wanted to create a scene, so no one else tried to go. However, the group became somewhat hostile and distracted. That experience taught me quite a bit about allowing students to go to the restroom. The facilitators were trying to demonstrate the origin vs. pawn concept (deCharms, 1976). They were showing us that when we force children to beg or wait for permission to use the restroom, we are teaching them to feel like pawns. Pawns feel like they are controlled by forces external to them, such as other people. It is more desirable to teach them to feel like origins, or that what happens to them is controlled from within them. Origins have an internal locus of control (Rotter, 1954) and feel that they have some control over their lives.

I found an effective way to allow my students to function as origins as they took care of their needs. I encouraged my students to view going to the restroom and getting water as a privilege that was theirs as long as they did not abuse it. They would have a morning break and an afternoon break where they could leave and come back without permission. The procedure was one person would go out at a time. They would exit by rows and as soon as one person returned, the next person could leave. The policy was flexible enough to allow more than one person to use the restroom in an emergency.

As adults we demand the right to have this private time to do as we please and students deserve the same right. Some teachers are reluctant to relinquish their power to deny some students access to the bathroom because they are afraid of potential discipline problems or some form of disruption.

When a child has an "accident," the teacher should know the school's policy for handling this emergency. If there is no school policy, the teacher should contact a parent for a change of clothing and remove the child from the audience to avoid further humiliation. The teacher should first remove the child from the classroom as inconspicuously as possible and entrust him or her to the care of the school nurse or other adult until the parent arrives. If the parents cannot be reached and the school nurse is not available, the teacher, in the company of another adult, could assist the child. Hopefully the teacher has anticipated toilet "emergencies" and has a second set of clothing for each child or instructions from the parents for what to do in this situation.

SCENARIO 13.7
Wait, Wait ... Too Late

My worst experience happened to me when I was in the third grade. The teacher's name was Mrs. A. The announcements came over the intercom and she was trying to listen to them. I went up to her and asked if I could go to the restroom and she said, "Not right now, go sit down." The announcements were still on, so I waited a few minutes and then I asked her again. I told her I really needed to go and she told me just to wait and go sit back down. I sat back down and I held it as long as I could and finally I wet myself and she felt so bad, she started crying and kept apologizing.

℞ In this scenario, the teacher was so preoccupied and distracted by the announcements that were coming over the intercom that she effectively blew off a student's pleas to go to the restroom. Her tears showed that she felt responsible for the child's accident. She did try to apologize but the damage was already done. As evidenced by this worst experience scenario, the student will not forget this incident.

The solution here is very simple: Whenever a child says, "I need to use the restroom," say, "Sure, go ahead." Caring teachers do not require children to ask for permission, especially if there is a restroom nearby. Effective teachers teach restroom etiquette, such as observing the "in use" or "open" sign and cleaning up after using the restroom. Hall passes are often necessary if the restroom is a long way from the class.

In teacher's college we were taught to encourage the student to sit down and wait a little longer. Meanwhile, the child squirms and writhes in agony, counting every second. The purpose of asking them to wait is to discourage the fakers. The assumption is that they will forget about going to the restroom if they really do not have to go. Insightful teachers that use this type of policy are careful to watch their students for any signs of discomfort. At the first sign, they send them to the restroom immediately. I know from firsthand experience how uncomfortable it is to have to wait to use the restroom. I was on a shuttle that was taking me from a New York airport to my hotel. It was late at night and I was unaware that the trip would take a couple of hours. Near the end of the trip, I was so uncomfortable, but I was reluctant to ask the bus driver to pull over on a dark, snowy, icy road so that I could use the restroom. I came dangerously close to having an accident. Understandably, I have much empathy for students' discomfort when they are forced to wait to use the restroom. My motto is "When they have to go, you have to let them go."

SCENARIO 13.8
Right of Privacy: None of Your Business

In sixth grade I had a teacher, Mrs. E., who refused to allow me to use the restroom when I desperately needed to. It was during my monthly and she tried to make me tell out loud why I needed to go. I walked out. She called the principal. He defended me!

℞ Why do some teachers insist on students making a bathroom broadcast to get permission to use the restroom? It is intrusive behavior that ignores a child's right to privacy. In this scenario, the teacher forced a power struggle by demanding that the student say what she planned to do in the bathroom. The teacher set herself up for the student to undermine her teacher power. The student ignored her and walked out to use the bathroom without disclosing what she was going to do.

I have heard of similar situations where teachers have devised ways for students to disclose their bathroom business. In one case, the teacher required students that wanted to use the bathroom to hold up one finger if they had to urinate and two fingers if they had to defecate. In another case, the color of the hall pass would indicate what the student had to do. Teachers do not really care about what the students are going to do, they simply either want to use these methods as a deterrent or a way to monitor the length of time a student will probably stay in the restroom.

Experienced teachers do not need a bathroom broadcast to be effective. They recognize children's rights to be protected from *intrusion* into their private bathroom business. Competent teachers simply allow a reasonable amount of time for the child to urinate or defecate and pad that with a little time to dawdle. The end result is that the students' private business remains private and there is little, if any, routine interruption of class time.

SCENARIO 13.9
Pass the Pass Pronto

The worst experience I ever had with a teacher was in third grade. I had a teacher who was an elderly woman and was extremely strict. Mrs. R. was her name. Well anyway, I really needed to go to the restroom and the policy at the time was one student at a time would be issued a hall pass. Well, as it turned out a student already had the hall pass so incidentally she told me I had to wait till the other student returned. When the other student returned I was in agony with holding my bowels. So anyway as I made my way to the restroom, I had an accident and never returned to her class that day. Instead I went to the office and complained of being sick so I went home.

℞ Apparently, the policy for using the restroom was strictly enforced. Only one student at a time was allowed to use the hall pass. Teachers use this policy to keep students from socializing in the restrooms. Unfortunately, in their efforts to restrict the number of students leaving the class, they may restrict a student who genuinely has to use the restroom such as the student in the scenario. Sometimes the school has a policy about the number of students in the hall at one time. Teachers should be aware of the policy and comply as long as it is reasonable to do so.

Experienced teachers can usually anticipate unforeseen events such as two students genuinely needing to use the restroom at the same time when there is only one hall pass. They have a plan B such as an emergency pass or an "act now and explain later" policy where students leave in an emergency rather than soil themselves trying to wait. Understandably, teachers would be concerned that students would abuse the latter policy. One way to minimize abuse would be to keep the emergency pass in the teacher's desk and allow students to get it without permission. Students who wanted to play might be deterred by having to get the pass out of the teacher's desk. A student who truly needed to use the restroom would welcome the flexibility in the policy. Resourceful teachers know that some abuse may occur but there are other measures such as bathroom checks to curtail undesirable activity. Most importantly, teachers should empathize with the agony children feel when they are trying to control their bladders or bowels for a long time. It is a difficult battle that children frequently lose.

Scenario 13.10
Toilet Tyrant

One semester at Southwest Texas State University I had a biology teacher whose restroom policy was ridiculous. On the first day of class he let us know that if we left class to use the bathroom he would flunk us from the course. There were absolutely no exceptions. He said, "I do not want any documentation of a bladder infection or an excuse of pregnancy." One girl spoke out against this nonsense. He proceeded to kick her out of class. As a freshman in college I was terrified to flunk a class so I never used the restroom during class.

R͟x Tyranny is the offspring of insecurity and a need for power. Teachers who establish such a heavy-handed authoritarian discipline policy need to control others to feel secure. Denying others a right that is theirs by birth, namely, the right to use the restroom whenever nature calls, provides the dictator of such a policy a heightened sense of power. This teacher's refusal to accept any excuse no matter how legitimate or urgent was his assurance of no possible threat to his self-constructed autocracy and his piteous outcry for power. He blatantly misused grades to enforce compliance to his absolute rule. Like many tyrants throughout history, he used extreme punishment to extinguish any threat to his tenuous power. His intent in using extreme punishment with a student was to incite terror in the other, the hope being that the rest of the students in the class would vicariously experience the consequences of the student that was kicked out of class. It worked; his ridiculous policy terrorized the author of this scenario so much that not only did she never ask to use the restroom in his class, but she never used the restroom in other college classes. Her fear of failing a class outweighed any sense of outrage that her rights as an adult student and human being were being violated. In this case, the student would never even request to use the restroom. This teacher accomplished his mission to the hefty price of his students' loss of freedom.

One easily overlooked fact in this scenario is that the teacher was a biology teacher which suggests that he should have been aware of the consequences of suppressing bodily urges. I believe this toilet tyrant's deep-seated need to sit on his tissue paper throne and rule his class may be deeply rooted in his low perception of himself as a capable adult instructor. It appears that he felt that his students would not take him seriously and recognize his legitimacy as a teacher unless he took a punitive stance in establishing classroom policy. This teacher would benefit from some professional development that focused on enhancing feelings of self-efficacy (Bandura, 1986) or feelings that he could handle the tasks inherent in being an effective teacher. Such training should alleviate possible fears of inadequacy and diminish his need to effect punitive policies. This scenario provides some evidence that abuse in education also occurs at the adult level, validating the need to enlighten teachers in higher education about establishing reasonable policies.

4

Classroom Management and Instruction

"Class, I've got a lot of material to cover, so to save time I won't be using vowels today. Nw lts bgn, pls trn t pg 122."

Mistake

14

Inappropriate Educational Strategies

SCENARIO 14.1
Gifted: One Who Walks on Water

In second grade I was told to write a research paper with reference notes and bibliography. One other girl and myself were in the GT [Gifted and Talented] program and we had to do this while everyone else got to dress up and give a book report as his or her favorite book character.

℞ The stereotype of the outstanding, highly motivated, gifted, and talented student can be detrimental to the social, emotional, and academic development of gifted students. One hazard is going overboard and giving assignments that are not developmentally appropriate (Elkind, 1989), such as the research paper assignment in this scenario. Developmentally appropriate instruction is designed to meet the social, emotional, cognitive, and physical needs of students. Years ago, teachers were accused of not providing challenging assignments for gifted students. Today it is important to strike a balance and make sure that their challenging assignments are developmentally appropriate. Teachers of gifted students should also consider their students' preferences in assignments.

Renzulli and Reis (1991) define giftedness as possessing a high level of creativity, a high level of general ability, and a high level of achievement motivation. Having a high level of creativity would explain why these gifted students would prefer to dress up and be their favorite character from a book rather than do a research paper. Gifted students enjoy "fun" assignments, too. An added caution is to let gifted children be themselves—do not expect them to be "perfect" at all times. Such expectations could lead to perfectionism, which can be detrimental to these students (Orange, 1997).

SCENARIO 14.2
I Don't Know, I'm Just the Teacher

I took a physics course in high school. We didn't get our teacher until one month after school started. The teacher was a seventh-grade math teacher who never taught physics. He developed this "oh well" attitude with us whenever we didn't understand. He would say things like, "oh well, that's what the book says." He couldn't justify the explanation in the book. Because of this my grades suffered, and my GPA dropped while others were allowed to take other courses. My class standing dropped.

℞ The school administrators share the responsibility for this twofold problem. The first problem is assigning a teacher to teach a subject that he or she is not qualified to teach. This strategy is doomed to failure. The second problem is not offering students who are forced to stay in the class some grade consideration and opportunities for remediation. The administration could have supplemented this teacher's instruction by offering tutors. The knowledge gaps that result from this poor-quality instruction could have long-lasting effects beyond the GPA, as these students attempt to take higher level physics courses.

The teacher's attitude is indefensible. Responsible teachers in such a situation would research the answers to the students' questions if they did not know the answer. They would put ego aside and enlist the help of other teachers. They also would make student learning the primary goal and top priority. A lesser response is a teacher luxury that students cannot afford. The results of poor-quality instruction are evidenced in the high prices this student had to pay, namely low grades, lowered GPA, and lowered class standing.

SCENARIO 14.3
Get Thee to the Second Grade!

I was in the fifth grade and had a history teacher by the name of Mrs. W. She made us read aloud in class. The boy who read before me could not pronounce one of the words correctly and so she made him stand up. She yelled at him and called him names like "stupid." Then she sent him to a second-grade class for a day to learn how to read with the young children. He was so humiliated and I felt sorry for him. He was my best friend and, even worse, she called on me to continue where he left off! I was so nervous, I felt like I had forgotten how to read.

R It is unfortunate that sending the child to a second-grade class was used as a punishment. It could have been a very effective strategy with proper implementation. The teacher could have made arrangements with a second-grade teacher to have the student experiencing difficulties come to the class as a peer tutor. I used this strategy with a third-grade student who needed remediation. The second-grade teacher worked with my student in exchange for his helping a second grader. It removed the stigma of going to a lower-level class. Peer-tutoring a younger student seemed to improve his self-esteem and the remediation improved his reading. A bonus was fewer discipline problems with this student.

Another very significant problem evident in this scenario is the inhibition exhibited by the author. Bandura (1986) defines inhibition as an event where observing a model being punished for a particular event will likely keep the observer from performing the same actions. In this case, when one child saw another child being punished for trying to read, the other child was so inhibited when asked to read that she felt as if she had forgotten how to read. There were probably other students who had the same inhibition. This is a serious consequence for the minuscule error of mispronouncing a word. Teachers have many options that would have been more effective. The simplest response, with the least disruption to the class, would be to assist the child by providing the correct pronunciation of the word.

SCENARIO 14.4
Standing the Test of Time

My worst experience was in eighth-grade math. My teacher asked me to go to the board to work a math problem. When it was obvious that I had a problem with the math problem, my teacher failed to offer any guidance or assistance whatsoever. After approximately twenty minutes of standing and staring at the blackboard, she told me to sit down. From then on I had a problem with math and have been intimidated by it. It is only recently that I have begun to become comfortable with it.

R It is difficult to determine this teacher's motive for having the student stand for an agonizing twenty minutes staring at the blackboard. What was the point? After the first few minutes, it was apparent that the child did not know the answer. Humiliating the child by spotlighting his lack of knowledge for a long period of time would not make the answer appear. Apparently, the teacher's motive was more sadistic than educative. Perhaps she wanted to make an example of this student or she felt that having to stand at the blackboard would be an effective deterrent to not knowing the answer next time. After class, the student said he had night-mares about this situation for a long time. Academic trauma, such as this senseless act, usually has a very high price tag. It is not worth the detrimental effect that it had on the student.

   Sensible teachers would have given the child some assistance at the board or would have invited another child to come to the board to help. One of the least threatening ways to use the blackboard is to have students work at the board in groups or with a buddy. Perhaps it is even more effective to ask for volunteers and make it clear that they can sit down at any time without penalty.

SCENARIO 14.5
Math Mania

I guess my worst experience was in elementary math. We always had to change class-rooms for math class and we were grouped according to the grade level and the week of the year that we were up to, so if you were in 4.5 you were fourth-grade math, fifth week. Math has never been my strong subject so I was always behind all my friends and was in classes with kids who were younger than I. This was always so devastating to me and made me so upset that it would make me ill.

℞ This is a multifaceted problem that stems from ability group-ing, where students are assigned to classes based on test performance or other achievements. First and fore-most, research has shown that ability grouping is not a particularly effec-tive teaching strategy because it tends to benefit high level students more so than low level students (Slavin, 1990). Teachers often have lower expectations, lower demands, and less tolerance for low-level classes. The quality of instruction is usually less for low-level ability groups, making it more difficult for them to break the cycle of underachievement and move to a higher group. In this process, students' self-esteem and self-efficacy or beliefs about their abilities are at risk. Low self-efficacy is evidenced in this scenario where the student said she was always behind all of her friends and her acknowledgment that math is not her strong subject. Gardner (1993) suggests that humans possess multi-ple intelligences, with strengths or weaknesses in one or several. If teachers seek out and recognize a student's strengths in other areas of intelligence, competence in those areas may focus a more favorable lens on a student's weak areas. Having a more favorable view of a student may encourage teachers to supplement a child's lagging perfor-mance with remediation and enrich-ment (Mason & Good, 1993) or with peer-tutoring. These strategies offer favorable alternatives to ability grouping.

SCENARIO 14.6
No Play, You Pay

I was kicked out of music class almost every day because I would not participate. My music teacher would make me take a chair outside and wait till class was over. This would result in missed recess time as punishment by my homeroom teacher.

Upon walking into my math class the instructor told me to sit outside today because she did not want to put up with me today. This was a shock because class hadn't even started.

℞ The key words in this over-played scenario are "punishment" and "every day." Obviously putting the child outside of the class every day was not effective because the undesirable behavior continued on a daily basis. Viewing this problem from a behaviorist perspective, putting the child outside the classroom is negative reinforcement that increases the likelihood that the behavior will occur. Perhaps the student enjoys being outside of the class more than he enjoys being in class participating. The teacher should try to find out why the student refuses to participate. If it is lack of ability, she could help the student develop an action plan for improving performance. If it is lack of interest, the teacher could solicit suggestions from the students and offer them choices to add meaningfulness and interest to the lessons.

If students are disruptive, teachers may be justified in removing them from the class. However, to make the removal of a student effective, teachers should eliminate the attractive aspects of removal, such as opportunities to socialize with friends.

SCENARIO 14.7
Prime Time

My worst experience was in eighth grade when Mr. E. yelled at me on my second day at a new school because I did not know what a prime number was. I became so upset that I threw up in the hallway and had to go home. My dad picked me up and taught me a prime number lesson.

℞ Teachers should not expect new students to come into a class knowing all of the answers. Prior assessment is usually necessary to ascertain a student's skill level. It is inappropriate and unnecessary to yell at such a student. This teacher's loud rebuke distressed the student so much that it caused extreme anxiety, which is often accompanied by a physiological reaction. The vomiting, an outward manifestation of this student's distress, underscores the importance of developing tolerance for students' mistakes and lack of knowledge.

Without tolerance and understanding, teachers may risk intimidating students. For new students, who are already insecure and uncomfortable, additional anxiety could interfere with their performance.

SCENARIO 14.8
Once More, With Feeling

In chemistry my teacher would always call on me knowing well how lost I was. Then she would roll her eyes, take a deep breath, and say something like, "Okay, let's go over this one more time since you obviously weren't paying attention." She would repeat it (the same way as before) and once again it made no sense to me.

℞ There is a euphemistic expression that suggests that pointing a finger of blame at someone leaves the other fingers pointing back at you. In this case, the teacher blames the student for his confusion and accuses him of not paying attention, when in fact she may be doing a poor job of explaining the material. It is a known fact that chemistry is a difficult subject for many students. Knowing this, the teacher should be prepared to vary her presentation of the material to accommodate the needs of her students that are having trouble.

Making a dramatic production of answering the question "once more" for the undeserving, inattentive student may be a way of masking her inadequacies. This tactic of giving students a hard time if they ask questions would protect her from questions that she might not be able to answer. The students would be so deflated and discouraged by her words and actions that they would not dare to ask a question. Her inadequacy is evident in that she presented the material exactly as she did before.

A better approach would be to vary the presentation and take into consideration student's learning styles and learning preferences, if possible. Students' learning styles determine how they approach the material. Snow, Como, and Jackson (1996) found that some students see learning as a means for understanding where others may be more concerned about surface learning rather than meaningful learning. My high school chemistry teacher required that we outline every chapter for homework. This seemed to "force" some understanding of the course material.

SCENARIO 14.9
Teacher, Can You Spare a Sign?

My worst experience with a teacher was during algebra. I loved math and really thought I knew and understood math. But my algebra teacher sent me home crying every day because she marked my homework and tests wrong because I used to get my positives and negatives wrong; I knew how to do the problems, but I would get my answers with the wrong sign.

℞ This teacher missed an opportunity for meaningful instruction and shifted the responsibility of learning the correct way to use signs to the student. It was obvious that the student could not learn the difference between the symbols without assistance. In his work, Vygotsky (as cited in Wertsch, 1991) identified a zone of proximal development, an area where a child cannot solve a problem alone but may be able to successfully solve the problem with appropriate assistance from an adult or skilled peer. As in this case, the student may be on the verge of solving the problem, but may need some cues, prompts, heuristics, or words of encouragement from the teacher.

Resourceful teachers would have provided their students with some simple tips or reminders for using signs. My math teacher made a little reminder chart for our class that really made using signs much easier:

+	•	+	=	+
–	•	+	=	–
–	•	–	=	+

This heuristic is a form of scaffolding (Wood, Bruner, & Ross, 1976) where skilled adults provide students with just enough hints and clues to guide them in their efforts to give a correct answer.

SCENARIO 14.10
Wait a Minute ... or Two or Three

A teacher asked me a question and made me feel embarrassed because I didn't know the answer. I felt stupid in front of the class.

℞ Calling on students at random is a good behaviorist strategy for keeping students on their toes. When calling on students at random, teachers should observe a questioning etiquette that allows students to say "pass" and save face if they do not know the answer.

After teachers have observed an appropriate wait time for an answer from a student (Rowe, 1987), they can offer to come back to the student, or can ask if there is anyone else who would like to answer the question. Teachers also may rephrase the question to assist the student in understanding the question and thereby increase the odds that the student can respond correctly. Hints and clues may jog the student's memory. To question students effectively, teachers must be willing to offer as much assistance as is reasonable.

SCENARIO 14.11
No Excuses ... EVER!

When I was in seventh-grade orchestra, attendance at all concerts was mandatory, which I perfectly understood. However, at the spring concert, I had to get a ride from my friend's parents because my dad worked swing shift and my mom didn't drive. At my friend's house, things were chaotic. Her mother couldn't find film and batteries for the camera. As time got closer and closer to the concert time, I got more and more anxious. "Your mom knows the orchestra is first?" I asked my friend.

Her mom insisted we would not be late, but we were. When we got to the school, I ran to the band room, grabbed my violin out of the case, and ran down the hall. I opened the door to the gym just as the orchestra played the first note of our first song. I knew I couldn't come running in and interrupt while they were playing. I burst into tears. The band members waiting to play next insisted the teacher would understand. "You don't know Miss J.," I bawled. "She said if we weren't here we'd fail."

When Miss J. came out in the hall, she looked like she could have killed me, even though I was still hiccupping from crying so hard. She said she'd talk to me about it the next day and that I could at least play in the finale. The next day she told me, "I realize that you were late for reasons beyond your control and you did play in the last song. So, in view of that I will not give you an F. You will get a C."

I'd had an A up until that point. To this day, I don't think I've forgiven her. As an adult, I wonder how she could punish a thirteen-year-old for something, knowing an adult had been to blame, not me. I had even brought a note from that parent explaining and apologizing. Fortunately, I still love to play the violin. (Amazing.)

℞ The teacher was understandably angry with the student for being late to the concert. However, her reaction to a situation that was obviously out of the child's control was extreme, punitive, and irrational. The student indicated that she brought a note confirming that it was the adult's fault that she was late. The teacher obviously ignored this acknowledgment and remained steadfast in her resolve to punish the student.

In extenuating circumstances like this, effective teachers are flexible. They show empathy and understanding for what was obviously an agonizing situation for the child. The teacher's intent was to have a mandatory policy that permitted no exceptions under any circumstances. Policies that are this rigid are bound to break somewhere. In this case, it broke the spirit of an innocent child. Teachers' policies should not be like dry, brittle, rigid sticks but more like green branches that bend in a gracious bow of forgiveness and understanding in extenuating circumstances. The teacher let the student play in the finale and she should have stopped there. The child had been punished enough. Lowering her grade at this point was more of a punishment than an assessment. It is reasonable that teachers should communicate rules to students, should expect that the rules be followed, and should have appropriate consequences if they are not followed. Teachers also should communicate that each case will be judged by its own merits.

The teacher's inflexibility about rules is reminiscent of Piaget's (1965) concept of moral realism where children see rules as absolute with no consideration of intent. In a similar childlike manner, this teacher did not consider her student's intentions.

SCENARIO 14.12
Competition Isn't Always Good

I hated being "bawled out" by teachers. I hated being forced to participate in competitive sports at school. I wasn't good at this and found it humiliating.

℞ Students are often required to participate in competitive sports. Forced participation becomes a shame-based activity because students who are reluctant to participate are usually poor performers. They are uncomfortable about their ability to perform and about their teammates' reaction to their performance. Reluctant students are usually the last to be chosen to be on a team. This agonizing form of rejection has long-lasting effects. It reinforces a child's feeling of inadequacy.

Although teachers cannot eliminate competition in sports at school, they can minimize its adverse effects on students by recognizing their good qualities. Gardner (1993) proposes a theory of multiple intelligences that suggests that different students may be intelligent in different ways. Versatile teachers will showcase the poor performers' talents in one of these areas. Behaviorists such as Skinner (1953) would argue that this student's dislike of competitive sports may be attributed to classical or operant conditioning, where the student associates the negative feelings of humiliation with the sport and subsequently becomes conditioned to hate competitive sports.

SCENARIO 14.13
Keep Working, Rain, Shine, Sleet, or Divorce

When I was in the third grade Mrs. L. was my teacher. I lived in Massachusetts and my parents were getting a divorce so I was quite upset most of the time. Mrs. L. would always make me read when I had been or was crying. I could never understand why but now I do. I believe that she was trying to deter my thoughts to something else, but at the time I hated her for it and will never forget it.

℞ This is an inappropriate strategy to expect some form of academic performance when children are visibly upset. This strategy may set children up for conduct problems or other inappropriate behavior. The children may either refuse to participate or, as in this case, be so anguished that they are scarred for life. This student was traumatized by this event, as evidenced by the strong emotional tone of the sentence, "I hated her and I'll never forget it," and underlining the sentence for emphasis. If children are crying, teachers should talk to them privately to find out if there is something wrong. Without being intrusive, they should try to keep a finger on the pulse of what's going on in each child's life and home and try to be attuned to recognizable signs of distress.

Divorce is an extremely traumatic event for most children. Helping the child make the adjustment is a better strategy than distraction. In this case, offering a child an opportunity for distraction through participation is fine only if the child welcomes the opportunity.

SCENARIO 14.14
I'm Writing as Fast as I Can

In first grade, [my teacher] used to make us copy paragraphs from a projector. We had a limited amount of time to copy these paragraphs. I was so scared of her that my hands would perspire so much that they would stick to the paper. One day I did not finish in time so she hit my hands with a ruler at least two or three times. I do not ever remember not finishing in time again. This was very unfair. Some students do not write as fast as others. As you can see, I'm the only one still writing. Well, almost.

℞ This punishment was only temporarily effective. The student wrote faster to avoid punishment but as soon as the threat of punishment diminished, the student resumed the slow writing and continues to write slowly to this day. The ominous persona presented by the teacher and the punishment made the student very anxious. The real question here is what is so important about rapid writing that it warrants high anxiety and physical punishment for the student. What is the objective of forcing a first-grade student to write rapidly when they may be hindered by limited manual dexterity at that age?

The effective teacher would allow ample time for students to complete the writing task. Of course teachers need to set limits on assignments, but they could give extra time to students who need it, especially first graders who are just learning to write. Timed writing could simply require only as much as the child is capable of copying within the time frame. This amount should increase as the exercise is repeated over time. Each student is different. Some students at this level need to work at a slower, more deliberate pace to form the letters correctly. A slow pace is certainly not a punishable offense. Teachers rarely hit students with rulers anymore, but any type of punishment for writing at a slow pace is inappropriate. A good teacher would create a nurturing, relaxed atmosphere that is conducive to learning. When I was in graduate school, I was a substitute for a first-grade teacher whose students had excellent penmanship. I was so impressed that all of the students had such good handwriting that I had to ask the kids how they became such good writers. They said, "Our teacher smiles at us and gives us a happy face when we write good." I talked to their teacher later and she agreed. She laughed as she explained that they hurry and line up for her to see their work. She thought it was important to smile at the children in addition to drawing a happy face. I agree with her: The proof is in the writing.

SCENARIO 14.15
Reading Reticence: To Read or Not to Read

In the fourth grade I remember my teacher making us read out loud in groups. I had a hard time reading because I had moved due to my father being in the military. So my first four years of school were hectic. This teacher made me read in front of my group, then I was laughed at because I had trouble. This still bothers me today. I have trouble reading, or even talking, in front of my peers.

℞ A student who was reluctant to read in front of the group always sent up a red flag for me. This reading reticence usually signals low self-esteem, poor reading skills, shyness, illness, and so forth. All of these conditions suggest that the student should not be forced to read aloud, but should be allowed to pass until the teacher has had time to investigate and address the problem. An effective teacher would be empathic and encouraging and would admonish the group for laughing at anyone who is trying to read.

The teacher could desensitize the student to reading before a group by having the student read one-on-one with the teacher first, then read aloud with a peer, next read aloud in a small group, and then read before the class. The effective teacher could teach the students to be supportive of each other when someone is having trouble. Sprinthall, Sprinthall, and Oja (1994) suggest that teachers are a potent force and by using social approval, they can shape the behavior of their classes.

SCENARIO 14.16
No Make-Up; I'll Take a Powder

I was a freshman in high school. I had the flu for about a week. When I returned to school, I inquired about taking a make-up test for a history class. The teacher said I could not make it up because he had to go hold a pep rally! I asked if I could make it up the next Monday. He said he would think about it. I told my parents that I probably would get a D or F. I ended up dropping out of school. I did go to another school, and had a good experience.

℞ This teacher was apparently very busy and preoccupied with some duties he had to perform.

There was no obvious malicious intent in his actions. His off-handed response of "I'll think about it" was either a result of his busy schedule and unwillingness to commit to a time, or his response was deliberately unaccommodating to cause the student some discomfort about missing the test. Whatever his intent, he misjudged the importance of the make-up to the student.

Teachers should establish a test and assignment make-up policy at the beginning of the school year clearly delineating if and when a make-up test is allowed. These make-up test guidelines should acknowledge extenuating circumstances such as illness, death in the family, and so on. The goal of the make-up policy should be to maximize student participation in class assignments. If a student has a tiny flicker of responsibility about a missed assignment, teachers have an obligation to fan that flicker into flames by helping the student make up the assignment. This teacher could have fanned this student's flicker by simply designating a better time to discuss the test and possible make-up. This simple act could have avoided the student's panic about getting a poor grade and subsequent dropping out of school.

SCENARIO 14.17
Can't You See That I Can't See?

I guess it had to do with first grade. The homework was always written in the corner of the blackboard. Because I was seated in the farthest row I could never see it or copy it before Sister M. A. erased it. So I repeatedly received hand slappings with a ruler because I did not have my homework completed. It was later discovered that I had a vision problem but the teacher still did not place me closer to the homework board or give me the assignments when I asked.

Rx   Apparently, the child was not the only one who had visual problems. The teacher obviously missed the signs that the child was having difficulty seeing the board. Children with visual problems often squint, strain their necks, use their hands to slant their eyes, or use other behaviors to improve their vision. An effective teacher would suspect that maybe the child was unable to see the board from the back of the room at an angle. A major clue that something was amiss was the incomplete homework assignments. How sad that the environment in this classroom was so unresponsive to the needs of the students. The student was obviously afraid and ashamed to say that she couldn't see.

To avoid this problem, teachers should be aware of students who show signs of having difficulty seeing the board. If there is any doubt, ask students if they are having trouble seeing and encourage those students to move closer to the board. Once it is a known fact that the child has a problem, change the seating arrangement immediately. To knowingly ignore a child's cry for help under these circumstances is malpractice. The teacher has an obligation to create a class environment that is conducive to learning and the child's well-being.

SCENARIO 14.18
Small but Mighty

My worst experience with a teacher occurred when I was in second grade. There wasn't one particular incident that happened; she was just a horrible teacher. She used to give the class an outrageous assignment like rewriting the Constitution, and then walk around the class clicking and tapping her fingernails on everyone's desk. She tormented us! She never let us get up from our desks unless we were leaving the classroom for some reason. I think she did this because she was only four feet tall and we not only outnumbered her, but we were taller than she was!

℞ This case reminds me of a teacher who worked as a permanent substitute for our school. She had a similar stature, about four feet tall, and a nice smile and long red fingernails. She was an enigma because the children were terrified of her. Many of the children towered over her, yet *they* feared her. They begged us not to have her come back. When I asked her what she did to the children, she just smiled with no answer. She always had control of her classes. I think these teachers must have felt the need to use extreme measures to control their children because of their short stature. These extreme measures would guarantee that the children would respect and obey them. Their tactics may control their classes but they also can stifle a child's sense of industry at this age.

Second graders need some autonomy and mobility to promote what Erikson (1963) refers to as a sense of industry. The development of a sense of industry demands that a child be allowed to make and do things and experience some success, as well as be encouraged to persist at a task. When children are not allowed to do this, they may experience a sense of inferiority. Woolfolk (1998) suggests that children should be given an opportunity to pursue realistic goals and should be encouraged to work responsibly.

Every aspect of this teacher's instruction counters these suggestions. She gave her students an unrealistic assignment. Good teachers have realistic expectations of student performance and try to give their students developmentally appropriate instruction.

SCENARIO 14.19
Anything Worth Doing Is Not Worth Doing Well

Mrs. C., third grade, looming over my desk (front row), ripping up the little yellow paper that was my math homework, yelling that it was a disgrace and asking what was wrong with me that I couldn't produce homework that was neat or correct. I had spent two hours the night before, working with my mom on that homework. We were only allowed one half sheet of paper. My writing was poor and there were quite a few erasures. Mrs. C. threw up her hands in dismay and gave up on me. This happened on a regular basis. I was frightened and came to associate that with math class.

℞ A person is not his or her performance. This seemingly novice teacher assumes that they are one in the same. She asks the child what was wrong with her that she could not produce neat homework. This statement absolves the teacher of any responsibility in the child's poor performance. The teacher's explosive outburst illuminates her frustration with dealing with the student's problem. She seems convinced that the child owns the problem.

Perceptive, responsible teachers assess their share of the problem and take action. They would begin by finding ways to improve instruction and by ascertaining alternate approaches to helping students. Effective teachers would focus their efforts on helping students improve their performance, which would eliminate the need for disparaging remarks and angry outbursts (Sabers, Cushing, & Berliner, 1991). Shaping (Skinner, 1987) is a behavioral strategy that effective teachers use often. Using shaping, teachers reinforce successive approximations or small steps of progress toward a specific behavioral outcome and offer praise and encouragement at each step. For example, they could praise the fact that the student brought in the homework, next praise the neatness of some of the letters, next note that the paper does not have erasures, and so on. The child is most likely to try harder to get some praise and approval and less likely to try harder for hurtful remarks.

SCENARIO 14.20
Ready, Willing, and Able

My worst experience with a teacher is one where I was singled out without my permission to "help" a student with dyslexia. I didn't mind helping at first, but the experience turned into one where I did all the work and the teacher did none and neither did the other student. I felt unappreciated and felt that the situation was unfair.

℞ Peer-tutoring has its merits, provided the tutor is willing and able to provide quality instruction. In this case, the child assigned to be a peer tutor was neither willing nor able. This child did not "agree" to tutor the student and this child was not trained to teach students with learning disabilities. The teacher passing the total responsibility for teaching the dyslexic student onto a resentful child compounds this problem. Apparently the dyslexic student sensed the teacher's abandonment and the tutor's frustration and opted out of that educational process.

Peer-tutoring has been shown to benefit the tutor and the tutee (Good & Brophy, 1997). Teachers should only use peer-tutoring if it is mutually beneficial to both students. Student tutors should be willing participants and should not be expected to work beyond their level of mastery. Caution should be exercised with students needing tutoring to avoid making them feel "less than" for needing assistance.

SCENARIO 14.21
Talk, Talk, Talk

My worst experience with a teacher was in eighth grade at St. L.'s School. Her name was Mrs. D. Even as an eighth-grade student I realized that she was a bad teacher, the worksheet queen, Ms. Boring!! She taught her class in the lecture style all year long and half the time I had no idea what she was talking about. She never smiled and never tried to make any connections with her students.

℞ Lecture can be an appropriate teaching strategy, but this strategy should be reserved for students at the high school level and above. The younger the students, the more disengaged they become as time goes on. If lecture is used, it should be interesting and include as much media as possible. Integrating video, audio tapes, visual aids, PowerPoint-type computer presentations, and other sensory sources will keep students engaged and will enhance the effectiveness of lecture as a teaching strategy. Kindsvatter, Wilen, and Ishler (1988) suggest three ways to enhance the lecture presentation: Use visual aids, present simple material before complex material, and use nonverbal behaviors to hold students' attention. This teacher missed the mark on all three points. She used worksheets, a less-desirable instructional tool, she used no visual aids, and she presented complex material most of the time. She never smiled. This simple non-verbal expression would have helped her to connect with her students and to minimize the gap that seemed to emerge from her ineffective use of the lecture method.

A more effective approach is articulated in the concept of connected teaching, proposed by Belenky, Clinchy, Goldberger, and Tarule (1986). They suggest that connected teachers function as a midwife who helps students give birth to their own ideas as opposed to functioning like a banker who merely makes knowledge deposits in a student's head.

SCENARIO 14.22
Here an "F," There an "F," Everywhere an "F," "F"

My single worst experience in school was my high school economics teacher. I had this teacher my last semester during my senior year. On the first day I had his class, he stood in the middle of the classroom and proceeded to tell us how he prided himself on failing students. From that moment on, I knew I was in trouble. He gave us two chapters to read every night and would lecture over things not in the book. His tests were hard because nobody ever knew what he would test us over. I had a horrible time making him happy with my projects. In the end, after working very hard, I made a B in the class.

℞ There is a degree of irony in the pride this economics teacher took in failing students. Little did he realize that failing a large number of students is a direct reflection of the inadequacy of his teaching. He entertained the misconceived notion that the goal of education is to fail students. His deliberate attempt to fail students was apparent in his practice of not communicating the objectives of his instruction to students and not relating his tests to those objectives.

Effective teachers would make every effort to avoid failing a student. There are a variety of strategies available to teachers to avert failure, such as providing cues, encouraging students, and offering multiple exposures to the material and multiple opportunities to learn the material presented.

Effective teachers would try to make sure that students understood what is expected of them. They would provide specific instructional objectives for students that would help students to direct their study efforts to meet the teacher's goals and objectives. Gronlund (1995) recommends objectives that focus on student behaviors and learning outcomes.

SCENARIO 14.23
Academic "Payday"

In 1985, I moved to San Antonio from Houston. The school placed me in an advanced math class. Though honors math wasn't new to me, I found the class learning aspects of math that I had never been introduced to. I fell behind. Feeling frustrated, I approached my teacher on several occasions for help. However, she never made time for me. Within six weeks, I was failing and felt demoralized. The school chose to put me in an average math class. On my last day, I told my teacher that I would ace the quiz. She said, "I doubt it." Well, I earned a 100. I showed it to her, left, and never spoke to her again. In case you're wondering, I made all As in my new math class.

While in the end, I believe that I came out triumphant, I find it a very negative memory. In my opinion, no one is permitted to doubt my ability. Not even me.

℞ This teacher missed her "payday" by failing to find time to help a student. Teachers often derive a psychic income from helping students who truly need help. In this scenario, the student's failing grade spawned a vengeful motive for achievement that was conceived in hostility and resentment. It would have been so much easier and productive to help the student or to provide help for the student. There are many help venues available such as computer-assisted instruction, tutors, peer-tutors, or one-on-one instruction. This teacher could have been a beacon of light for this student; instead, she became a lasting negative memory. This lost opportunity was truly her loss.

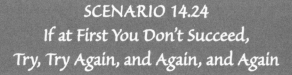

SCENARIO 14.24
If at First You Don't Succeed,
Try, Try Again, and Again, and Again

I was a very sensitive child, easily hurt. Probably the worst times with teachers were when I felt ostracized or made a spectacle of. Sometimes teachers would have no regard for how much they can embarrass a child in front of his peers.

One particular time when I was in eighth-grade PE class (the worst year of my life), we were practicing batting the softball. The teacher had us line up and each had to stay until we hit the ball. Everyone else hit it after a few tries, but I had to stand there and swing and keep missing. After about ten to fifteen tries, he let me pass. That class was also bad for letting the kids pick teams. I was, all through school, the last one picked. I will never intentionally let that happen to a child.

℞ This student sums up the problem in his statement that some teachers "have no regard for how much they can embarrass a child in front of his peers." This teacher crossed the boundaries of reasonableness when he forced this child to keep trying to hit the ball for an excessive number of tries with no apparent hope for success. The child obviously did not have the skill set to hit the ball. This teacher crossed the boundaries of decency when he made an example and spectacle of this child and allowed the classmates to witness the agonizing event.

Effective teachers would set a reasonable limit on the number of attempts students would be allowed to make before they could pass. If a child cannot perform after several tries, teachers, as trained professionals, should diagnose students' weaknesses and reteach those skills until the students succeed.

Physical education classes are notorious for creating anxiety by fostering the anxiety that accompanies "picking teams." Insightful teachers can anticipate the stress and anxiety that students who are at the bottom of the pick list will feel. If teachers used a lottery system or a similar method of selection to assign teams, the stress level would be significantly reduced, if not eliminated.

Mistake

15

Inappropriate Assessment

My worst experience was starting private school in sixth grade and being told that I should repeat fifth grade based on some test scores. Later I found out I had been given the wrong form of a test so I didn't have to repeat fifth grade.

Rx The teachers in this test situation made a serious error that could have resulted in misplacement, stigma, and retarded academic development if the student had to repeat the fifth grade.

Prudent teachers know that placement of students should not rely on one test score. Glaser and Silver (1994) contend that testing has become separated from instruction. Messick (1984) says that testing should be a last resort and quality of instruction should be a primary concern. If it appears that the classroom performance is average and the test score is low, give students the option of moving up to the next grade level or repeating the grade. In this scenario, there was no mention of class performance so it is difficult to determine if instructional outcomes were taken into consideration. The quality of instruction should be considered before a student is tagged, labeled, and shipped off to a lower grade.

In eighth grade my English teacher was awful! She hated me. I would do a paper and get an F. I even had a certified teacher, who was our neighbor, help me on one paper.

I still received an F. We changed teachers for one six-week term, and I received an A that time. My parents finally had me transferred to his class, so I could have a chance to pass. I ended up with As in his class, where I had made Fs in her class. I did nothing different. I can honestly say it was just a personality conflict. I guess there was something she did not like about me. I know I will do my best to never let myself be influenced like that so that I would fail a student. I hope to be fair to all of them and will strive hard to achieve that goal.

℞ Teachers who wield a big sword with an F on it intend to hurt someone. They are no longer evaluating grades; they are carrying out a vendetta of unknown origin. Perhaps as a child, this teacher felt the sting of getting an F, maybe even an undeserved F. Knowing the power of the failure, perhaps this teacher was identifying with her oppressor when she consistently gave Fs to a student she disliked. She effectively used the bad grade as a weapon.

Emotion is often a barrier to effective student assessment. Some teachers allow their personal feelings about students' academic potential, attitudes and beliefs, personal appearance, social class, race, or gender to bias their grading or assessment. Teacher bias seems apparent in this scenario but the factors underlying the bias are not clear. When a teacher's assessment of a student embraces bias, the grades or scores are useless; they only reflect the inaccuracy of bias and offer no meaningful feedback on student achievement. The inaccuracy of biased grading is evident in this scenario where the student consistently made Fs in one class and made As upon transferring to another class. The disparity in grading is a red flag that perhaps the student was right. The teacher probably disliked the student and tried to use grades as a punishment.

Fair-minded teachers have high expectations for all students. They are aware of their responsibility to set appropriate achievement goals for all students, including students they dislike. Delivering quality feedback is virtually impossible in the presence of bias. Using appropriate assessment to identify student needs allows teachers to target instruction to address those needs, which effectively enhances the achievement of all students, particularly low achievers (O'Connor, 1998).

Informed teachers realize that the purpose of assessment is to provide quality feedback that can be used to improve student performance. They know that a grade of F is only a form of feedback. They also realize that using grades for punitive reasons is pure folly that is doomed to end in failure for the student . . . and the teacher!

SCENARIO 15.3
I Am Not My Brother's Keeper

When I was in high school, we were taking our exit tests. We were placed three at a table in the library to take our tests. The day we got our results back, the boy who sat at my table came up to me with his score. He told me he was so relieved that he passed because he had copied all of my answers and then found out we probably had different test forms. Luckily for him we didn't, so he passed his test and graduated because of me. When I complained to the counselor and they said they couldn't do anything, I flattened his tires!

℞ Improper management of a testing session permitted a student to cheat and capitalize on another student's scores. Experienced teachers use preventive measures and adequate proctoring to discourage cheating. Preventive measures include but are not limited to using parallel forms of the test, spacing students to make it difficult for them to see each other's tests, scrambling test questions and creating corresponding answer keys, or giving scrambled electronic versions of the test. Wise teachers know that proximity is often a deterrent to cheating. Frequent proctoring and scanning the room should minimize or stop cheating activity.

SCENARIO 15.4
Caustic Critique

I was a freshman in college, and I thought I had made it. I wanted to be a writer, and I thought I could. I had been given so much positive reinforcement in high school. I felt on top of the world. I handed in my first English paper to professor P. (I'll never forget his name). I anticipated greatness. As he handed my paper back, I flipped to the back page, anxiously awaiting the glorious comments. The simple red print asked, "Is English your first language?"

℞ This scenario has two possible angles: The student was deficient in self-evaluative techniques and the teacher was deficient in effective assessment techniques, or the student was a good writer and the teacher was a sadistic critic. In the first instance, the student possibly had an overinflated sense of her writing ability and the teacher's grade was justified but the comment was unduly harsh and disparaging. In the second instance, the grade was undeserved and the comment disparaging. The consequences of a disparagement model of assessment are many. Foremost, a personal attack on the student's competence directs the attention away from legitimate concerns about the manuscript to personal characteristics of the author. This tactic contributes nothing toward the improvement of the manuscript. In fact, a personal attack may close the mind of the recipient to constructive criticism, destroy the writer's confidence, and discourage aspirations of being a writer.

Encouraging educators would instinctively know that sarcasm and ridicule are not effective for improving student performance. In lieu of the disparagement model, they would opt for a germination model of assessment where the topic is the seed and students' first attempts at writing are viewed as the planting of the seed. Teacher feedback on specific errors and strategies for improvement help to cultivate and weed the growing seed. Helpful comments and suggestions water the seed. Encouragement and praise provide the sunshine. Rewrites of the paper simulate stages of germination. A finished paper that is well-written is the blossom of the endeavor. A caustic critique can nip the germination process in the bud.

SCENARIO 15.5
Being Taught Red-Handed

In third grade our teacher Miss Y. decided to give us a quiz on our multiplication tables. The day before the test she told us that if we didn't make a 100, we would get a spanking (with a yardstick) on our hands. So of course I was upset and nervous. The day after the quiz Miss Y. went up and down the rows. When she came up to me all I got was my paper with a grade of 100 percent. I was relieved but upset because some children actually got the spankings in front of the whole class.

℞ The multiplication assessment in this scenario is reminiscent of the Gestapo tactics of old. In this case, having 100% on the quiz was the equivalent of having "papers." Going row by row and systematically spanking those who did not have 100% may be likened to stopping people to ask for their papers and arresting or punishing those that did not have them. Some of the teacher's misconceptions that are apparent here are that threats of punishment can guarantee outcomes or that assessment should be used to determine who needs punishment. The teacher seems unaware that assessment can be used to determine who needs remediation.

The teacher's terroristic tactics polluted the classroom climate with stress and anxiety that possibly affected everyone. The student in this scenario reported being relieved but upset because the class had to watch the children get spankings. The class probably experienced the spankings vicariously. The pressure to perform and the potential for punishment also contributed stress and anxiety to the classroom climate. Wigfield and Eccles (1989) warn of the perils of this combination.

Knowledgeable teachers know that assessment should provide feedback for students in need of remediation. These teachers know that using fear and punishment as a motivator is not as effective as using remediation, praise, and encouragement. They also recognize that having students compete with themselves and strive for improvement is much more effective than giving students one shot at a perfect score and punishment if they miss. Good teachers are cognizant that the quality of instruction may be a factor when students miss learning goals. They evaluate their instruction and reteach concepts if necessary. They realize that spanking has no role in the improvement of instruction. On the contrary, it has more potential for injury. Students need remediation, not punishment.

SCENARIO 15.6
Group Consequences: All or Nothing

In my senior year in high school, I had a group project in my sociology class. When the time came for our group to present our findings, one of our group members didn't show up. The teacher proceeded to tell us that we would all get zeros on the project. I then burst out of the room, went to the principal's office, and waited to see the principal. I was not going to allow my teacher to give me a zero. My teacher walks in and starts to scream at me for walking out of the class. I was humiliated, but we got an extension on our project.

℞ The potential for unfairness and inequity is an implicit problem in the assessment of group projects. In some instances, one student does all of the work and in some instances one or more students do very little or no work. Assessment becomes problematic when students' grades are contingent on the work of other students. The teacher had a rigid, high-stakes, all-or-nothing grading policy. All students had to be present for anyone to get a grade. It was not apparent that the teacher had communicated these grading criteria to students in advance because they seemed surprised by it.

Understandably, such a rigid, unfair policy precipitated a number of undesirable consequences. One of the students was vehemently opposed to the teacher's grading practice. The student's anger was possibly rooted in a fear of the impact of the grade of zero on being able to graduate. The teacher had a tangential tantrum about the student walking out of class but seemed oblivious to the looming fairness issue.

Proficient educators establish guidelines for group assessment in advance and make students aware of their criteria for grading. They realize the importance of basing individual grades on individual effort. Grades are not contingent on the performance of others. Perhaps a separate grade evaluates group effort and collaboration, but students are not penalized for criteria that are beyond their control. Effective teachers are mindful that students' grades should reflect their attainment of instructional objectives. They encourage students to do self-evaluation to become more self-regulating (Stiggins, 1994). They know that peer models are useful for teaching self-evaluation and other self-regulatory skills (Orange, 1999). These teachers model good evaluation when they grade fairly and follow these guidelines.

SCENARIO 15.7
Inflexible, Indifferent, Illogical, and Inaccurate

In third-grade math we took a test. I had all the answers correct, but I missed a space on the test so all my answers were off. The teacher placed me in the "lower" math group. She did not listen to me when I tried to explain what happened.

R̽ There are a number of assessment-related problems embedded in this scenario. One is using a single test score to place students in groups. This practice has many flaws, one of which is incorrect placement, as depicted in this scenario. The teacher's indifference to the student's mistake resulted in an illogical placement and inaccurate feedback. Such an inflexible environment leaves little room for students to make an error.

Clifford (1990) posits that the assessment environment should be conducive to risk taking and freedom to make mistakes without undue penalty. Astute teachers avoid the one-shot opportunity that discourages risk taking and opt for a more flexible form of assessment that allows students to make some mistakes with minimal, if any, penalty. An environment where students are not allowed to make mistakes impedes learning and hinders critical thinking. Good teachers may give practice tests or bonus questions to allow mistakes without penalty. If a student makes a simple error on a significant test, experienced teachers consider helping students to reconcile the mistake and obtain their actual score. In this scenario, the student had all the correct answers in the wrong places. Helping the student make the correct placement is more important than penalizing the student for the mistake. Moreover, the effective teacher is aware of the ills of ability grouping and is wary of placing a student in a low group using one criterion, a test score, even if it is a standardized test. There are a variety of forms of assessment that could supplement a test score and help teachers make a more informed decision if they insisted on grouping by ability.

SCENARIO 15.8
Tragedy on the Classroom Stage

In my senior year of high school, I had to take either band or theater arts to be the first valedictorian to graduate under the advanced diploma plan. I chose theater arts even though I was shy and really dreaded it. I asked the teacher for exemption from the Christmas play for religious reasons. (She seemed to take this personally.) During the many weeks preparing for the play, the only thing I was asked to do one day was go to the local craft store and get some materials. One Wednesday she told everyone that they would have a dress rehearsal. Well, I didn't think that applied to me because she had me stuck off behind her when she said it, plus the fact she never gave me anything to do. So I didn't go. I went to church. My best friend tried to call me when she arrived and found out I was going to get a zero for not being there. She actually had to lie to the teacher and sneak across the street because the teacher wouldn't let her call me. (She didn't reach me.)

The next morning, I was in history class and the principal came and got me. I couldn't imagine what was going on because I was never in trouble. When we got to his office, the teacher was there and she started literally screaming at me for not going to her practice. She then told me that she had given me specific duties to do when in fact she had not. She gave me a zero with no way of making it up. I was devastated.

℞ This scenario had the makings of a tragedy rooted in religious drama from the beginning. The setting is a dreaded drama class that the student is forced to take. Next, she opted out of the play for religious reasons. Her shyness may also have influenced her decision. The teacher was not pleased, possibly because the play was a major part of the grade. The student seemed to think the teacher took her exemption from the play personally. The plot thickens, as the student is truly exempt from the production because she has no specific duties or responsibilities. The turning point in the story is when the student skips dress rehearsal because of some miscommunication about her role in the rehearsal. The cliffhanger is that a friend tries to warn her of the impending danger of getting a zero, but the teacher will not let her. BOO. HISS. The teacher emerges as the villain, going after the student with a vengeance. She enlists the help of the administration to bring in the student. Foul play and suffering is heaped upon the student as the screaming teacher lies about the student's duties. In a moment of high drama, the teacher gets her revenge by giving the student a zero with no opportunity to make it up. The student endures the suffering and accepts her tragic lot. Tragically, she may not have made valedictorian. She is doomed to remember and relive this event for many years.

Discerning teachers would suspect that fear and shyness were protagonists in this classroom drama. These teachers would have alternative duties and ways of assessing the performance of a shy student. They would also respect the student's religious decision and offer an alternative assessment. These experienced teachers would inform the student of expectations, specific alternative responsibilities, and grading criteria in advance. There would be no reason to use grades to punish the student because there would be no misunderstanding. A potential tragedy would become an ordinary classroom performance with the potential of a happy ending.

5

PERSONALITY AND PROFESSIONALISM

"Looks aren't everything. It's what's inside you that really matters. A biology teacher told me that."

Mistake

16

Teacher Insensitivity

My English teacher offered to help students with their papers before they handed them in. As a student eager to do well, I went to her for help. She basically destroyed the essay as well as my self-confidence in my writing. I can still vividly see my introduction crossed out in red. I had spent so long working on it that to see it all rejected felt horrible. While she was supposedly trying to help me rewrite it, more of her ideas and words were going down on the paper. I can't remember her exact words, but I know for years afterwards, I had horrible writer's block. It took me several years to accept the idea that I might be a good writer. I still can't put words and sentences down unless I think they are perfect. Additionally, since then, I have never asked a teacher for help with a paper.

℞ Traditionally, red ink was used in accounting procedures to record debits and losses. Perhaps educators borrowed from this practice and used red ink to grade student papers to note deficiencies and mistakes. The practice of using red ink for grading has been so overused and misused that red ink has become symbolic with failure. When students see returned papers covered with red ink, they often see red. After their anger subsides, they are left with diminished self-confidence and fear of failure or of making mistakes. Some teachers, like the one in this scenario, are insensitive to the effect red ink has on students. Although her intent was to help the student, the teacher in this scenario was not sensitive to the student's reaction to the grading. It seems suspect that so much of the student's paper was crossed out in red.

Effective teachers know that they need to clearly state the objectives and expectations for the assignment. Brophy (1982) attributed some student failure to a lack of clarity about what they're supposed to be doing for the assignment.

Good teachers know the importance of balancing criticisms with positives. They praise student effort and hard work as they make suggestions for improvements. Skilled teachers avoid imposing their words and ideas on students. Instead, they encourage students to critically evaluate their own work and edit and revise it as needed. This helps students to appropriately attribute their successes and failures (Weiner, 1979). An alternative is for both the teacher and the student to edit and critique the paper, then compare their edits. If there are any discrepancies in the edits, the student is responsible for using references to look them up and determine which is correct. Finally, a good way to keep students from seeing red is to use other colors to grade papers, such as green or purple.

SCENARIO 16.2
And the "Winner" Is . . .

My worst experience with a teacher came when I was in junior high, and there was an awards ceremony in PE. All the students in three classes were sitting in the bleachers, and the three PE teachers were down on the gym floor. They would call each student receiving an award individually to come down to receive their ribbon, certificate, letter, etc. I was never good at sports, so I knew my name would not be called. I was very surprised when I heard, ". . . and the next award goes to (my name)." The award was for "BIGGEST PHYSICAL RETARD."

They meant this to be funny. I have no actual physical disabilities. All the students laughed. I tried to take it in good humor, but I felt humiliated. My adult perspective is that it's a terrible idea to make fun of an adolescent in public. Even if the child knows that it is a joke, no big attention should be made that is derogatory—especially in front of a large group!

R̶x̶ Award ceremonies are usually held to recognize students for their accomplishments. At award ceremonies, there is usually an air of goodwill and anticipation, as students wait to see if they have won something. When students win, emotions are high and joy prevails. When students lose, hope often informs the determination to do better next time. When students are ridiculed for their efforts, hope becomes humiliation and pain prevails.

The insensitive coaches had no regard for the student's well-being. They all had a good, hearty laugh at the student's expense. Students have a difficult time in school when they are different in any way. In this case, maybe the student had poor coordination or a physical problem. Whatever the reason, it did not warrant the humiliation of a student under the guise of a gag award. To make matters worse, the student felt compelled to laugh with the crowd to conceal the depth of her pain.

Good teachers would only use an award ceremony for that which it was intended . . . to recognize achievement.

They would never use the ceremony as a forum for humiliation and shame. Woolfolk (1998) decries anything that draws attention to a student's physical differences, which includes physical performance. Instead of looking at a student's effort as half bad, it is more helpful and productive to view it as half good. An award that recognizes effort is much better than a nonproductive attempt at humor.

SCENARIO 16.3
Name Sweet Name

In third grade I was adopted and my last name changed during the middle of the year from M. C. to M. B. My teacher refused to change my name. I was so excited to be adopted by my stepfather and it deeply upset me that she would not acknowledge it. She insisted on calling me by the wrong last name.

℞ The adoptive process is centered on the welfare of the child—the physical and psychological welfare. Adoption obviously boosted this student's self-esteem and sense of belonging. Having a new last name was symbolic of the love and acceptance she had been granted. The teacher threw cold water on her happiness by refusing to acknowledge her new name. It's difficult to determine if the teacher's inaction was rooted in malice or ignorance. There is no excuse for either.

Insightful teachers would sense the feelings of happiness and pride that being adopted gave this student. They would make a conscious effort to remember the new name. Many teachers would take the opportunity to help the child celebrate the new name by reintroducing her to the class, using her adopted name. Another way to acknowledge the student would be to put the child's picture on the wall with the new name underneath and the word "congratulations" over the picture. These acknowledgments should only be done with the child's permission.

SCENARIO 16.4
Exit Front and Center Stage

In first grade I had an accident in class during naptime and the teacher made it obvious. I sat in the back of class. There was a back door out of the room, but she made me first sop up my mess with paper towels, then leave the room out the front with the wastebasket to go to the principal's office.

R̸ The problem in this scenario is that the teacher treated a young child's accident as if it was a misdemeanor that warranted shame and public exhibition. Having the child clean up the mess, carry the trashcan containing the soggy mess, and, as a finale, take the trashcan out of the front door was a demeaning, covert form of punishment.

The insensitive teacher had no empathy for the child and made a conscious effort to make the situation obvious. Perhaps the motive for this less-than-empathetic response was that the teacher felt she could not let the accident go unnoticed because it may encourage others to do the same.

Empathic teachers would respond to the child's accident with minimal attention and class interruption. They would send for the janitor to do a quick clean up while they directed their students' attention to other relevant instructional matters. Students would learn the valuable lesson that accidents happen and maintaining dignity is a better approach to handling an accident than is invoking shame. Children should not be sent to center stage for unintentional acts of behavior that are better known as accidents.

SCENARIO 16.5
Eye to Swollen Eye

My PE teacher completely ignored me when I told her my eye was bitten by an ant and was swollen. By the time I got back to regular class, my eye was swollen shut and I couldn't see. The main thing I was mad about was that she completely ignored me and didn't even look at me.

R̸ The teacher in this scenario didn't bother to look at a student who was complaining of an eye injury. This reckless act of indifference could have endangered the injured student. If the teacher had at least made eye contact, she could have readily seen that the student's eye was swelling rapidly. The student could have had an allergic reaction or serious injury to the eye. Prompt attention to an injury is necessary to protect the well-being of the child. This teacher's lack of response borders on negligence.

Prudent teachers investigate all student complaints of injury immediately. Although some complaints may be trivial, to ignore them may risk ignoring a serious or life-threatening injury. Sometimes just acknowledging students' injuries makes them feel better. It's human nature to want to tell someone where it hurts. Good teachers are willing to listen.

SCENARIO 16.6
Diagnosis: Faking

My worst experience was in the fourth grade. My teacher made fun of me and called me names like "baby" because I was very sick with migraine headaches. She would accuse me of faking just to go home. I used to cry all the time, especially when I was sick, because I was scared. I never ever faked. To this day, I am a migraine headache sufferer and I go through a lot of treatments that include daily medicine, therapy, and Demerol. But that teacher was the poorest excuse for a teacher that I ever had. My mother was furious and had a real long, LOUD talk with her one day and then she changed her ways.

℞ The unsympathetic, insensitive teacher in this scenario is not trained to diagnose illnesses, but she presumed to diagnose faking an illness. She taunted and ridiculed a sick child because she thought the child just wanted to go home. She labeled the child a baby because the child cried about her illness. Migraine is a serious illness that involves headaches, severe pain, and visual disturbances. The severity of the migraine varies by individual. For a fourth grader, intense pain and visual disturbances can be very scary.

Sensitive, compassionate teachers would respect the student's illness, show concern, and offer assistance.

Teachers should never assume that a student is not ill. If they don't want to take the student's word for it, they should request doctor's statements or other documentation to verify the illness. Consulting parents about the legitimacy of the illness is a good alternative.

I am a lucky migraine sufferer. I have migraines with visual disturbances but without the pain. They began when I was a sophomore in college. It was very scary for me and I was an adult at the time. Good teachers know that illness is scary, and they make efforts to calm students and to make them more comfortable.

SCENARIO 16.7
When the Bough Cracks

I was sick and had ulcers. I went to class and I had to get up and leave the classroom. I felt ill and knew I was going to be sick. When I got up and was walking toward the door, my teacher chased me out and yelled at me for leaving. He embarrassed me in front of everybody. I told him I was sick and was going to the bathroom. He just turned around and said he was going to mark me absent.

℞ The new green twig on the branch of a tree is full of life, supple and yielding as it bends to withstand the winds of change. In contrast, the dead, dry twig is hard, unyielding, unbending, often cracking under the forces of change and nonconformity. In many ways, the teacher in this scenario is like the dead, dry twig. He is hard and calloused in his attempt to punish a sick child. When the sick student breaks the rules by abruptly attempting to leave the classroom, the teacher turns a deaf ear to the student's explanation. The teacher finally cracks and starts yelling and chasing the student. His cracked, irrational behavior shatters the peace of the classroom. His punitive action has embarrassed the student, created an inaccurate attendance record that could cost the school some dollars, and encouraged truancy.

Like the green twig, reasonable teachers easily bend and sway with change. If there is a change in routine or a disruption in class because a student is ill, these teachers skillfully handle the emergency without losing momentum. They would keep the disruption to a minimum by giving some gesture of approval to assure the student that leaving is permissible. Caring teachers would follow up to make sure the student was feeling better or to provide further assistance. They are flexible and willing to relax the rules in times of crisis.

SCENARIO 16.8
The Bereaved Must Leave

When I was in fourth grade, my grandmother had just passed away. Since we were very close, that was a difficult time for me. I would cry in class sometimes when I began to think about her. One day I was crying, and Ms. H. sent me out into the hall.

℞ Bereavement is a state of loss of a loved one. Grief is the overwhelming feeling of anguish or sorrow that accompanies bereavement. Crying is a natural expression of that grief. Children and adults cry over the loss of loved ones. Crying is therapeutic for some people. If crying is so natural, healthy, and therapeutic, why is the teacher so bothered by it? The teacher's discomfort with the child's display of grief may be attributed to the conventions of our society. A public display of grief, outside of funerals, is viewed as disconcerting and sometimes inappropriate. As a society we are uncomfortable with tears. We are quick to offer a tissue to sop them and stop them. Sending the child to the hall for crying was an insensitive act that may give a child the impression that she had done something wrong.

Compassionate teachers are tolerant of tears. If a child is crying, these teachers feel compelled to investigate the cause of the crying and to offer comfort if necessary. Gelman (1983) contends that people should be allowed to work through their grief. Understandably, teachers might have a problem with crying if it disturbs the class too much. They might involve a counselor or social worker when the child needs to cry. Resourceful teachers would seize the occurrence as an opportunity to discuss bereavement, grief, and expressions of grief. Caring teachers may be tempted to touch or hug a crying child. Teachers, if they must hug, should know that they do so at their own risk. An alternative would be to have a volunteer hugger or a close friend of the student offer comfort. This may be effective for young children. Explaining the nature of grief and providing comfort for the student could reduce a potentially disruptive occurrence down to a minimal distraction.

SCENARIO 16.9
Children Must Be Seen and Heard

When I look back at grade school and think about my worst experience, Mrs. P. immediately comes into my mind. She was the PE coach, and I always thought she was so mean. One day in PE class, I was talking too much, well at least in Mrs. P.'s eyes I was. To be honest, I do not even remember if I was talking a lot that day, I was always so quiet and never got in trouble. After PE class that day, Mrs. P. told me, "A., you have not shut your mouth today at all!"

As I walked away, I was so hurt and wanted to cry. What hurt even more was when my third-grade (and all-time favorite) teacher told me that Mrs. P. said I misbehaved that day. I admired Mrs. B. so much. She was so disappointed in me, and I will never forget that day.

I hope that one day I will meet Mrs. P., and let her know that I am going to be an elementary teacher very soon, and that I have learned and experienced so much. PE class should allow young children to be free and expressive to a certain extent. I do not think talking should be punished with such harsh and personal words. They could remain with a child for a lifetime. I can still hear her voice so well in my head, even today. I lived through the experience, but it scares me to think of the other little kids who will not live through it.

℞ The last part of the student's scenario is a fine response to the first part. He is about to join the ranks of good teachers who would agree with him. Young children should be free and expressive in classes like art, physical education, and music.

SCENARIO 16.10
Stripped of Protective Coating

In Mrs. D.'s class I was wearing an overcoat over clothes that didn't match. I was overweight and wore hand-me-downs and she made me take off the coat. I cried because I felt insecure even though she thought I was probably just hot and sweaty. I was made to feel naked and exposed; the teacher did not have a clue or did not care.

℞ This scenario is a twist on the children's story, "The Emperor's New Clothes." In that story, the Emperor was duped into believing he was wearing a fine suit of clothes when in reality, he was actually naked. He felt happy and proud and paraded himself before his subjects. In contrast, the young girl in this scenario was wearing clothes, yet she felt naked and exposed. She was not happy or proud; in fact, she was ashamed and vulnerable. She was psychologically exposed once her coat or "shame cover-up" was removed. Middle-school and high-school students typically experience a period of vulnerability as their bodies are developing and they become overly conscious of their appearance. Students with perceived flaws will go to great lengths to camouflage them. These students prefer to keep a low profile at school, particularly if they are likely to draw unwanted attention to themselves. A student wearing an overcoat out of season should send up a red flag for the astute teacher that is paying attention. A sensitive teacher would make a private inquiry and ask the child if she is uncomfortable and if she wants to remove the coat. Such a teacher would intuitively know that the child is trying to hide something, particularly when the child refuses to take the coat off in adverse conditions.

The student in this scenario may be correct in her belief that the teacher just did not care. In our society and schools, there is much bias directed toward overweight, poor children. This probably was not the first time the child wore hand-me-downs that heralded her lower socioeconomic status. The teacher's behavior toward the student may reflect her personal bias or perception that children of low socioeconomic status are not worthy of respect and gentle treatment. Tirri (2001) contends that a teacher's personal preferences or biases can override their sense of professionalism and cause them to make moral mistakes. A more foreboding perspective suggests that the teacher knew what she was doing and derived some pleasure out of humiliating the student. Most likely, the teacher was just insensitive and unable to read the telling signs of student distress. This teacher could benefit from lessons, such as valuing the student to improve children's self-esteem, offered by Canfield and Wells (1976). I believe the key to avoiding a problem like this is for teachers to make every effort to respect a student's right to privacy. They should be sensitive to the struggles of overweight and poor children, supporting whatever means their students might employ to protect their young, vulnerable self-image and self-esteem.

SCENARIO 16.11
Turning a Deaf Ear to Bullyragging

When I was in the sixth grade I was attending a new school and found it difficult to fit in. I was constantly tormented by a group of girls. They started calling me Miss Perfect and soon it caught on and everyone in my class was doing it. I told my mother about it and the next morning she was talking to the teacher about it. I'll never forget the lack of interest that the teacher showed. Needless to say, she did nothing about putting an end to it. That was the worst year of my life and I was 12. I transferred to another school the following year. As a teacher, I will never tolerate this behavior and will try to put a stop to this type of "bullying."

℞ Bullying has two faces as evidenced by this scenario. Calling the student "Miss Perfect" seemed on the surface to be harmless, but considering the context in which it occurred and the student's impervious pleas for help, this places this namecalling in the same category as other offensive forms of bullying. This form of bullying is sometimes referred to as bullyragging. Turning a deaf ear and a blind eye to bullying is a luxury that teachers can no longer afford. Bullying has many negative consequences such as teen suicide, student alienation, school violence, and an increasing drop-out rate. Society is demanding that schools become more accountable in dealing with a bullying situation.

Caring, conscientious teachers recognize that bullying manifests in a variety of forms. It is not just fighting or calling students bad names, sometimes it's calling students good names that are meant to be uncomplimentary. Bullying is any behavior that makes a child feel tormented such as in this scenario. Bullying is where a child endures continuous harassment or student-perceived aversive behaviors on a regular basis. This includes but is not limited to namecalling, particularly special names coined for a certain child, such as "Miss Perfect" in this scenario. Matters are worsened when no one intervenes. It is typical of bullying situations that bystanders seldom say or

do anything to intervene because they are afraid, they don't want to get involved, or they are afraid that their intervention will not make a difference. Some bystanders don't intervene because they enjoy the tormenting and aggression. They are often empowered by the bully and some of them join in the tormenting behavior. Teachers who don't intervene are a part of this bystander effect. They allow bad things to happen to children because of their indifference. The astute teacher knows that intervention is the key to dismantling a bullying situation.

Savvy teachers are constantly on the alert for less-popular children that are the outsiders and are not a part of the school's "in crowd." Students in the in crowd are often cruel to outsiders and those perceived to be weaker than they are. Thompson, and Cohen (2005) suggest that there is a culture of cruelty in American schools that perpetuates stress and anxiety for the victims of the in crowd. Teachers that recognize the less-popular victims of the in crowd can alleviate the plight of these victims by befriending them and giving them positive recognition. As the adage points out, "You are nobody until somebody loves you."

Caring teachers have a moral obligation to recognize and stop bullying immediately. They should make it clear that there will be no tolerance for bullying and there will be severe consequence for those engaging in bullying behavior. There is no margin of error for failure to address bullying. The damage resulting from constant bullying can be permanent and in some cases, deadly. Persecuted, alienated children have been known to strike back in violence or to turn their pain inward and end their lives. Teachers must take up arms, in a sense, and aid students in the psychological battle against powerful peers who wish to victimize others. These teachers effect change by teaching students to love and respect each other, by empowering the disempowered, and by dousing any flickers of bullying behavior immediately, whenever, wherever, and in whatever form it appears.

Mistake

17

Academic Shortcomings

SCENARIO 17.1
Shame and Punishment

My worst experience with a teacher was my first-grade teacher. She sent me to the corner and didn't allow me to be a helper (chalkboard cleaner) because I could not write my name correctly. I was devastated and felt ashamed of my incompetence. I also was extremely nervous the remainder of the year.

℞ This teacher is confused in her assumption that "not learning" is a punishable offense to be punctuated by shame and deprivation. According to information processing theory, several exposures and repetitions of material are necessary to encode information into long-term memory (Woolfolk, 1998). Good teachers know that some young children have more difficulty learning skills and concepts than do others. They are aware that cognitive development varies in children (Piaget, 1952) so they expect variation in children's classroom performance. There are so many traditional and innovative ways to help children learn to write their names that punishment need never have been an option. Effective teachers are aware that shame is not an effective motivator. Competent teachers would have used some writing readiness activities or some one-on-one instruction to help their students practice. They would try not to discourage their students by shaming them. Instead, these teachers would empower their students by praising their efforts and inspiring them to do better the next time.

SCENARIO 17.2
Ducking the Stoning Incident

When I was in second grade I had a problem with two young boys who were in another class. During my PE class they would throw rocks at me. One day I told my teacher what they were doing and she did not believe me. She told me to stop acting like a baby and she did nothing to help me out.

℞ In biblical times stoning, or throwing rocks at a person, was an act of violence that was used to kill someone. Although the students' rock throwing is on a smaller scale, it is still an act of violence. The teacher ducked her responsibility in the rock-throwing incident and blamed the victim. Her lack of action sent some negative messages and paved the way for some serious consequences.

One negative message was that the student was unimportant and not worthy of protection. The teacher's indifference added psychological insult to the victim's physical injuries. The teacher's indifference sent a message to the young men that there were no consequences for their violent, antisocial actions. This message has serious potential consequences for the young males. By successfully participating in minor misbehaviors, they may get the impression that it's acceptable to engage in inappropriate behavior. Kauffman (1989) found that boys are more likely to be discipline problems than are girls. Ignoring the young boys' behavior places them at risk for engaging in more serious delinquent or criminal actions.

Although the teacher managed to duck the rock-throwing incident, she might have had a little more difficulty ducking a lawsuit if the young men had injured the student. The school has a responsibility to protect students by preventing or punishing serious discipline problems. The teacher placed herself, the school, the victim, and the perpetrators in jeopardy by ignoring this act of violence.

Sensible teachers act on misbehavior immediately. Gottfredson (1984) stressed the importance of communicating to students that they must obey school rules. Otherwise, schools run the risk of communicating to errant students that misbehavior is sanctioned. Responsible teachers know it's important to act immediately, before misbehavior escalates into delinquency. Good teachers try to prevent misbehavior; they punish inappropriate behaviors and get parents involved as much as possible. Creative teachers can find ways of teaching prosocial behaviors that effectively diminish antisocial behaviors.

When I was teaching elementary school and students hurt other students, they had to apologize and make their victim feel better. I would have them wipe their victim's tears, get their victim a drink of water, and in some cases, rub the child's hand and ask if he or she felt better. Most of the time, both students would end up smiling or laughing. Sometimes, I would make the perpetrator the victim's protector for the rest of the day.

I tried to do this in a humorous way. It worked for me. Sometimes students would give their own genuine apology and they would play together at recess.

Years ago I visited a classroom that had a rule posted that said,

"Hands are for hugging and for loving." I was really impressed with the prosocial message in this rule. My hope is that more teachers will adopt prosocial rules for their classroom that extends beyond the traditional "Don't do this and don't do that."

SCENARIO 17.3
A Know-a-Little and a Know-It-All

I cannot pinpoint a specific negative experience. The general ideas that come to mind include a teacher who did not know her content area as well as I did as a student. We often had arguments about answers that I would win. Another teacher told students they were "misguided and wrong" if they did not agree with his interpretations of history.

℞ Some above-average students have an overinflated sense of what they think they know. In some cases they're not teachable because they think they know more than the teacher knows. On the other hand, sometimes these students are correct; sometimes they do know more than the teacher knows about the content area. Some teachers have an overinflated sense of what they know about their subject and fail to adequately prepare for their lessons. I was supervising a student teacher who found herself in the embarrassing predicament of not knowing some fifth-grade math. She informed me later that she was so sure that fifth-grade math would be easy that she didn't bother to prepare for the lesson.

Wise teachers seldom take content for granted. If they have been teaching for awhile, they know that content may reflect new developments, techniques, concepts, and understandings. Most teachers know that nothing is constant but changes, and

that it pays off in instructional dividends to be prepared. Advanced preparation of lessons helps teachers pinpoint areas of weakness before they present the information to students. Resourceful teachers make productive use of this advanced warning to correct any deficiencies that are apparent.

The second example in this scenario features a very authoritarian approach to instruction. The teacher seems to think he's all knowing and students are misguided and wrong if they don't agree with him. Constructivist teachers know that it's important to help students construct their own meaning to make sense of the world (Anderson, 1989). They are aware that it's difficult to do that if they discount their students' contributions. These teachers realize they must let students have a voice and a choice in instructional matters. Belenky et al. (1986) suggest that teachers learn to trust and respect each student's experience.

Wise teachers attach value to their students' responses and interpretations although they might not agree with them. Good teachers want their students to become more self-regulated learners, which means that they are willing to become less involved in lessons and become more of a facilitator of learning. These teachers encourage students to participate more in their own learning, and to assume responsibility for what they learn and to rely less on the teacher.

SCENARIO 17.4
Academic Inquisition

One of the experiences that happened to me in grade school was during Halloween. Trying to act like my mom (who is a Jehovah's Witness), I went to school and did not participate in the Halloween party. My teachers asked me why and I explained that my mom doesn't celebrate the holidays. The teacher phoned my mom to tell her my position and when I got home my mom did not say it was good or bad which was very confusing for me. I wasn't mad at the teacher, just confused.

℞ One definition of inquisitions is an investigation that violates the privacy or rights of individuals (*American Heritage Dictionary,* 1992). This kind of activity dates back to the thirteenth century when the Roman Catholic Church used inquisition to combat heresy (*Concise Columbia Encyclopedia,* 1995). This teacher's actions are reminiscent of the actions of the old tribunal. She dared to question and interfere with a student's religious preferences. Calling the mother about the mother's religion and her son's choice was clearly a violation of the family's privacy.

Sensitive teachers respect a student's religion and culture. If students choose to adopt their parents' religion, which is often the case, teachers should respect that choice. It seemed that the mother did not try to impose her religion on her child, which possibly explains why the mother had nothing to say about the child's decision. The mother appeared to respect her child's right to choose and the teacher should do no less.

SCENARIO 17.5
Jumping to a Gender-Biased Conclusion

I was in fourth grade and in all of the "A"-group classes. I made As in everything except math, but got thrown into "honors" math because I was in this group. I remember making a failing grade on a test. When my mother went to parent–teacher conferences, the teacher had us sit in with our parents. My mom asked her what she could do to help me and the teacher said, "Nothing, she is just not a math person and will never be." To this day I have a phobia of math!

℞ "Never" is such an absolute term. Imagine a child hearing that she is "not a math person and will never be." Such a label of hopelessness could easily become a self-fulfilling prophecy (Rosenthal & Jacobson, 1968). Why would a female teacher make such a disparaging remark about a young girl? One guess is that she may be echoing comments that were once made to her or her female classmates. If she is unaware of the gender bias in math classes against girls, she may see nothing wrong with her comments. When I was in high school, I can remember a math teacher saying to me, "You should never take any more math classes, you're too careless." I internalized this opinion and I freely told people that I was not very good in math. I only took the required math courses in my undergraduate studies. I only aspired to a C because, after all, I wasn't very good at math. I nurtured this belief until I applied for graduate school. I froze when I saw that statistics was a required course. I was very upset when I realized I couldn't get through the educational psychology degree plan without taking that statistics course. Fortunately, I had a great professor, Dr. Linda Stewart, who was a visionary. She was aware of mathematical gender bias long before the study that revealed that girls were often short-changed by schools (AAUW, 1992). She encouraged me to enroll in the program and wait for her to teach the statistics course. She already knew that I had been told I was not suitable for math and had been advised not to take any more math courses. She assured me that I would do well in her course because she had a systematic way of teaching that made it easier for women. I received an A in statistics and I was elated, not so much because of the grade, but because I could dispel the myth that I wasn't good in math. I regained my confidence, but I was one of the lucky ones. There are many young girls that never regain their confidence, as evidenced by the author of this scenario.

The first step toward eliminating bias is to become aware of it. Encouraging teachers are necessary to imbue young girls with the confidence they need to take more math courses. The American Association of University Women (1992) found that boys have better math scores than girls on the SAT. They attributed that discrepancy to girls taking fewer math classes rather than to a lack of ability. Maple and Stage (1991) found that girls are now taking more math classes and the gender gap on math scores is closing.

Good teachers never say never, especially when trying to predict a student's success in an area. Possible is a better word than never; it's a word that fosters hope. We can empower students by telling them that anything is possible.

SCENARIOS 17.6 and 17.7
Tread Lightly, but Do Tread

All through school I was always labeled as a hyper child so I labeled myself as a hyper child who had a hard time in school and it was not till I was twenty-two years old I was discovered as being ADD. It really frustrates me still today that my disability was not discovered until two years ago! However, I am dealing with it and, for the first time in college, I made an A on a test with the help of Ritalin, and last semester I got a 2.0— the closest I have ever gotten to a 3.0.

Another experience was my junior year in high school and I was in Advanced Geometry, the first advanced class I ever attempted and I was studying with my mom and my boyfriend, C. After turning the homework in, C. and I both missed the same problems and he was a straight-A, advanced student and I was a B, C, regular student, and she called me a cheater!

In third grade I visited the orthodontist over Christmas vacation and was fitted for a retainer. Anyone who has experienced this knows it can be humiliating, especially in the speech department. It takes some getting used to. When school resumed I was still having some difficulty. My teacher, obviously hoping to be awarded "teacher of the year" for noticing this defect, placed me with a speech pathologist.

℞ Trying to determine if a student has a learning disability or a physical disability is a difficult, sensitive process. Teachers should tread lightly in these areas, being careful not to misdiagnose, but tread they must, lest they miss a diagnosis or condition. Scenario 17.7 is a misdiagnosis. The teacher jumped to the erroneous conclusion that the student had speech difficulties and remanded the student to a speech pathologist without further investigation. If she had treaded lightly and talked to the student first or obtained further evidence of a problem, she could have avoided misdiagnosing the student. The teacher does deserve credit for trying to act on the student's behalf.

Scenario 17.6 is a case of missed diagnosis. For about twenty years, no one suspected the student had attention deficit disorder. This disorder is making its way to the forefront of research on exceptional learners, as increased knowledge of the disorder becomes available.

Diagnosing attention deficit disorder (ADD) may be difficult because it mimics attention problems in other disorders (Slavin, 1994) and in some cases, children may have difficulty paying attention and not have ADD or any other disorder.

To avoid missing a diagnosis of a disorder or misdiagnosing a disorder, effective teachers will proactively arm themselves with knowledge. They learn how to identify learning disabilities according to their school district's rules, regulations, and requirements. They learn characteristics of students with learning disabilities or physical challenges. They become knowledgeable of the legal ramifications of serving exceptional learners. Effective teachers tread lightly in recommending students for special education to avoid contributing to the disproportionate number of males and African Americans that are overrepresented in special education (U.S. Department of Education, 1991).

SCENARIO 17.8
All Talk and No Teaching

My worst experience with a teacher occurred with my dance instructor my senior year. She taught the dance class the dance team was required to take. I was the colonel of the team and therefore had to work very closely with the teacher. It was her first year at the high school; however, she had been a teacher for another Texas school for two years before. She was totally unprofessional with her job. Days that we were to practice a dance routine for competition, she would sit the whole team down and explain how her house was haunted with ghosts. She wanted to be everyone's friend instead of teacher. She was eventually fired about three-fourths of the way through the year. Being that I was the colonel, an unbelievable amount of stress and responsibility was placed on me. I should have been paid for doing her job. There are so many stories I could tell you that you wouldn't even believe. It's really sad when I look back to my senior year as being the worst. I truly believe that if I hadn't gone through what I did, I would have gone on to become a professional dancer. This teacher just took my will to dance and crushed it.

R̥ A favorite source of recreation for many students is to get the teacher to go off on the proverbial tangent, in other words, to digress from the subject matter. Students find it more difficult to get experienced, prepared teachers to digress. This teacher was inexperienced and obviously unprepared. She presented very little challenge to students; as a matter of fact, she made it very easy for students to deviate from the subject matter. She totally abdicated her responsibilities as a teacher to talk about ghosts in her home. Perhaps she wanted to entertain her students, or there is always the possibility that she was mentally disturbed. Whatever the problem, she was not functioning as a competent teacher. She shifted her responsibilities to her student assistant. Her student suffered much psychological harm as a result.

Competent teachers know that first and foremost, they should put their students' instructional needs before their own personal needs. Most teachers like to interact with their students. They are well aware that teachers should be friendly but not necessarily the students' friend. Effective teachers will entertain their students occasionally but they realize that entertainment is no substitute for structure, organization, and quality instruction. These teachers will have instructional objectives that will keep them focused on the lesson and make it harder for students to distract them or direct them to some tangential topic. Finally, most conscientious teachers do their own teaching and rarely shift that responsibility to a student.

SCENARIO 17.9
Don't Know Fall From Autumn

My worst experience was in kindergarten. I was asked, "What are the four seasons?" I replied, "Winter, Spring, Summer, Fall." The teacher said, "No, it's not Fall, it's Autumn." I was mortified and never went back. I wouldn't tell my mother why I was so upset. It's a wonder I learned to enjoy school when I started first grade the next year!

℞ The student had a rather extreme reaction to the teacher correcting the student's response to the question. Perhaps it was because the teacher's "correct" answer was incorrect. Apparently, the teacher wasn't aware that autumn and fall are used interchangeably. In the dictionary, autumn means fall (*American Heritage Dictionary,* 1992). If the teacher was aware that they were the same, she didn't have to embarrass the student to express her preference. Experienced teachers would not have missed the opportunity to let the child know that fall is also referred to as autumn. However, those teachers would be savvy enough to praise the student's response first and introduce the idea of autumn as a bit of extra information. An idea-friendly environment would encourage meaningful exchange of information between students and teachers. Students should be encouraged to give added information when it is appropriate. This scenario should encourage teachers to proceed with caution when correcting students with such absolute certainty. Good teachers are prepared to admit they are wrong if they make a mistake, or if they are not sure an answer is correct, they put it on hold until they can research it.

SCENARIO 17.10
Teaching Solo Students Can't Hear You

I was in tenth grade. I had this teacher who was from somewhere else other than the United States. She always wore long sleeves and a long dress or pants. She also wore a scarf over her head. Her whole body was covered. Anyway, she had no control in the classroom. Everyone was always loud and she would teach from an overhead and talk so softly that no one could hear her. I did not learn geometry at all that semester. To this day I have a lot of trouble with it. She just did not know how to teach well.

℞ Effective communication is a critical component of effective instruction. How can students learn if they can't hear the lesson? Students can't hear if the class is disorderly. Judging from the student's account, the teacher had no control of her class. Her soft-spoken attempt at instruction was rejected by the students, as evidenced by the disorder and chaos and the lack of participation in the educational process. This teacher was truly teaching solo. She lost her students when she opened her mouth and nothing came out but whispers and snatches of academic information.

Experienced teachers would use what's commonly referred to in academia as the "teacher voice." Developing this voice is an art that requires practice. A good teacher voice is audible, clear, purposeful, commanding, and can usually project across the room. Skilled teachers know that using the teacher voice appropriately minimizes discipline problems and effectively enhances instruction. Voice inflection, volume, accent will help communicate the teacher's messages and desires to the students. Expert teachers are able to use their voices to command student attention and to communicate a no-nonsense approach to their lessons.

SCENARIO 17.11
The Incarceration of Originality

The worst experience ever with a teacher was in kindergarten when a substitute teacher asked me to color a worksheet that had a witch on it. I decided to color my witch orange. After I had finished coloring my picture I proudly went to show it to my substitute and she proceeded to tell me how ugly it was and that witches were supposed to be black, so she made me color it over in black.

℞ Primary students are known to make nontraditional uses of color in their artwork. The proud student did some creative coloring and tried to share it with a teacher. Under the guise of a mindless art critic, the teacher assaulted the child's competence and incarcerated her originality. She forced the student to change the bright orange witch to traditional black. She committed the ultimate sin of artistic evaluation: She called the student's artwork ugly.

Diplomatic teachers know that it's considered ill mannered and in bad taste to call an adult artist's work ugly, so why say that to a child? These teachers know that beauty and ugliness are both in the eye of the beholder. Teachers who seek to inspire budding artists celebrate their freshness, creativity, and originality. They limit their criticism of children's work because a budding Picasso may be among these children. Torrance (1972) found that teachers' judgment of children's artwork was not necessarily a good indicator of the creativity these children exhibited later in life. Astute teachers seek to foster creativity and encourage originality. They will encourage students to go where their vision takes them. These teachers embrace nonconformity and are amenable to divergence. Caring teachers seek to ignite and sustain the creative spark in all students.

Mistake

18

Poor Administration

My worst memory of school was in high school, my sophomore year. That year I joined the drill team because the instructor said they were going to change the image by using dancers and better costumes. So they hired a guy to choreograph the dances and design the costumes. Well, the dances were just awful and when the first game came to be, no one had seen our costumes. At the first game, the guy gave us our costumes just before we were supposed to go on. Those costumes were ugly and didn't fit anyone. The smallest one they could find to put on me still had to be wrapped around me three or four times. Everyone was so embarrassed that we thought we were going to die.

℞ The drill team instructor did not live up to the students' expectations. Perhaps he thought the dances and costumes were fine, but he did not have to wear them and perform in front of the crowd. The entire operation seemed poorly orchestrated. There was no evidence of either planning or preparation.

Experienced teachers know the value of planning. A lack of planning makes the outcome a product of chance and vulnerable to random happenings.

Efficient instructors would not wait until the night of the performance to give students their costumes. They would order the costumes early enough to allow ample time for several fittings. An added benefit would be to allow students to vote on several designs before costumes are ordered. This same approach should be used for the dances. Student input would boost morale and possibly improve the quality of the dances. Finally, instructors should not make promises that they cannot or do not intend to fulfill. In this case, the outcome was terrible. The instructor should have owned the mistake and given students the option of wearing the costumes or wearing something else. Forcing students to wear ugly, ill-fitting costumes at the last moment, leaving them no choice, undermines the instructor's credibility and sense of integrity.

Mistake

19

Teacher Reputation

SCENARIO 19.1
Fearsome Reputations Often Precede People

The worst experience with a teacher that I can remember was in sixth grade. This was the first year that I had more than two teachers so I was already intimidated. She was my math teacher. She was known to be very mean. I never even spoke to her one-on-one, but just her looks and reputation made me tremble. Being in her class was so hard because I was afraid to even move. I felt if I moved she would see me and give me a bad look. Some kids in the class loved to make her scream and turn all red. I wanted to have nothing to do with her. The simple fear of being in her class made it so stressful that this was my worst experience.

℞ Teachers' reputations are developed by the characteristics or traits ascribed to them by their students and peers. Their reputation is based on how they teach, how they grade, and how they interact with their students and peers. Most teachers behave in consistent ways with each class. Eventually a pattern of behaviors, expectations, and reactions becomes evident and becomes a general estimation of the teacher. Reputations can be good or bad. Teachers' reputations usually precede

them, especially if the reputation is bad. The academic grapevine is a fact of student life. Students warn each other about teachers and offer recommendations of who to take and who to avoid if they have a choice.

The teacher in this scenario had developed the reputation that she was intimidating or someone to be feared because she was very mean. The teacher's reputation and looks filled the student with fear and debilitating stress. The teacher's screaming and raging behavior compounded the student's fear. It is very difficult for a student to learn under these conditions.

A variety of factors may be responsible for the teacher behaviors that precipitate a bad reputation. In classroom management courses, preservice teachers are taught not to smile before Christmas.

Teachers who follow this advice may be perceived as mean. Preservice teachers are encouraged to use voice and demeanor to prevent discipline problems. They run the risk of intimidating some of their students. When teachers have low expectations of students, they may treat these students poorly and gain a bad reputation from their actions. Teacher burnout is another factor. Unfortunately, some teachers who have a reputation for being bad teachers may, in fact, be bad teachers.

Effective teachers usually develop a reputation for being approachable, fair, consistent, good teachers, and good coworkers. They usually have high standards and expectations for their students.

Good teachers who discover they have a bad reputation can work to develop a warm, supportive environment that fosters mutual trust and respect. These efforts should dispel students' fears. Ormrod (1998) suggests creating an environment where students feel free to take academic risks. Stress management courses would be very useful for teachers who feel they are suffering from teacher burnout.

Mistake

20

Teacher Misjudgment

SCENARIO 20.1
Shrinking Violet or Conceited Prima Donna?

When I was in sixth grade we were to do some sort of assignment that required us to stand in front of the class and speak. I was a very shy person at that point in my life and when I jokingly told my teacher I was scared of doing the assignment because I was scared, she told me that it wasn't fear, it was conceit. I felt so dumb and hurt that she thought I was conceited. I was in student council and sometimes did have to speak in front of the school, and I was in choir, so I suppose audiences shouldn't have intimidated me. However, in speaking to them I had a written dialogue that was not my own creation and I never stood alone, but technically I was still scared, not CONCEITED!

℞ The teacher erroneously confused a student's shyness with conceit. Her misdiagnosis may be based on her definition of shyness. By its very nature, shyness suggests a focus on or an awareness of self, whereas conceit suggests a preoccupation with self. However, there are many factors that influence a student's tendency toward shyness. Fear is a legitimate factor; fear of failure, fear of success, fear of strangers, fear of making a mistake.

Teachers with an understanding of child development know that fear is an integral part of growing up. Conceit is an overinflated opinion of one's abilities or sense of self-efficacy. Fear on the other hand is a deep-rooted psychological and physiological reaction to a perceived threat to the self. The reaction can be so intense that it can immobilize a person and at the very least hinder performance. It is presumptuous for teachers to think that they can discount labels that students put on their feelings. The presumption is compounded when teachers change the student's label, especially if the teacher's label is negative.

Informed teachers know that their opinion of students' personal characteristics have a powerful influence on students' self-esteem, self-confidence, and ultimately, on their performance. These teachers exercise extreme caution when making personal statements about students. If a student is fearful or shy about talking in front of a group, I think the teacher should be empathic and try to encourage the student in such a way that the student's feelings are validated but not encouraged. To discourage shyness or fearfulness, teachers can help desensitize shy students by having them practice being before a group as they approximate speaking before the group. For example, the shy student can pass papers to the group, can stand in front of the group with other students and participate in a discussion, can be selected to assist the teacher, or can call on other students by name. Students should know that some fear is a normal accompaniment of the uncertainty of growing up.

SCENARIO 20.2
Damsel in Distress?

I was at lunch in sixth grade and a girl hit me with her purse repeatedly. I chased her down and thumped her in the arm. The lunch monitor took me to the vice-principal and called my mom and said I would have to serve ICS, in-class suspension. My mom took me out of that school and transferred me to private school.

℞ In this scenario, in which a male student was involved in an altercation with a female student, there are several problems. One problem is a failure to acknowledge that there are two sides to every story and that both sides should be heard. Assuming the lunch monitor was another student leads me to the second problem, the problem of delegating such an important responsibility to children. Piaget (1965) points out in his theory of children's moral reasoning that young children may not consider a person's motive or intent when judging that person's behavior. Another problem is the possibility of gender bias. When a young male and a young female are involved in a conflict, educators and administrators frequently assume that it is the male's fault. Even if a young woman starts a fight and the young man retaliates, he is perceived as picking on a "defenseless" female. A fourth problem is the harshness of the punishment. Males, minority males in particular, tend to receive harsher punishments and more frequent suspensions than do females (Gibbs, 1988).

Fair-minded teachers listen to both sides of the story when there is conflict. These teachers consider the merits of each argument without letting race, gender, or socioeconomic status influence their judgment. If they cannot settle the conflict with verbal reprimands, they make sure that any punishment administered is appropriate and equitable. I do not think a student should be responsible for reporting another student to the vice-principal. A teacher as the lunch monitor may have been able to stop the problem and may never have had to report the incident. Teachers are usually more of a deterrent to misbehavior than are student monitors.

SCENARIO 20.3
Trust Me at Your Own Risk

My worst experience with a teacher was in high school. I was taking a government class at night and was receiving As on all exams. The last night of class the teacher said we could leave early. When I left the class I had an A. I was apprehended by a school guard on my way out and the teacher was reprimanded for letting me leave. After the guard left, the teacher handed me my grade, which was now a C. When I asked her why my grade had dropped, she accused me of cheating.

Rx The teacher violated school policy and dismissed her students early. This heedless act spawned a multitude of academic sins. The first sin was possibly jeopardizing the students' safety. Having a guard on the premises suggests a need for precautions. She exhibited displaced anger—anger at the student rather than at the guard or with herself. She did not accept the guard's reprimand gracefully. She did not take responsibility for her actions. She took her anger out on her student who was caught. She lowered that student's grade and finally, she justified the lowered grade by accusing the student of cheating. Unfortunately, her response to being reprimanded undermined her integrity.

Responsible teachers try not to let situations get out of hand, as this one obviously did. The mistake would not have happened if the teacher had observed school policy. Teachers may unintentionally violate policy because they are unaware of

school rules, but responsible teachers make it their business to know school policy on important issues. Teachers with integrity take full responsibility for their actions. Good teachers would not let their students suffer any consequences for their own misdeeds. They would not consider lowering a grade or accusing a student of cheating in retaliation for their being reprimanded.

When I was in eighth grade, our home economics teacher let us go home early. We were bussed to the school so we had quite a distance to walk to get home. There was a large group of us, so we stopped at a little candy shop that had a jukebox and we danced and talked and went our separate ways. It was all very innocent but the next day seemed ominous. I had never been in trouble in school before.

The principal came to our room to collect all of the students that left early. The administrators treated us as if we had skipped school. There was talk of suspension, and I was mortified. I do recall looking at my teacher, imploring her to intervene, but she did nothing but look away. I do not think she ever took responsibility for letting us go. She certainly never apologized to us for setting us up for trouble. Fortunately, we were not suspended. I did learn years later that the seemingly innocent "candy shop" was really a front for drug dealers who sold drugs to kids. As I reflect back on my experience, I see the importance of rules and policies that are designed to safeguard children. Teachers should not knowingly violate school policy no matter how well intentioned the situation might be.

SCENARIO 20.4
The Whole Is Greater Than Its Parts

Mrs. W. called me up in front of the class to reprimand me for a 68 in spelling on a scholastic achievement test, when I had made a 99 cumulative score overall.

R_x A classic mistake that teachers and parents make is focusing on the negative and effectively discounting the positive. In this scenario, the teacher virtually ignored the high cumulative score and zeroed in on the low spelling score. The public reprimand was perceived as a punishment. The high cumulative achievement was neither recognized nor rewarded. This is confusing for the student. It is not clear if the student was a success or a failure at the task.

Savvy teachers know that if they feel they must criticize some aspect of a student's performance, it should certainly be put in proper perspective. In this scenario where the child was weak in spelling but overall did an excellent job, a word of encouragement to improve in spelling and a jubilant focus on the overall accomplishment would be appropriate. Weiner (1979) proposes that we help students to properly attribute their successes and failures to their ability and effort. If a child is confused about his or her successes and failures, he or she may never learn to attribute appropriately.

SCENARIO 20.5
Excluded!

In my sixth-grade drama class after the script was written and handed out to the students, I looked on the character listing and I wasn't even in the script! She had to write me in.

R_x Sometimes teachers make honest mistakes that can be perceived as having malicious intent. In this scenario, the author obviously believed that the teacher had an ulterior motive in writing her out of the script. Although the teacher wrote her back in, the student was unable to let go of the initial omission. The student apparently internalized the slight, nurtured it, and hung on to it for years. There is no evidence that the teacher was aware of the impact of the omission.

Astute teachers know the importance of apologizing to a student when they make mistakes. I think it is important to preface that apology with an acknowledgment that teachers make honest mistakes and to assure the student that it was not personal. To soothe ruffled feathers, teachers can ask students what else they can do to make them feel better.

SCENARIO 20.6
To Err Is Human, to Admit It Is Divine

When I was in sixth grade my English teacher gave me a C on a project. That isn't a bad grade, it could have been worse, but I disagreed with it. The assignment was to make a poster showing the difference between "good" and "well." He said I got the concepts backward and gave me a C. I was so sure I had them straight. I remember every week in elementary school telling my teacher, "I don't feel good," and she would say, "Well, you don't feel well."

And so I was positive that my picture of a man's face that I put on my poster with a thermometer and sad, droopy, watery eyes saying, "He doesn't feel well" was correct. Wrong, my teacher said. I still believe that I was correct. Even today, I am confused as to how I feel. So I mostly say I have a headache or my stomach hurts. And I seldom correct others on their use of good and well, fearing I might correct them the wrong way and traumatize them for life. I am not really traumatized, but I will never forget all of my hard effort I put into that poster and joy I felt, thinking I finally used the word correctly, only to find out I was wrong and had been misguided.

℞ This is a scenario of "the student is right and the teacher is wrong." *Well* can be used as an adjective or adverb to mean in good health, satisfactory, or to appear well dressed; whereas, good is only used as an adjective and it is never used to modify a verb (Warriner & Griffith, 1977). Either the teacher was unaware that he was wrong or was reluctant to admit that he was wrong. Erroneously, some teachers believe that because they are the teachers, they must know all of the answers all of the time and never make mistakes. They think that if they admit that they are wrong, their admission is a sign of weakness that undermines their credibility.

The smart, confident teacher realizes that saying "I don't know" and being ignorant for the moment is preferable to never saying "I don't know" and remaining ignorant for all time. When children are so sure they are right, effective teachers investigate and tell them that teachers make mistakes and that sometimes the student is right. If the student is right, these teachers readily admit their errors or shortcomings. Teachers can save face and validate the child by thanking the child for the gift of the new knowledge.

SCENARIO 20.7
It's Gobbledygook to Me

About the only thing I can remember was my kindergarten teacher. She had an accent but I can't recall where she was from. The problem was that I had trouble understanding her and when she would give directions, I'd do something different. As a result, I'd always get in trouble. This was a daily thing and it got to be a real chore just to go to school. One day, as soon as my mom dropped me off, I ran back home because I was lost with the teacher.

Rx Clear directions are imperative for student success. The teacher was apparently unaware of her accent and the disorienting effect it had on her oral instructions. Unfortunately, she penalized her students for her unintentional error. It is human nature to be aware of someone else's accent and be oblivious to our own. Unfortunately, she penalized her students for not being able to follow her confusing directions.

Discerning teachers monitor their students' body language, expressions, and tone of voice continuously to detect any signs of miscommunication or misunderstanding. These experienced teachers know the importance of asking the students if the directions are clear. Language or accent may not be a problem, but the difficulty level of the content may make directions confusing. Difficult material should be broken down into manageable chunks and explained one step at a time. The classroom climate should be warm and friendly enough so students feel free to say they do not understand the directions. Teachers should speak slowly and deliberately and use visuals if possible when they are giving directions. They can demonstrate or model what is to be done. An example and a visual are especially helpful when language is a barrier. If there is still some doubt about the clarity of instructions, teachers can ask other students to explain the directions in their own words or to demonstrate the steps in the directions.

SCENARIO 20.8
Your Crime, My Time

I had a Spanish teacher in high school and she had left for maternity leave and she gave me an F because I did not turn in my notebook, but I did. And my mother still put me on restriction. It turned out I got a B.

Rx If we can assume that the author of this scenario did turn in the notebook assignment, then it is reasonable to assume that the Spanish teacher misplaced or lost the assignment. The teacher's lack of organization became a serious consequence for the student—a failing grade and undeserved punishment. I had a similar incident in my sophomore English class. I turned in a paper and the teacher said I did not turn it in. She wanted me to redo the paper. I was very upset because that meant retyping the paper without the benefit of either a correcting typewriter or a word processor. I remember telling her that it was our job as students to do the work and turn it in and it was her job to keep up with the work. Coming from a teenager, that was considered an impudent remark. Today, as an adult educator, I would echo that remark with gusto.

Well-organized teachers have routines for collecting assignments, storage of papers, grading, and recording grades. Experienced teachers realize that if they do not have a system and papers are turned in or collected haphazardly or improperly stored, the odds of losing papers increases. If a teacher has lost or misplaced a student's paper, the student should not be penalized in any way. The teacher should take responsibility for the lost paper. If there is even a remote possibility that the student turned in the work, the student should receive the highest possible grade. The rationale is that the student may have earned the highest grade, although that remains an unknown. If it is not too much trouble, teachers can offer students extra credit to resubmit an assignment. When in doubt about whether or not a student turned in an assignment, leave parents out. This avoids providing parents with a reason to unnecessarily punish their children.

6

TEACHING STYLE
AND BEHAVIOR

"Teachers are fighting back against kids who cut class.
Today I was the victim of a drive-by math quiz!"

Mistake

21

Teacher Bias or Expectations

SCENARIO 21.1
Once a Clown, Always a Clown

The second semester of my junior year of high school, having been the class clown in Mr. H.'s social studies class, I had determined that I was going to turn over a new leaf with my new teacher. On the first day of class, Mrs. C. immediately announced, "Where is so and so?" I raised my hand and she stated, "I have heard all about you, you need to sit up here!" She then sat me at a desk next to hers. So much for a fresh start.

℞ Even a class clown deserves a clean slate with a new teacher. The classic study by Rosenthal and Jacobson (1968) suggests that having negative expectations for a student can become a "self-fulfilling prophecy." This action by the teacher was apparently very disheartening for this student who wanted to change. In lieu of a reformed, mature student, this teacher would most likely get a repeat performance of the old disruptive behavior and the student would become a discipline problem as expected. When I was teaching, I intentionally avoided reading any comments about my new students.

I preferred to form my own opinions of my students, giving each of them an opportunity to change.

In fact, I had a fifth-grade class that I was able to turn around using this strategy. As I recall, there were four teachers on the team. Their policy was to select their classes from the pool of new students. One of the classes did not have an assigned teacher. The team came up with the brilliant idea to place all of the "undesirable" students into the class without a teacher. I was returning from maternity leave and I had the great fortune of inheriting this class. One of the teachers was a close friend of mine. She warned me about my students and apologized for the nightmare class that the teachers had created. I ignored the warning and decided to use the "self-fulfilling prophecy" theory to my advantage. When I met my students for the first time, I was very enthusiastic and excited. I told them how pleased I was to have them as students, because I had heard that I had one of the best classes in the school. I was amused by the way they looked around as if to ask, "Who is she talking to?" This class far exceeded my expectations and certainly those of the other teachers that year.

SCENARIO 21.2
Dark Comedy of Gender Bias

In my eighth-grade industrial arts class, there were only two girls in the class, including me. The teacher would always take our work and say, "C'mon guys, if a girl can do this good, you guys better at least try to do better than they do." His low expectations because of gender bias could have been devastating, but although irritating, it proved to be humorous too.

℞ The secret is out. Research findings have shown that teachers' expectations tend to favor males (Block, 1980). This teacher's comments support evidence that traditionally, girls have been expected not to perform as well as boys in predominantly male activities such as industrial arts and sports. When males are not performing up to par, they are called "girls" in a very derogatory manner. As this student indicated, these messages are often delivered with humor, but gender bias is dark comedy with lasting effects.

Insightful teachers encourage their students to be more androgynous in their thinking and behavior, meaning that they do not favor masculinity or femininity but respect both. Resourceful teachers use every opportunity to encourage androgyny. They encourage girls to participate in male-dominated activities and boys to embrace more female-oriented activities. Students are always praised for their efforts. These progressive teachers might one day make gender bias an obsolete term.

SCENARIO 21.3
Justice for All

My worst experience was staying after school in the first grade. I do not remember the rest of the year. All I know is, my mom had to pick me up from school at least once a week because I had a fever. When I got home I was fine. The fever was gone.

In seventh grade I had a math teacher who was very unfair. If there were a group of us talking in her class, I would get in trouble. When she separated the class I was moved to the very back. She would just treat me more unfairly than the rest of the students.

℞ Most students are very perceptive about how a teacher feels about them. They keep a watchful eye and constant surveillance of the teacher's actions and reactions, looking for telltale signs of like or dislike. When children conclude that a teacher does not like them, the focus shifts from learning and education to feelings and motives. When a teacher is unfair, children know it.

Master teachers know that fairness is a sterling quality in teachers. Children want their teacher's approval and they deserve to be treated fairly. Caring teachers critique their own behavior frequently to assure themselves that they are not singling out a student for punishment or unfair treatment. Impartial educators insist on fairness for all students, including the ones that they do not like.

SCENARIO 21.4
Extraterrestrial Terror

My worst experience in school was no doubt with my kindergarten teacher. She plainly didn't like me and she let everyone know about it every day with her actions.

I think it all started when my mother brought my lunch to school for me. We lived close by, so my mom liked walking over and giving me a nice, warm lunch. My teacher obviously disliked pampered kids, but this was beside the point. She began to treat me more harshly than the other kids. Her voice and tone seemed to be different with me. Every minimal accident on my part, such as spilling paint, called for severe punishment. She constantly threatened to send me to the principal for a paddling. I was always in time-out.

The teacher had an inflatable E.T. that she would place on the table of the quietest student. Knowing that I was deathly afraid of the E.T., she always placed it on my desk, whether I had been quiet or not. I noticed her anger toward me as we filed past her into the room. She patted everyone as they walked past her, but she always skipped me. It got to the point that I refused to go to school. My father took me to school and even though I was crying, she didn't bother to get up and attempt to soothe me. That's when my dad saw her lack of effort.

℞ The obvious bias described in this scenario is curious. Why would an adult teacher make such overt gestures of unfair treatment to such a small child? What pathology would motivate such actions? Unfortunately, some unbalanced teachers manage to infiltrate the teaching profession. Many professions are hosts to similar unfortunate souls. In most school districts there are no screening processes in place for new teachers that are sensitive enough to detect deep emotional or mental problems. Maybe the rare instances of getting this type of teacher do not warrant mental screening.

Good teachers are sensitive to a child's need for acceptance and fair treatment. Caring teachers would never do anything to terrorize children, such as constantly showing them a feared object. Caring teachers are always willing to comfort a distressed child, but they wisely regard the legal limitations of their school district. If the district has a hands-off policy, they soothe and comfort with words.

SCENARIO 21.5
Liar, Liar, Your Habit's on Fire

I was educated in Catholic school all of my life. With that in mind, I had a bad nun experience. As a young student I was always fearful and intimidated by the older women in their scary black hoods and gowns. This time period would have been in the late sixties when they still wore the full-length battle dress. In my opinion they more closely resembled witches, like the one in the *Wizard of Oz*, than saintly women who had devoted their lives to the church.

Well, there was this one nun who always had it in for me. No matter where I went or every time I was about to do something she was always there, so I never really had the opportunity. Then one day while in sixth grade, another classmate came running to tell me that my sister, who was a fifth grader, was in a fight with a boy, so I better get over there, which I did, but there was no sign of a fight, just a mob of kids surrounding my sister and this boy. I quickly got to the center of the mob; as I was about to ask my sister what was going on, I felt some huge force pulling me from behind. When I turned to see who was pulling me toward the outside of the mob, I was surprised to see it was the nun who was always after me. She was grabbing me, saying, "Don't hit that boy anymore." The principal, who was also a nun, then came up and asked what happened and why did this nun have me in a police chokehold. The bad nun then said I was beating up the fifth grader and she had to pull me off of him before I did any more damage. I had no say in this field trial. I was given the mandatory amount of demerits and put on probation, as well as having to do a month of work detail during recess, lunch, and after school. I have never looked at nuns the same after this travesty of justice.

Rx Are the nuns above lying? If we believe this student's account, then clearly they are not. Nuns are people, not saints. They have the same character defects as anyone else. It is certainly plausible that the nun in search of an offense manufactured this story and took advantage of the situation. This "I've-got-my-eye-on-you" behavior is not limited to nuns. Teachers and administrators frequently have this attitude toward problem students. Although some students truly bear watching, for others it is a setup, a misdeed waiting to happen. Effective teachers have high standards of integrity and honesty and would never lie about a student. Competent teachers work on helping students to change undesirable behavior. They never perpetuate bad behavior by setting a student up, by falsely accusing a student, or by manufacturing an offense.

SCENARIO 21.6
Cheater Watch

My worst experience was in high school when I was a junior. I believe the class was physical science and there were about eighteen students in my class. We would go over a couple of chapters and then have an exam. Our teacher gave tough exams—essay type, fill-in-the-blanks. Anyway—not to brag—but I usually got one of the top scores on the exams. This made a few girls angry or jealous, so they told the teacher that I was cheating. Well, I found this out from one of my friends and I confronted the teacher. I told her that I study for the tests and I DO NOT CHEAT. I told her that she could watch me and sit me close to her every time we take a test. Well, she did this—but for some reason I always thought she labeled me as a cheater. I graduated salutatorian of my class, but to this day because of some jealousy and hatred I was labeled a cheater. I did not like the teacher before and I still don't.

℞ When students decide to blow the whistle on a student for cheating, teachers have an obligation to follow up on the charge. Accusing a student of cheating is a serious offense that invites serious repercussions. It is imperative that teachers consider the motives of the accusers and look out for hidden agendas. The teacher in this scenario took the word of the accusers at face value with no evidence. She communicated her beliefs to the accused student by agreeing to observe that student during the test.

Astute professionals know that high grades are not *prima facie* evidence of cheating. The risks of falsely accusing a child of cheating and of showing an expectation that the child will cheat are great. Accusing a child of cheating is a good way to extinguish the good behavior of making high grades. Students can be expelled for cheating, their reputations can be ruined by rumors of cheating, and they can become disenfranchised by a teacher who thinks they are cheating. Teachers need to tread lightly in the cheating arena, unless they witness the cheating. If a teacher suspects cheating but has no evidence, the best action is no action until there is indisputable proof. In the interim, it is prudent to remind students of the consequences of cheating and to use measures that are incompatible with cheating such as parallel forms of the test. Teachers should never communicate to students that they expect them to cheat or single a child out for strict surveillance. Proximity and movement around the classroom are effective cheating deterrents for most students. Teachers should circulate among students rather than focus attention on one possible cheater. Keep in mind that most students are responsible learners that do not cheat. Trust is a great motivator.

Mistake

22

Unethical Behavior

There are two incidents that stick out in my mind and they were with the class as a whole and not just me. My sixth-grade year I was put in an English class with a bunch of troublemakers. The teacher had a breakdown and quit and the rest of the year the class watched movies and read books out loud.

When I went into my seventh-grade class (it was in a different school district), I had a wonderful, but hard, teacher for English, who taught me more than I ever learned before or since.

My second experience was during my senior year of high school. I was taking two English classes with two different teachers, because I was pregnant the previous year. The teacher for my sophomore English class is who I am about to talk about. My sophomore English class was with a bunch of "lower levels" and troublemakers. The teacher told us that none of us would ever go to college. I could not believe this teacher was telling us that. She was a teacher!

The worst experience I remember having in school was during my senior year in high school. I had just found out I was pregnant with my daughter and had been absent several days from school. I was placed on "homebound" by my doctor. In order to be on homebound I would have to change from my computer course to an elective I could study at home. I went to speak to my computer teacher about dropping the course and she told me, upon finding out I was pregnant, "Why don't you just drop out?" That was the worst thing a student could be told by a teacher.

℞ In both of these scenarios, the teachers were less than encouraging. They actually discouraged their students by communicating their low expectations for their students. Suggesting that a student drop out of school or that a group of students will never go to college is unethical behavior. Our mission as educators is to try to give every child a good education. We would be appalled if a doctor told a patient, "Why don't you just die, you're probably not going to get any better?" We would think that a doctor's duty is to do everything possible to help the patient get better and to keep the patient alive. The teacher's charge is no less important. The teacher has a duty to help students become better students and to keep hope alive.

Encouraging teachers have high hopes and expectations for their students and communicate their feelings to their students in very loving ways. They make their students work hard and they teach them to believe in themselves. Encouraging teachers help students get enthusiastic about learning and they teach students to persevere. Encouraging teachers seek to inspire students to stay in school and would never suggest that a student drop out, especially a pregnant student. It is imperative that a teenage mother obtains an education. The quality of her baby's future depends on it. Dinkmeyer and Losoncy (1980) offer some strategies for becoming better encouragers in *The Encouragement Book.*

SCENARIO 22.3
Out in the Cold

The winter of 1972, the ground was covered with snow. I got in trouble for talking, I think. The teacher told me to get my coat, take a chair, and go stand on the chair in the hallway, which was outside. I stood there the rest of the day, even through lunch. When my sister came to pick me up after school the teacher said I couldn't go. My mother had to come up to the school to get me. Because I was standing in the hallway other classes walked past me on the way to lunch. Other teachers would stop and tell their classes that this is what happens to bad children.

I met this teacher's ex-husband about six years ago (small world). He told me that when she was teaching at that school, she wasn't even certified. When she did get certified, she got kicked out of a school district for having sex with students, went to another school district, and did the same thing again. Now she can't teach anywhere, thank God! The teacher did many things that were humiliating and devastating to a child's self-esteem.

℞ This scenario conjures up an image of a small, bewildered, frozen child, huddled on a chair, informing the masses of her misbehavior by her presence. The teacher obviously wanted to make an example of this child, but she chose a very unethical approach. It is unethical to leave a child outside of the class most of the day for a minor offense. It is particularly offensive to make that child stand outside in cold, freezing weather for a long period of time. Forcing the child to stand out in the cold placed the child at risk for frostbite and other cold-related illnesses. The irony of this intense punishment is that the child was unaware of the offense, which renders the punishment ineffective. The pathology evident in this teacher's behavior underscores the need for better screening of teacher applicants.

Rational teachers are aware that social isolation is more effective if they specify the misbehavior and communicate the desired behavior.

Social isolation is not recommended for more than ten minutes. Experienced teachers know that the setting should be somewhat isolated from the class, but the student should be visible at all times. The alone time without reinforcement gives students an opportunity to think. The astute teacher does not use time-out as punishment; instead time-out is an opportunity to regroup and resume appropriate behavior. Qualified, responsible teachers would use tactics that make the punishment fit the crime. They would never put a child in such a risky, inhumane situation.

SCENARIO 22.4
Bloody Secret

In the fourth grade I had a female teacher whose name I cannot recall. I do recall that I was acting up on the way out of the room for recess and she grabbed me. She had long red fingernails and when she grabbed me, she dug them deep into my arm. As she did, I jerked my arm and left a considerable amount of flesh under her nails. My arm was bleeding and she wouldn't let me go to the nurse. She just gave me a wet paper towel to put on it and made me sit in the room during the recess period. I never forgot her!

R̞ The overzealous teacher in this scenario accidentally clawed a student with her long, red, and possibly dirty, nails. The scratches were deep enough to draw blood and if the nails were dirty, there was the risk of infection. Injuring the child was terrible, but when the teacher failed to acknowledge that she had hurt the child, that made her offense worse. Denying the child medical attention elevated this offense to unethical status. It seems that the teacher was trying to cover up the incident to avoid

any negative repercussions such as a lawsuit or losing her job. Her efforts to protect herself placed her student at risk for infection and for further discomfort. She made no effort to comfort the student. She tried to act as if the incident did not happen and she probably secretly hoped that the student would do the same. Then again, maybe she felt that the injury was the child's fault because he pulled away. On the contrary, she was the adult in charge. She inflicted the wound. She was responsible.

The responsible teacher would have apologized to the child immediately and let the child know that she did not mean to hurt him or her. She would take the child to the nurse if possible, acknowledge what happened, and point out that the child pulled away and precipitated the accident. She would make sure the child's injury was attended to and that the child was comfortable before returning to class. If necessary, she would be willing to acknowledge the accident to the class to assure them that the child would be fine. The smart teacher would learn from her mistake and cut her nails or keep her paws off her students as long as she has claws.

SCENARIO 22.5
A Lesson in Deception

The worst experience I can remember is plagiarizing my entire senior research paper. My teacher was a man whom I highly respected and thought of as being very scholarly and astute. When he returned my paper, he made a note on it that he could tell it was plagiarized, but still gave me a C and did not make me rewrite it. I learned that subaverage work was acceptable and enough to get by. I also learned that "scholars" could look the other way and lower their standards.

℞ A high-school senior with a developed sense of right and wrong realized that "giving" a student a grade is unethical. Teachers are supposed to model moral and prosocial behaviors. The astute student was quick to detect the dishonesty in the way the teacher graded the paper. He realized that the grade of "C" was not a gift. It was a lesson in deception. The student was obviously disenchanted with the teacher's willingness to look the other way. It suggested that the teacher had low expectations for the student. The teacher's motive could have been to seek the approval of his students. Perhaps he was giving the student the benefit of a doubt. Whatever the motive, the action was inappropriate.

The best "gift" a teacher can give a student is honest feedback that will help to improve the student's performance. Expecting students to do the right thing is an added bonus. Discerning teachers are unwilling to accept anything less than a student's personal best. If they suspect that they are getting less, they send students back to the drawing board for a redo. These caring actions teach children to strive for excellence and to take "good enough" out of their performance vocabulary. Most of all, wise teachers make their students accountable. Plagiarism carries heavy consequences. Students who knowingly plagiarize should have consequences that are not rewarding. Good teachers only give students grades that they earn, no more and no less.

SCENARIO 22.6
Sneaky Snacking

In sixth grade a friend and I made cupcakes for our third-period class. The teacher accused C. and me of each stealing one cupcake. Two were missing. Well, she accused us in class and we told her we didn't do it. I then proceeded to tell her that she probably ate them. I was sent to the office but I stopped by my uncle's room (he was a teacher at the school), told him what happened, and we both went to the principal. We went back to the teacher's room and found the wrappers in the trashcan under her desk.

℞ Teachers are not immune to the frailties of man. The teacher's behavior in this scenario appears to have been deliberate unethical behavior on the surface, but closer inspection suggests an eating disorder. People who steal food, sneak and eat it, then lie about it may have an eating disorder. If the food substance is a carbohydrate, that is usually a telling sign. Sometimes people with eating disorders eat compulsively and need food, much like an addict that needs a drug. This eating disorder is often known as food addiction. Food is the food addict's "drug" and like other addicts, they will do whatever they can to get their substance, even lie about little sixth-grade children.

I often caution my preservice teachers to empty their emotional baggage before they enter the teaching profession. Claudia Black (1991) and other researchers have found that children from alcoholic households usually develop addictions themselves and flock to "helping" professions as adults. Teaching is a helping profession that attracts adult children of alcoholics (ACOAs). There is a body of literature available on the subject of ACOAs. I recommend that preservice teachers from alcoholic homes read this literature and visit the ACOA support groups where they can learn to break the cycle of addiction and counter its ill effects. Prudent teachers recognize the value of working on their issues before they enter the classroom. Awareness and action would make situations like lying about students and stealing food unnecessary and nonexistent. Wise teachers know that they destroy their credibility if they lie to or about their students. It is critical to the learning process that students perceive their teachers as trustworthy. The quality of teacher–pupil relationships affects how students learn (Flanders & Morine, 1973).

SCENARIO 22.7
Teacher Goes AWOL

My bad teacher experience occurred when I was in the ninth grade and we had a big earthquake (1987). During the earthquake my teacher decided to run out of the room.

The students were scared to death, yet no one spoke. We stayed inside the classroom until the evacuation team came to inspect the room. They were shocked to find us still inside. About fifteen minutes had passed. We never saw our teacher again.

℞ The most difficult aspect of a crisis is the critical period of indecision that usually triggers the fight or flight response. The teacher in this scenario made the inappropriate choice of running away from the crisis and abandoning her students. As a result, her students were not evacuated immediately. This teacher's actions could have put her students' lives in jeopardy.

Skilled teachers know that in a crisis situation, flight is not an option, especially when children are involved. The nature of the relationship of teachers and students places the teachers in *loco parentis* (in the position of the parent) as dictated by common law (Reutter, 1975). Competent professionals recognize the serious nature of their charge and act reasonably to protect the welfare and best interests of the children. Sometimes the call of duty dictates that teachers place their students' best interests before their own. In this scenario, the teacher had a responsibility to stay with the students and make sure that they were evacuated safely. Parents have a right to assume that schools will do everything in their power to protect their children. Most teachers are good, dedicated people who would do whatever is necessary to protect their students. In the 1999 Littleton, Colorado, shooting crisis (Shore, 1999), a teacher sacrificed his life for his students. The teacher in this scenario was not prepared for this aspect of teaching— that's probably why she was never seen again.

SCENARIO 22.8
Sleepy Slacker

I had a second-grade teacher that had a heart condition and required medication for it. This medication made her sleep through most of the class. She would have the students write to 100 over and over again while she slept. I missed out on so much learning that year, that for many years I was labeled "slow" or "poor" student. This resulted in my dislike and fear of school.

℞ In teacher's college, my preservice classmates and I were warned that if we had any visible tics, twitches, defects, or other idiosyncratic behaviors that we might not be suitable material for teaching because we would distract our students. At the time, I thought that was a bit extreme, although in support of that notion, my entire class often focused, for much of the class period, on the tic that resided in the left eye of one of my English professors. My professor's tic was distracting but very minor compared to what the students in this scenario experienced. The teacher in this scenario had a major medical problem that rendered her no longer qualified to do the job she was hired to do. In fact, she had become a potential liability to her school; while she was sleeping, the children in her charge were technically unsupervised. She indirectly robbed students of precious instruction time by giving them tedious, repetitive tasks to keep them busy while she slept. The most obvious mistake in this scenario was the complete absence of instructional objectives that clearly articulate intended learning outcomes for students (Gronlund, 2000). As a consequence, the children received little if any meaningful instruction during this teacher's tenure and they suffered severe academic deficiencies.

A conscientious teacher that is committed to acting in the best interests of her students would have voluntarily sought a different job that would better accommodate her illness. This mistake could have been avoided if the administration randomly visited classrooms to observe. Classroom teachers and staff should always be on the alert; they have a professional and moral obligation to report unusual behaviors that may negatively impact students. So it seems prudent that schools should implement a policy that requires the reporting of consistently unusual behavior, such as sleeping, for further investigation. The administration, once aware of unusual, potentially harmful behavior should do everything in their power to meet the needs of students and hopefully of the teacher in their efforts to solve the problem.

Mistake

23

False Accusations

SCENARIO 23.1
Do Send a Girl to Do a Man's Work

My vocational drafting teacher accused me of not doing my own work because years prior to my being in his class, two of my brothers had him as their teacher. He thought all of my projects had been done by them.

℞ Current research suggests that schools shortchange girls in many ways (AAUW, 1992). The male teacher in this scenario provided evidence of one of those ways. He refused to give his female student credit for her work. His obvious gender bias prevented an objective appraisal of his student's work. He thought that her work had been done by her brothers. It seems that he was acting under the influence of gender stereotypes rather than accusing her of cheating. Whatever his motive, his behavior was clearly a strike against the equal treatment of males and females. It is less probable that he would tell a young male that a female did his work for him. Failure to give female students credit where credit is due diminishes the self-esteem and motivation of female students.

Progressive male teachers are aware of the negative effects of gender bias. They seek to promote the accomplishments of both male and female students. They try not to promote sexual stereotyping. Instead, they encourage students to assume nontraditional roles and expect them to do well in those roles. These teachers would not go so far as to accuse a student of having someone else do her work simply because the teacher's views are firmly entrenched in gender stereotypes.

SCENARIOS 23.2, 23.3, 23.4, and 23.5
Arbitrary Scapegoats

It was in sixth grade, we were working on an art project and someone lost the project. The teacher (Sister A. we called her sister Asusta—it means scary) accused me of stealing it and basically humiliated me in front of the class. I started crying and kept on telling her that I had not taken the vase. We were making a paper-maché vase. The vase turned up from someone else. She never apologized to me about what she had said.

In orchestra we had to perform our tests, sometimes live, this time on tape. The next day, the teacher was angry because the tape machine was used incorrectly. She blamed me and reprimanded me in front of the class as the one who messed it up. It wasn't me. J.W. did it and he admitted it later. I was made to feel embarrassed in front of everyone when I wasn't at fault. She never apologized to me privately or publicly.

I was in kindergarten when I was accused of throwing rocks on the playground. I had to sit down the rest of recess. My teacher went on the word of her pet student. I was not a troublemaker in class so I was really upset. I remember that I just sat there and cried.

The teacher that I least like to remember is Ms. M. She was my sixth-grade homeroom teacher. I really didn't like her because it seemed that she was always in a bad mood. She seemed to always take it out on us. She would never let us go to the restroom. Well, I guess the real reason that I didn't like her is because she wanted to punish me for something I didn't do. This girl who sat next to me, M., was throwing staples across the room. One accidentally hit Ms. M. on the neck. She asked the students who it was and they said it came from the direction that I was sitting in. So I was accused of this. I kept telling her that it wasn't me. Even M. denied it and said it was me, but it wasn't. So, I was sent to the office. My mom was called and I told her what happened. My mom believed me, but the vice-principal didn't. The only reason they didn't punish me is because my mom swore she wouldn't let the issue rest. After that I didn't like Ms. M. much.

℞ The students in these scenarios were all impulsively selected to bear the blame for someone else's misdeeds. None of the teachers actually saw the accused student do anything wrong. They would each have to examine their consciences or biases to determine why they arbitrarily selected the students they accused. Teachers who make accusations without any evidence or proof have a number of reasons for justifying their accusatory actions: The student looks sneaky, guilty, nervous, or suspicious; they don't like the student; or maybe they don't trust the student. In some of these cases, students are guilty by association or by proximity.

When these teachers feel personally touched by a wrongdoing, they look for someone to blame. When there is doubt, they will settle for a scapegoat.

Prudent teachers only make accusations when there is unquestionable proof. They usually rely on what they see and hear, but they are aware that sometimes they can be mistaken. These teachers tread lightly when there is uncertainty. They avoid making oral or written statements about a student that they can't prove because they could be sued for libel or slander. In Scenario 23.2, a teacher accused the student of stealing a vase. She made the accusation in front of a third party, the class. Froyen (1993) contends that the teacher's comments could be construed as slanderous if they subjected the student to the scorn of a third party, namely the class. Teachers can also be sued if they spread this information and damage a student's reputation. Good teachers are hypervigilant about what they say about students in the presence of the class.

Mistake

24

Inappropriate Reactions

SCENARIO 24.1
Volunteer or Else!

My worst experience was with my fifth-grade teacher, Ms. F. I remember it was my first oral report and everyone, including myself, was terrified. We had been working for quite some time on the assignment; learning all about library research, how to set up a presentation, etc. She asked for volunteers and one student presented. Then, she asked for volunteers again and no one raised their hand. I will never forget how that woman flipped out! She started yelling and told us all we were cowards and everyone would be receiving an F. I lost all respect for that teacher. Everyone had worked so hard. She offered no encouragement for us and didn't give us the opportunity for success.

℞ An important principle of classroom management is that teachers should provide an environment that is conducive to learning. An important principle of assessment is that teachers should provide meaningful, relevant feedback. An important principle of behavior modification is to use praise rather than punishment and humiliation because studies show that praise and encouragement are more effective. An important principle of motivation is to give students an opportunity to experience success, to promote future success. The teacher in this scenario violated all of the above principles. She provided a punitive environment that was not conducive to learning. She threatened to give everyone an F, which was meaningless, false feedback. She punished her students by yelling at them, calling them names, and giving them a bad grade. She effectively denied the students an opportunity for success by ignoring their hard work.

Knowledgeable teachers are very cognizant of these principles and employ them at every opportunity. They would know that something was amiss if all of the students were reluctant to volunteer. Perhaps the students needed practice or needed to be desensitized to speaking before a group of people because it was their first time giving an oral report. Wise teachers would take into consideration that fifth grade heralds the onset of puberty for many students, which adds a new variable to the shyness equation. Sensible teachers would recognize the futility of punishing students for their reluctance and would know the consequences of denying the students an opportunity for success. They know that they would extinguish the good, productive behavior of their students by failing to recognize their hard work and effort. The teacher in this scenario should have resisted an angry, ineffective outburst and exercised patience, understanding, praise, and practice to achieve desirable outcomes.

SCENARIO 24.2
Silence Is Not Always Golden

When I was in second or third grade I experienced a very embarrassing moment that I have never forgotten. My class was in the lunchroom with all of the other classes. Because the noise level had reached a high level, the principal, who monitored the lunchroom daily, had called a "silent lunch." This meant that no one in the lunchroom was supposed to be talking, for any reason.

For about twenty-five minutes the room had been quiet, and my class was about to be dismissed. As I packed the remains of my lunch back in my lunchbox, I dropped a napkin and whispered to the person next to me, asking them to pick it up. At this moment the principal came up behind me and screamed, "Young lady, do you know what silent lunch means? I suggest you shut your mouth." I was very hurt and embarrassed and have never forgotten that experience.

R̟x̟ The concept of a "silent" lunch as a punishment for talking is a throwback to the tactics used in character education or moral education that was popular during the late nineteenth and early twentieth centuries (Sprinthall et al., 1994). The assumption was that children learn best when everything is quiet. "Good" teachers with "good" control had the quietest classrooms. This obsolete approach presumed that teachers had an obligation to keep students quiet. There was no flexibility and zero tolerance for noncompliance. This obsolete practice of "no talking and I mean no talking" still contaminates many classrooms today.

Informed teachers have abandoned the penal model of education where children are treated as if they are in jail. They realize that they cannot teach children to be independent, self-directing, and responsible by insisting that they be docile, dependent, and controlled by teachers

(Sprinthall et al., 1994). Sensitive teachers recognize that children are humans, not pawns. It is human to want to communicate and enjoy other people. It is inhumane to demand silence from children all day. Most adults would balk at such treatment. Flexible teachers would never insist on absolute silence and certainly would not embarrass or humiliate a child for such a minor breach as whispering. Recess and lunch periods should belong to the children; it is their free time. Teachers and administrators should respect that.

SCENARIO 24.3
Abandoning the Band

The worst experience that I can remember from my high school years took place when I was drum major of the high school marching band and I was conducting a practice on the football field during class time. In the middle of practice, the band instructor threw up his hands and left the field for the rest of the period. I was left to fend for myself in front of the entire band. Although I was used to doing this, I had never had to conduct the band when the disagreement between the director (the real person with authority) and myself had been so blatantly obvious. It was really hard for me to retain my authority among my peers when the person who was supposed to be backing my authority had abandoned ship, so to speak.

In this particular situation, I felt that the instructor handled things in a really unprofessional manner. As a kid, I felt confused and wondered what I had done that was so wrong. In retrospect, I feel that the instructor (as the adult in charge) should have controlled his emotions and dealt with the problem in a more reasonable and adultlike manner.

℞ The band director who threw up his hands and left the field seemed to be very frustrated and stressed. One explanation for his abandonment of his students may be *selective avoidance* (Charles, 1983). Selective avoidance is when a person who is highly stressed simply avoids anything and anybody that causes stress.

A professional educator knows that leaving a source of stress may be appropriate for some situations, but it's not always prudent or advisable. Although the drum major is frequently in charge of the band, the teacher is ultimately responsible for the class, not the student. He should have stayed unless there were other adults present. Most teachers realize that delegating students to help with some of the tasks of teaching can reduce stress. Effective delegation is good; shifting responsibility is not. Wise teachers know that it is unwise to leave a class, including a band, unattended with a student in charge. There are unpleasant legal consequences if something goes wrong and the teacher was not there to assure that every effort was made to prevent the occurrence. As the student suggested, the band director should have faced the music in a more adultlike manner by telling the student what was wrong and by working with the student for a solution.

SCENARIO 24.4
Oops! Too Bad for You

One day another student knocked over my desk. The teacher watched and snickered. I had to pick up my desk myself and tried not to cry. There were no apologies from teacher or student. It was difficult to concentrate the rest of the day. I thought I had done something wrong.

℞ Every person has a radius of personal space that encompasses their person and their belongings. When an outsider trespasses in their personal space, the person is entitled to an apology. This is in accordance with the conventions of our society. Failure to give an apology or to show contrition is considered bad manners or rude behavior. It also sends a silent message that the person who is violated is not valued. When teachers condone rude behavior and fail to demand an apology for bad behavior, they rubberstamp the lack of value for this person.

Teachers who laugh at a student's misfortune communicate that they do not care about that student.

Effective teachers are aware of the obligation to model and expect good behavior. In this scenario, the teacher should have demanded an apology for the student whose desk was knocked over. Insightful teachers would realize the importance of making the child who knocked over the desk go back and pick the desk up and put it back. Teachers have a professional duty to suppress any bias they might feel and to insist on fair, courteous treatment of all students.

SCENARIO 24.5
The Smoke Detector

My worst experience with a teacher was in fourth grade with Mrs. D.; I swear this lady hated me. I was home sick for three days, maybe a week, so I had a lot of take-home work to complete. Back then my mom smoked, and my papers must have stunk with cigarette smoke. Well the day I got back to school, I went up to the teacher's desk to turn in my papers. I don't know if it was one of her bad days or not, but she goes and just throws my papers on the floor. I was so embarrassed. I wanted to cry. The class got real silent. No one liked what she did. She told me to pick up my papers and put them on the windowsill to air out. This happened before lunch, and at lunch everyone in my class was sympathetic.

When I got home I told my mom about the incident and she called Mrs. D., who said that she was allergic to cigarette smoke and that was why she did what she did and she said she was sorry. However, I think she could have handled the situation better. The reason I don't believe she liked me was because throughout that year she would do or act in such a way that you knew she didn't like you. I could feel it. A few years later I came across her again when she was a judge for a science contest. Her attitude let me know that she didn't like me.

℞ Children are very insightful. They also are very sensitive to whether a teacher likes them or not. In this scenario, it is apparent that the teacher did not care too much for this student. It is conceivable that the teacher might have an impulsive knee-jerk reaction to cigarette smoke, but this reaction should have been tempered by concern for the student's feelings. Her cold, callused reaction of having the student pick up the papers she threw down screamed out her disdain for this poor student. She did not bother to explain her actions to the student, which clearly revealed her contempt. The teacher managed to indulge her scorn for this student at a tremendous cost. She lost the respect of her class and she undermined her credibility as a good teacher.

Caring teachers exercise tact in dealing with troublesome situations that have the potential to harm or humiliate students. In the process of trying to resolve the problem, they are sensitive to the child's feelings and seek to speak and act in ways that are not offensive. Sensitive teachers would not say anything to the child because the smoke was not the child's fault. Instead, they would find an inconspicuous way to air out the papers, preferably not in the child's presence.

SCENARIO 24.6
What's My Name?

My seventh-grade science teacher was absent for the day so we had a substitute. When it was time to call roll she mispronounced my name. I corrected her in a nice manner and she told me to either say here or present and then she told me not to correct her. She said my name wrong again so I corrected her again. Then she moved me to the back, wrote me up and sent me to the principal's office. The principal was busy, but the next day my science teacher apologized and I did not get in trouble.

℞ This scenario appears very innocent and straightforward on the surface. Important variables here are the student's tone of voice and intent. Was the student being rude? Was the second correction an attempt to test the limit? Was it an innocent attempt to get the teacher to pronounce the name correctly? The answers to those questions are not apparent. What is apparent is that regardless of the student's motive or intent, the teacher overreacted and imposed some stiff penalties as a consequence.

Experienced teachers know that student rudeness appears in a variety of forms; tone of voice, body language, pitch and inflection of voice, backtalk, defiance, and so on. A default reaction to rudeness is anger, aggression, punitive behavior, and so on. However, competent teachers manage to handle rude responses in a professional manner, suppressing any urges to lash out. In this scenario, the teacher could have avoided the power struggle over the name by apologizing and by making a concerted effort to pronounce the name correctly. If the name is too difficult, the teacher could promise to work on getting it right. Students have a right to expect that their teachers will attach enough value to them as a person to pronounce their name correctly.

SCENARIO 24.7
Copycat?

One of the most humiliating moments in high school was when my senior year English teacher accused me of plagiarizing. I had spent several days working very hard on a research paper. When I received the paper a week later I was surprised because I had received a C on the paper. I spoke with the teacher about my grade. He told me that he thought I had copied an article or some sort of publication. The fact of the matter is that I used vocabulary in the paper that I was not accustomed to writing and since I took an effort to increase my vocabulary skills, I was punished. I felt humiliated.

℞ Behavioral learning theory (Skinner, 1950) makes it clear that in operant conditioning, an organism will not persist in a behavior if reinforcement is withheld. In this scenario, an appropriate grade is the reinforcer. The teacher apparently had low expectations for the student and effectively penalized the student for improvement. He gave the student an inappropriate grade of C as punishment for what he believed was plagiarism. Getting a lowered grade for improved performance could extinguish efforts to improve performance in the future.

Wise teachers are not willing to jeopardize student improvement by failing to give credit where credit is due. They would prefer to err on the side of giving too much credit rather than not enough. This is especially true when there is not enough evidence to warrant the latter. A teacher should only accuse a student of plagiarism when there is indisputable proof.

Mistake

25

Sexual Harassment

SCENARIO 25.1
Scratch My Back, I'll Scratch Yours

The worst encounter I had with a teacher was when I joined Number Sense, a UIL competition, and I was hit on by my algebra teacher. I felt that if I didn't comply I would not pass the class. I hated to go to my algebra class because he always called on me and never acknowledged the other girls. I was always teased and everyone would always ask me where's my boyfriend, the algebra teacher, Mr. C. I hated my sophomore year in H.S. because of this. What made matters worse was that on Fridays as a cheerleader I had to wear my uniform with my little skirt and that made me feel very uncomfortable!

℞ Teachers like this teacher clearly violate sexual harassment laws. Sexual harassment is not limited to unwanted sexual advances. It includes words or acts that demean a person on the basis of sex. The Equal Employment Opportunity Commission recognizes two types of sexual harassment that can conceptually be used in claims of harassment. "Quid pro quo," or something for something, occurs when a superior seeks sex in exchange for a decision. In this scenario, the teacher is the superior and the quid pro quo is the course grade. A second type of harassment is "hostile environment," where unwelcome sexual advances create an offensive environment

(Huston, 1993). The student said she was uncomfortable with the teasing of other students, wearing short skirts around the teacher, and his overly attentive response to her in class. Title IX of the Education Amendments of 1972 guarantees students protection from sexual harassment in schools (Crumpler, 1993). New legislation that holds schools liable for sexual harassment will trigger a more aggressive response to these types of claims. Schools will not want to invite lawsuits. A new ruling allows sexually harassed students to collect monetary damages from schools and school officials if they know of the harassment and ignore it. Schools have to show that they took some action and tried to alleviate the situation. An easy, acceptable action would be to suspend or fire the offending employee. This teacher is not just flirting with a child; he's flirting with disaster. He may end up in a full-blown love affair with disgrace and dismissal. True professionals would never misuse their position to take advantage of vulnerable students. Teachers have a duty to report any sexual harassment that is reported to them.

SCENARIO 25.2
Let the Student Beware

I was sitting in band class in the front row when a boy came up behind me and sprayed my butt with a water gun. I had on light-colored pants with blue polka-dot underwear. I was a freshman and he was a junior.

℞ The male student in this scenario sprayed a female student with a water gun. It seems like an innocent prank but the sexual overtones of his act puts him, his school, and school officials in danger of sexual harassment charges. Unfortunately, playing around will not be an adequate defense. Schools will no longer turn a blind eye or deaf ear to claims of sexual harassment; they will act swiftly and assertively if they are made aware of it.

Competent teachers will be aware of the new ruling that protects students from sexual harassment under Title IX. These teachers will make sure their students are aware of the dos and don'ts of interacting with other students. Teachers may use role playing to help students understand which behaviors step over the line into sexual harassment territory. It is imperative that students are taught that they can no longer tease or ridicule or touch or engage in unwanted sexual conduct with other students.

SCENARIO 25.3
Biting Remarks Beget Big Bucks

I was in geometry my sophomore year in high school. I sat around several guys and yes, we did talk a lot. This one particular day my pencil fell off my desk and landed under one of the guy's desks. I asked him to get it for me. Well, guess who heard us talking? I tried to explain that my pencil had fallen under his desk and she said, "Why didn't you just get it?" I said, "Well, because it's under his legs." Then she made the comment, "I'm sure you've been there before." I did discuss this with the vice-principal because I was an aide for them. Of course, nothing came of it, it just blew over.

℞ This teacher made a lewd, sexually suggestive comment that could cause her to lose her job in today's environment. The new Supreme Court ruling would hold the school liable because they ignored the student's complaint and did nothing. They might bring themselves into compliance if they established policies that prohibit any form of harassment.

Competent teachers would encourage students to come forward without retaliation or repercussions. These teachers would actively investigate and try to remedy the situation immediately.

Skilled teachers would offer conferences with students in a confidential manner that preserves their anonymity. However, no school personnel should be encouraged to take corrective action without previous investigation. These suggestions are adaptations of EEOC guidelines (Huston, 1993). The teacher's remarks and the school's indifference toward them could cost the school a great deal of money if they are sued. Schools and teachers must become hypervigilant in their efforts to combat harassment in any form.

SCENARIO 25.4
Bottoms Up

The classroom was long and narrow with long tables pushed together down the middle. The students sat in a row on either side of the tables. I guess I was up on the chair with one foot, to reach something on the other side. Leaning over a table, the teacher slapped me on the bottom. I had a dress on. I guess my panties were showing. I was embarrassed and humiliated, and it is the only thing I remember from first grade, except that I learned to read from a book about Dick and Jane and Spot. I don't remember having any other interactions with the teacher.

℞ It is not clear if the teacher in this scenario is a man or a woman. It really does not matter because sexual harassment laws do not discriminate; males and females are equally liable. Slapping a child on the bottom can be construed as a form of sexual harassment. It was probably an impulsive act, but because the slap was on the little girl's somewhat exposed backside, the slap could be perceived as having sexual connotations. Astute teachers know that touching students on the private parts of their bodies is taboo, forbidden, prohibited, and any other word that conveys the serious nature of this offense. Smart teachers know that the cost of such an act can be prohibitive in terms of financial and professional capital. These teachers are not willing to sacrifice their careers or the school's budget to indulge an impulsive act of impropriety. Knowledgeable teachers would have simply told the student to sit down and that would have solved the problem.

Scenario 25.5
Chest Nut Roasts Student

When I was in the eleventh grade, a counselor, Mr. H. told me that girls with big chests would do better in secretarial jobs, so college was not even discussed.

Rx This sexist, stereotypical remark is a frightening testimonial that incompetent counselors are alive and well. Although incredulous, Mr. H. may have believed that he was giving the student some good advice. His reference of women using their "wiles and wares" was not an uncommon view many years ago. Unfortunately, Mr. H. and many like him appear stuck in a time warp of sexist practices of yesteryear, when it was somewhat acceptable to stereotype women and make risqué comments about their bodies. Today is a new day; such comments are considered a form of sexual harassment. Mr. H. could have made the comment to open the door to his making a sexual pass or a solicitation of intimacy or to make further comments about her body, which is again, illegal. If Mr. H. thought he was saying something useful or complimentary, whatever his motives might have been, the actual damage he cost his student may be assessed by her last statement. She obviously felt diminished by both his low expectations for her and the fact that he did not bother to mention college or offer her strategies or tips for succeeding in college. Mr. H.'s comment was illegal, immoral, and sexist. But more so than that, it provided evidence of his obvious incompetence as a counselor. Whatever his motive . . . firing him would be justified.

The truly professional counselor would be laden with information about careers, colleges, college entrance exams and criteria, in preparation for a career advisory meeting with the student. There would be little time for personal remarks. Informed counselors would fear to tread in any area of conversation that has any hint of sexual innuendo or sexual harassment. Caring, competent, counselors would have the students' best interests as a priority and offer sound, effective career guidance. The law forces schools to assume some of the responsibility for sexual harassment. The school's job is to prevent sexual harassment and to guarantee a workplace that is free of harassment of any type. To avoid subjecting students to an incompetent counselor, like Mr. H., the school district should shore up their screening policy to include questions for the applicant about any charges of sexual harassment of students and/or colleagues. Eligibility for hiring should be based on the applicant providing acceptable responses to these questions.

All schools should conduct mandatory annual training to help employees stay abreast of current developments in sexual harassment policy and laws. Finally, students should be encouraged to evaluate the usefulness of the counseling session. The counselor could be required to put any recommendations in writing and both parties sign it. The student's signature would be an acknowledgment of receipt of acceptable advising. Accountability may be an effective deterrent for sexual harassment.

7

TEACHER CONFESSIONS OF WORST TREATMENT OF A CHILD

Their Motives and Feelings

"I'm going to hypnotize you to find out why you feel the need to arm
wrestle kindergarten children until they cry 'teacher.'"

Why Good Teachers Mistreat Students: Their Motives and Feelings

In this fast-paced sophisticated society of the new millennium, it defies belief that some teachers are still committing egregious acts of aggression, humiliation, harassment, and so on, such as those in the scenarios presented in the preceding chapters of this book. In these scenarios, students have collectively suffered myriad abuses due to teacher mistakes. The occurrences are so widespread and frequent, that many questions arise and demand answers, such as why did the teachers do what they did? What were they thinking and feeling when they committed their misdeeds? Did they regret their mistakes? What would they do if they had a second chance? To get some insight into teacher mistakes, I asked about 50 teachers to discuss their worst treatment of a student. Six of those teachers said they could not recall any mistreatment of a student; 44 teachers did recall mistreatment and were willing to share their situations and their feelings. The 44 participating teachers were surprisingly candid in their "confessions" of their worst treatment of a student. To do an in-depth probe of the underlying motives for their admitted poor treatment of their students, I asked them the following questions:

1. Describe the scenario of your worst treatment of a student.

2. Describe the problem and your specific role in it.

3. Why did you do what you did?

4. What emotions or feelings were you experiencing at the time?

5. Was your behavior justified?

6. Do you regret your action(s)?

7. If faced with the same or a similar situation, what would you do?

Their responses are presented below as motive probes. After each motive probe, I offer prescriptive commentary that further illuminates the why of the misdeed and, where appropriate, makes recommendations for avoiding the precipitating event and resultant mistreatment. The teacher-reported explanations of their behavior, the motive probes, and the commentary are sorted by the 25 biggest mistakes to shed some light on the possible whys of those types of mistakes.

Mistake 1: Inappropriate Discipline Strategies

Teacher # 1

A Scenario of a Teacher's Worst Treatment of a Student

While student teaching, I would often yell at the students when I felt they were not "in control."

Motive Probe

1.1. Describe the problem and your specific role in it.

I did not yet have control of the class.

1.2. Why did you do what you did?

Frustration.

1.3. What emotions or feelings were you experiencing at the time?

I was just frustrated that the kids would not listen.

1.4. Was your behavior justified? If so, why?

No.

1.5. Do you regret your action(s)?

Yes.

1.6. Do you ever think about this incident? If yes, approximately how often since the occurrence(s)?

Not really. It was just a rookie mistake.

1.7. If faced with the same or a similar situation, what would you do?

Well, hopefully I would not have a classroom that was completely out of my control.

Commentary

This teacher appears to be in denial, wistfully hoping that she will never have a similar situation. To avoid making the same mistakes, she should make an effort to improve her classroom management skills to increase the likelihood that her classes will be under control in the future.

Teacher # 2

A Scenario of a Teacher's Worst Treatment of a Student

I have not had any problem of that nature, but I have seen teachers punishing students. One day this little boy was interfering with the class. The teacher decided to put him by the corner of the classroom facing the wall for the entire day. This was not a very good way to teach the boy. After that day almost three times a week this boy was assigned to this corner. According to the teacher, the boy needed a lesson.

Motive Probe

2.1. Describe the problem and your specific role in it.

The boy was moving around all the time.

2.2. Why did you do what you did?

The teacher probably thought that a better way to teach a class was without problems.

2.3. What emotions or feelings were you experiencing at the time?

I wanted to talk to the teacher because that was not fair to the boy.

2.4. Was your behavior justified? If so, why?

No, her behavior was not justified. There are boys that are very active.

2.5. Do you regret your action(s)?

Yes.

2.6. Do you ever think about this incident? If yes, approximately how often since the occurrence(s)?

Three years and every time . . . (no further comment).

2.7. If faced with the same or a similar situation, what would you do?

(No response.)

Commentary

This teacher apparently did not want to admit to her mistreatment of this child, so she blamed it on an imaginary teacher. However, her admission to regretting her actions and saying that she still thinks about it, gives her away. Another clue that she is probably the teacher in the scenario is that she was aware that the boy was facing the wall the entire day. How did she know that if she was busy minding her own class? It is good that she has regrets and that she shows signs of being more knowledgeable about child development and behavior, noting that little boys are naturally very active. It is a common occurrence to put disruptive children in a corner or outside the room and forget about them. Not having to deal with such a child's behavior will certainly make the job easier for the teacher. To avoid this mistake, teachers should have a specified maximum time-out that is just enough time to allow students time to regroup and rethink their actions before rejoining the group. Otherwise, the child should be engaged in some form of learning activity.

Teacher # 3

A Scenario of a Teacher's Worst Treatment of a Student

When I first began teaching at a small school in East Texas, paddling was the accepted method of discipline. I was appalled by the idea, but by Thanksgiving, I asked my husband to make a paddle for me. I practiced on a blanket that was thrown over a clothesline. I am not proud that I participated in this form of discipline.

Motive Probe

This teacher did not respond to the motive probe.

Commentary

This teacher's guilt and remorse are obvious in her last statement. Corporal punishment, although still legal in some states, is the least desirable form of discipline. To avoid resorting to paddling, this teacher could have ignored the actions of her peers and acquainted herself with other, more acceptable forms of discipline. She should consult successful veteran teachers in her school district to find out what they do in lieu of paddling.

Mistake 2: Physical Aggression

Teacher # 4

A Scenario of a Teacher's Worst Treatment of a Student

One of my students went to bite another student in the back. When I saw her, I hit her on top of the head and yelled, "NO"! I quietly looked around to see if anyone saw me. She was screaming from the blow. I tried to calm her down so no one would ask me why she was crying.

Motive Probe

4.1. Describe the problem and your specific role in it.

  I was stopping a child from biting another.

4.2. Why did you do what you did?

  It was a reaction.

4.3. What emotions or feelings were you experiencing at the time?

  None.

4.4. Was your behavior justified? If so, why?

  Yes, I needed her to stop because she kept biting the other kids.

4.5. Do you regret your action(s)?

Now I do.

4.6. Do you ever think about this incident? If yes, approximately how often since the occurrence(s)?

Yes, every time a student does something wrong.

4.7. If faced with the same or a similar situation, what would you do?

Probably the same thing; it was a split second reaction.

Commentary

It is apparent that this teacher feels justified, and not responsible for her actions. She fails to realize that her behavior just exacerbated the problem. She modeled the aggressive, physical behavior that she was trying to deter. To avoid defaulting to a physically aggressive response to student behavior, teachers should react to problem situations with restraint, knowledge, and understanding. Impulsivity just makes problems worse; teachers must think before reacting.

Teacher # 5

A Scenario of a Teacher's Worst Treatment of a Student

During my first year of teaching, I had six language arts resource classes, with about 20 kids in each class. I had no assistant. The students were majority male, with abilities ranging from prekindergarten to fourth grade. Additionally, sixth, seventh, and eighth were combined in each class, so I had kids ranging in ages from 11–16. Being that I was a first-year teacher, I thought being nice, I could get the kids to behave and achieve. Was I ever wrong? On the day of the incident, I had had it. The kids were being disrespectful, throwing things, fighting, and so on. I finally snapped. From the front of the class, I hurled an eraser across the room, barely missing 2 students. At the same time, I screamed for everyone to "shut up."

Motive Probe

5.1. Describe the problem and your specific role in it.

I had not set up a good discipline program in my class.

5.2. Why did you do what you did?

I was trying to send a message that I was about to snap.

5.3. What emotions or feelings were you experiencing at the time?

Anger, frustration, and a feeling of failure.

5.4. Was your behavior justified? If so, why?

No, although the kids were out of control I should have set guidelines from the start and the kids might have done better.

5.5. Do you regret your action(s)?

Somewhat.

5.6. Do you ever think about this incident? If yes, approximately how often since the occurrence(s)?

Yes, many times a year for 1–2 years.

5.7. If faced with the same or a similar situation, what would you do?

I would take a deep breath and walk out of the room for a second. This is what I have done since the incident and it works pretty well.

Commentary

The author of this scenario acknowledges that she was unprepared, that she had failed to set up a good discipline program. A lack of preparation is a lesson doomed to failure. This scenario teacher has not learned much from the experience, she does attempt to manage her anger, but she does not address the real issue, her lack of classroom management strategies, to prevent discipline problems. To avoid future problems, she could take some professional development courses on classroom management and effective pedagogy (teaching methods). She can also observe other classrooms where the teachers are successfully managing their classes.

Teacher # 6

A Scenario of a Teacher's Worst Treatment of a Student

I hollered at a student to get out of my class after I specifically asked her to put up a Gameboy® (portable videogame player) while we were discussing the day's math lesson.

Motive Probe

6.1. Describe the problem and your specific role in it.

I asked twice and when I tried to take it away she snarled, "Don't touch my f. . . . . g (profanity) stuff."

6.2. Why did you do what you did?

Anger.

6.3. What emotions or feelings were you experiencing at the time?

Anger.

6.4. Was your behavior justified? If so, why?

No.

6.5. Do you regret your action(s)?

Yes

6.6. Do you ever think about this incident? If yes, approximately how often since the occurrence(s)?

Ten–fifteen times a year for one year.

6.7. If faced with the same or a similar situation, what would you do?

Try and maintain my composure.

Commentary

The most obvious problem in this scenario is screaming at a student. This method of discipline is so ineffective. My forewarning to preservice teachers is "Once a screamer always a screamer" because students will enjoy pushing a teacher's buttons to make her scream or yell. To avoid this screamfest, the teacher should revise her class rules to make bringing in an inappropriate object or toy, an infraction. She can include students in the plan to determine the consequences for an infraction of this rule. However, it is wise to try to guide students to decide that anyone violating the rules should lose possession of the item for a specified period of time, if that's appropriate. Additionally, the offending student would be required to turn the item in after receiving a warning the first time. This would eliminate the need to physically take the item from the student and risk inciting aggression in the student that invites a power struggle. The student may be more apt to comply if reminded of classroom rules and mutually agreed-upon consequences. If the child refuses, it will be easier to maintain composure without the explosive situation that results from the physical aggression of taking something from someone. To avoid a serious confrontation, teachers should learn to gauge potentially explosive situations by being aware of these types of situations; student personalities, their personal circumstances, the collective persona of the class are all critical factors.

Teacher # 7

A Scenario of a Teacher's Worst Treatment of a Student

One of my students was one of those children who refused to make an effort. He would be off task, talk back with statements like, "I wasn't doing that" or "you let him" or "my other teachers let me." Often when he was asked to do something he would say "I am doing it," but he was not, and did not; he just ignored the directive. He would be standing; I would say "sit down"; he would say "I am." Then he would remain standing. I tried moving his seat, calling home, and writing office referrals. Nothing worked; to top it off, he is reading way below level and he was in denial. One day I had enough. I grabbed him by the arm and forced him to sit down, while yelling at him.

Motive Probe

7.1. Describe the problem and your specific role in it.

I forced a student to sit down, while yelling at him.

7.2. Why did you do what you did?

I was frustrated and wanted to communicate with him in a language he could understand.

7.3. What emotions or feelings were you experiencing at the time?

Anger.

7.4. Was your behavior justified? If so, why?

Yes, the boy needed to know his behavior was going to hurt him in the long run and "conventional" means of telling him that was not working.

7.5. Do you regret your action(s)?

Only that it was illegal.

7.6. Do you ever think about this incident? If yes, approximately how often since the occurrence(s)?

No.

7.7. If faced with the same or a similar situation, what would you do?

Now, I don't get as angry because I have come to accept that some children will be failures and there is nothing I can do about it. So I do all I can.

Commentary

What appears to be misbehavior may in fact be a student's defense tactic to mask an embarrassing learning disability. The child's misbehavior, talking back to the teacher and being off task, may be distracters designed to redirect the focus off real problems such as his reading deficiencies that interfere with his ability to perform at the level of his peers. It is easier and face saving for the student to act as if he does not want to do the work. To avoid misdiagnosing chronic misbehavior, note when, where, and why it occurs. Teachers should try to clearly distinguish between behavior disorders and intentional misbehavior. To make the distinction, teachers should try reading student behavior for hidden messages—that is, to see what is not apparent and to hear what is not being said.

Teacher # 8

A Scenario of a Teacher's Worst Treatment of a Student

There was a child in my class who had severe mental challenges. It was his first year in school. So my only alternative was to document his behavior for a referral. He had ADHD, and possibly Asperger syndrome, a form of autism. He couldn't sit still; he would bother others by talking, playing, or hitting. One day, I just got so frustrated with his daily behavior that after he was acting up and hurting another child, I pulled his arm by his hand and sat him down in a chair.

Motive Probe

8.1. Describe the problem and your specific role in it.

I told a student to sit down, while yelling at him.

8.2. Why did you do what you did?

My frustration with his daily behavior and fear for the safety of the other children.

8.3. What emotions or feelings were you experiencing at the time?

Anger, frustration, and disbelief.

8.4. Was your behavior justified? If so, why?

Yes, the point was that I removed a student from an unsafe situation.

8.5. Do you regret your action(s)?

Somewhat.

8.6. Do you ever think about this incident? If yes, approximately how often since the occurrence(s)?

One year.

8.7. If faced with the same or a similar situation, what would you do?

I would be more gentle in my actions.

Commentary

A premature judgment and labeling can unnecessarily mar a student's record and influence other teachers' expectations and perceptions of that child. This teacher rushed to judgment and labeled a kindergarten student before getting a formal diagnosis. Additionally, she had less than 3 years of teaching experience which translates into limited ability to recognize exceptionality in children without the assistance of experts in that area. What is worse is that she was aggressive with the student, although she believed he was not totally responsible for his actions. To avoid misjudgment and misdiagnosis, teachers need extensive training with special needs students. Teachers must not forget that special needs students have feelings and they should not be mistreated.

Teacher # 9

A Scenario of a Teacher's Worst Treatment of a Student

It was not a student, per se, it was a player on my basketball team. It was the fourth quarter of a game late in the year. The player was on the bench because we were ahead by a large margin. The players in the game at the time were having problems. I walked down in front of the aforementioned player and told him to check in for another player. He just sat there for a few seconds. When he finally decided to get up, I gently pushed on his chest (so he remained seated) and I said, "Fine, I'll get someone else." Things would have been okay except he decided to leave the bench before the game was over. I did not know until we were in the locker room and he wasn't there. I met with his parents and him after the game to clear up the problem. He was great the rest of the season.

Motive Probe

9.1. Describe the problem and your specific role in it.

A player failed to comply with my request immediately. I overreacted a little.

9.2. Why did you do what you did?

He should have jumped up and checked in the game. He was feeling sorry for himself because he did not play in the entire fourth quarter.

9.3. What emotions or feelings were you experiencing at the time?

Anger, because the kid was being selfish and not a team player. He should have been cheering for his teammates who rarely got to play.

9.4. Was your behavior justified? If so, why?

Yes, it is my decision who I substitute and when. I guess I could have waited until the next practice to speak with him and/or punish him.

9.5. Do you regret your action(s)?

No.

9.6. Do you ever think about this incident? If yes, approximately how often since the occurrence(s)?

One–five times for 5 years.

9.7. If faced with the same or a similar situation, what would you do?

The same thing.

Commentary

This teacher suffers from the omnipotent-teacher syndrome. He acts all-powerful and all-knowing. He's in charge and a mind reader, knowing what the player was thinking. He is authoritarian, expecting immediate obedience to his request; when he did not get it, he passed judgment and administered punishment in a split second giving the child no opportunity to explain. The child could have been hesitating for another reason. Although the coach felt that he was correct and the child was wrong, I question his unwillingness to examine his behavior and seek alternatives, particularly when he admitted he overreacted and he used physical force to make the student sit down. To avoid the omnipotence syndrome, teachers can adopt a more authoritative or diplomatic way of dealing with students that does not demand unquestioned obedience. Whenever possible, teachers should give students an opportunity to explain their behavior.
Mistake 4: Public Ridicule

Teacher # 10

A Scenario of a Teacher's Worst Treatment of a Student

I told the students in my class to get in groups for a project. There was one student who nobody wanted to work with because she was "weird." I made another student get out of his group and work with her. I yelled at him and ridiculed him in front of the class. He was so angry at me and embarrassed that he turned bright red and wouldn't look at me for the rest of the class period. Previously, he would come to my classroom after school and help me in class. After this incident he never did it again.

Motive Probe

10.1. Describe the problem and your specific role in it.

I didn't consider his feelings. I took out my anger on him.

10.2. Why did you do what you did?

I felt badly for the little girl and I also wanted everything to be my way.

10.3. What emotions or feelings were you experiencing at the time?

Anger, confusion, and overwhelmed with my job. It was my first year.

10.4. Was your behavior justified? If so, why?

No, I keep thinking I should have put my students' feelings first but I didn't. I really believe in the saying "no one has the right to hurt someone else."

10.5. Do you regret your action(s)?

Yes.

10.6. Do you ever think about this incident? If yes, approximately how often since the occurrence(s)?

Ten times for 2 years since the event happened.

10.7. If faced with the same or a similar situation, what would you do?

I have completely changed the way I handle my groups—I either assign students to groups, allow them to work alone, or work it so that everyone is ok with the way they are grouped.

Commentary

This is the wrong, wrong, wrong approach. This scenario presents a lose–lose situation for the girl who needed help and the student who was forced to help her. This teacher took her male student for granted, mistaking his niceness for weakness. She thought she could manipulate him more easily than the other students that did not come to help her after school. She could have avoided the disastrous situation by first treating her students with the same respect that she would give an adult friend. She could have asked him privately to help which would avoid a scene that would embarrass the girl and she could have treated him well in the process. The good news is that she has acknowledged the wisdom of the ages that simplifies life . . . being aware that she always wants her own way and that is not always possible or desirable.

Teacher # 11

A Scenario of a Teacher's Worst Treatment of a Student

I think my worst treatment of a student was when one of my boys was refusing to do his work in class and his homework assignments. I was so frustrated that I embarrassed him in front of the class.

Motive Probe

11.1. Describe the problem and your specific role in it.

I tried to make him feel badly about what he was doing.

11.2. Why did you do what you did?

Out of frustration.

11.3. What emotions or feelings were you experiencing at the time?

Anger, frustration, and disappointment.

11.4. Was your behavior justified? If so, why?

No, because I could have approached him in a different manner.

11.5. Do you regret your action(s)?

Yes.

11.6. Do you ever think about this incident? If yes, approximately how often since the occurrence(s)?

Ten times a year.

11.7. If faced with the same or a similar situation, what would you do?

I would try to do something different to motivate him to do his work.

Commentary

Some teachers embrace the misconception that making someone feel badly about what they are doing will motivate them to stop their behavior. To avoid making the student feel badly, a request to do the work could be in the form of a logical appeal, and explain to the student the benefits of completing assignments or doing homework (Orange, 2005). This appeal to the conscience could possibly work if it were not done in public. In a public forum it becomes humiliation.

Mistake 6: Physiological Discrimination

Teacher # 12

A Scenario of a Teacher's Worst Treatment of a Student

This treatment happened during my first year of teaching; actually during my first month of teaching. There was this little girl in my class. She was the tallest and biggest in the class. She had a severe attitude with everyone and anyone. One day she came back from lunch and was very disruptive. She kept interrupting and talking back. I had put up with her for a while and finally broke and just made her sit outside of the class in the hall with the door closed. I continued with the lesson and forgot about her. Twenty minutes later, a student reminded me she was outside. She was still waiting, standing up and I had forgotten. I felt really badly.

Motive Probe

12.1. Describe the problem and your specific role in it.

I made a student sit outside the class and I forgot about her.

12.2. Why did you do what you did?

For both of us to have a cooling-off period.

12.3. What emotions or feelings were you experiencing at the time?

I was so upset that I could not even look at her. I just wanted her out.

12.4. Was your behavior justified? If so, why?

Probably not.

12.5. Do you regret your action(s)?

Yes, I could have handled it differently.

12.6. Do you ever think about this incident? If yes, approximately how often since the occurrence(s)?

No, I just remembered it once since it happened, now.

12.7. If faced with the same or a similar situation, what would you do?

Just give the student a referral and have the counselor talk to him or her.

Commentary

Discrimination manifests in a variety of way. In this scenario, it seems that the teacher has a negative bias toward this student because of her size. She points out that the girl is the biggest and the tallest student with a severe attitude, in that order. The order suggests that the girl's size is more important than her attitude. Actually, size is irrelevant when considering a student's behavior, unless the student is using his or her size to intimidate others. Comments the teacher made such as not being able to look at the student, suggests further evidence of bias. Teachers can avoid discrimination based on physical attributes by setting personal standards that will not tolerate such bias. They can limit their judgment and subsequent treatment of children to the quality of children's work, behavior, participation, and productivity in the classroom.

Teacher # 13

A Scenario of a Teacher's Worst Treatment of a Student

I commented to a young girl about her weight. At that time I was working in a residential treatment center/children's home.

Motive Probe

13.1. Describe the problem and your specific role in it.

As a counselor-in-training, I hurt a young girl's feelings.

13.2. Why did you do what you did?

I was not thinking. I usually think before I speak . . . but not this time.

13.3. What emotions or feelings were you experiencing at the time?

Feelings of frustration for other reasons, not because of anything she did. I was frustrated with another situation in the children's home.

13.4. Was your behavior justified? If so, why?

The behavior was unacceptable.

13.5. Do you regret your action(s)?

Yes, absolutely.

13.6. Do you ever think about this incident? If yes, approximately how often since the occurrence(s)?

One time per year at least.

13.7. If faced with the same or a similar situation, what would you do?

I certainly would not make comments regarding sensitive issues such as weight, height, age, and so on.

Commentary

Childhood obesity is a serious problem that is nearly epidemic in the United States. A side effect of obesity is fat discrimination evidenced by people who apparently believe that fat people are subhuman and thereby are not entitled to the respect and courtesy extended to their slimmer counterparts. These people feel, do, and say whatever they want to an overweight person. To avoid this type of bias, teachers have an obligation to respect student boundaries, particularly those concerning student weight, gender, and ethnicity. Better teachers try to embrace student differences and help them with their challenges.

Mistake 7: Personal Attacks

Teacher # 14

A Scenario of a Teacher's Worst Treatment of a Student

While tutoring, I told a student he was being a smart mouth and if he was really smart, he would be quiet and do his work instead of being lazy.

Motive Probe

14.1. Describe the problem and your specific role in it.

I would tutor this child Tuesday and Thursday.

14.2. Why did you do what you did?

Because after meeting with his parents two times a week, the student did not change his attitude or become motivated regardless of how much I talked to him or how many varieties of instructional methods I used.

14.3. What emotions or feelings were you experiencing at the time?

Anger.

14.4. Was your behavior justified? If so, why?

No, anger is never justified. You should keep calm and try one more strategy or look for a solution.

14.5. Do you regret your action(s)?

Yes.

14.6. Do you ever think about this incident? If yes, approximately how often since the occurrence(s)?

(No response.)

14.7. If faced with the same or a similar situation, what would you do?

Think things through and remain calm.

Commentary

When the teacher makes the attack on a student personal, it suggests that the teacher feels threatened in some way and sees the student as a source of threat. This teacher obviously felt inadequate because she had run out of options for changing the student's behavior. She resorted to failure-breeding tactics such as name-calling, labeling, and criticism of students for talking. The teacher is obviously misinformed as evidenced by her apparent belief that being quiet is being smart. That's not necessarily true. Vygotsky (1993) proposes that children's private speech helps them to organize their thoughts when they are working. Being quiet would rob them of the opportunity to engage in this process. Perhaps she could have avoided the problem if she asked the student to tell her what he thought would be helpful to his learning in the tutoring session.

Teacher # 15

A Scenario of a Teacher's Worst Treatment of a Student

My son was in his room and I was upset to find that he was making faces as I asked him to read a book that his teacher sent home for homework. He continued to roll his eyes, to sigh, and fiddle as he attempted to read. I became increasingly frustrated because he seemed to be giving up and not trying after doing just a few school assignments, reading, and sports/extracurricular activities. He continued to stumble on words and act out and I became tense and increasingly upset. After many prompts, I exploded and told him he was lazy and not a hard worker.

Motive Probe

15.1. Describe the problem and your specific role in it.

See above.

15.2. Why did you do what you did?

I was frustrated and I felt guilty.

15.3. What emotions or feelings were you experiencing at the time?

I felt upset that he was giving up and seemed to not be trying. I also felt guilty because I may not have been encouraging enough in the past to instill a better work ethic in him.

15.4. Was your behavior justified? If so, why?

No, I don't believe yelling at a child and calling him lazy is any kind of motivation to develop a better work ethic, especially for a 5-year-old.

15.5. Do you regret your action(s)?

Yes.

15.6. Do you ever think about this incident? If yes, approximately how often since the occurrence(s)?

About ten times a year for about 2 years.

15.7. If faced with the same or a similar situation, what would you do?

Take a breath, walk away to collect my thoughts first.

Commentary

It's ironic that the mother was upset and angry because she felt the child was not trying hard enough and that he was giving up too soon, when in fact, that is exactly what she did. She gave up on her 5-year-old. A reluctance to read suggests that the child may have a reading problem or a developing learning disability. This mother is a teacher, but she forgot to use her teacher skills at home and give her son the same consideration that she would give a reluctant reader. As a parent, she felt more fearful and anxious about the possible outcome, namely that her son would always be a poor reader. Her frustration was a direct result of her feelings that she was powerless over that possibility. To avoid repeating this behavior, the mother should allow herself to be teacher at home when necessary and work patiently with her child. Patience and kindness will remove the need for the child to make faces and act out; instead, he will be more likely to work with his mom-teacher to remediate his reading deficiencies.

Teacher # 16

A Scenario of a Teacher's Worst Treatment of a Student

I don't recall the specific details of this incident. I was speaking to a boy out in the hall after I sent him there because of his perpetual, persistent misbehavior. I had tried many times before to be kind and reasonable with him. But this day, I had it with him. I ended up calling him a loser and told him to quit dragging everyone else down with him because that was one thing I wouldn't tolerate.

Motive Probe

16.1. Describe the problem and your specific role in it.

The problem is that I used harsh words and demeaned a student.

16.2. Why did you do what you did?

I was frustrated with his persistent, mischievous behaviors.

16.3. What emotions or feelings were you experiencing at the time?

I felt total frustration and anger. I remember being really mad that he wasn't responding to my kinder, gentler efforts.

16.4. Was your behavior justified? If so, why?

No, he really did not need one other person telling him he was worthless. If I had lived his life, I wouldn't care about school either. He is probably clinically depressed.

16.5. Do you regret your action(s)?

I regretted it immediately. This boy has been virtually abandoned by his mother, who should be arrested. His dad is already in jail.

16.6. Do you ever think about this incident? If yes, approximately how often since the occurrence(s)?

Yes, maybe twice since it happened.

16.7. If faced with the same or a similar situation, what would you do?

I did apologize to him afterward. I think I told him how frustrated I was. I am not sure if it was a good idea to burden him with that.

Commentary

This teacher is obviously a believer in the old adage—the apple doesn't fall far from the tree. She clearly sees the child's parents as losers and has the same low expectations for him. She assumes he does not care about school and that he's depressed, as if she has X-ray vision that can probe the interior of his deepest thoughts. Teachers must tread lightly through the muck and mire of low expectations and assumptions, lest they make them a reality. They must remember that some of those apples that fall close to the tree make great apple pie.

Teacher # 17

A Scenario of a Teacher's Worst Treatment of a Student

I had all three second-grade classes and no one was following directions or paying attention and this had been going on for a week or so. I had a visitor come in and had to stop and talk briefly. While I was talking, all control of my class was lost. You would have thought you were in a cage full of wild monkeys. When the visitor left, I started yelling at the students. I told them they were acting like idiots and if they did not know what an idiot was, all they had to do was to look in a mirror. The next day I was called into the principal's office to face the principal and an irate parent of one of those idiots. I apologized to my students, but I also made them copy down all the rules and practice them for 45 minutes.

Motive Probe

17.1. Describe the problem and your specific role in it.

I had had it.

17.2. Why did you do what you did?

I had had it.

17.3. What emotions or feelings were you experiencing at the time?

Anger and frustration.

17.4. Was your behavior justified? If so, why?

Not really.

17.5. Do you regret your action(s)?

No.

17.6. Do you ever think about this incident? If yes, approximately how often since the occurrence(s)?

Only when I see the parent—maybe once or twice a year.

17.7. If faced with the same or a similar situation, what would you do?

I would make them all sit down in time-out.

Commentary

Unfortunately for this teacher, the reflection the kids will see in the mirror will not be theirs, it will be hers. Her lack of planning and establishing procedures or rules when there is a visitor is evident in her students' poor behavior. Being prepared is the only way to handle unexpected visitors. Good teachers expect and plan for the unexpected.

Mistake 9: Deliberate Mistreatment

Teacher # 18

A Scenario of a Teacher's Worst Treatment of a Student

When I was a teacher trainee, I sent one of my students to go play soccer with my ex-boyfriend who is a national soccer player. I told my ex to keep him on the field as long as he could. They ended up spending time playing soccer for almost 4 hours. My ex was fine, but my student did not come to school the next day. I felt so badly about that, but after that day, he had never skipped my class anymore.

Motive Probe

18.1. Describe the problem and your specific role in it.

He always skipped my class, and went to play soccer.

18.2. Why did you do what you did?

I wanted to fatigue him and I was hoping he would stay in the class.

18.3. What emotions or feelings were you experiencing at the time?

Frustration and being upset.

18.4. Was your behavior justified? If so, why?

(No response.)

18.5. Do you regret your action(s)?

Yes, I realized I should not have done so.

18.6. Do you ever think about this incident? If yes, approximately how often since the occurrence(s)?

Three years.

18.7. If faced with the same or a similar situation, what would you do?

Sit down and talk to the student.

Commentary

The discipline strategy that the teacher's trainee attempted to use was "satiation" or having a child repeat a behavior until he is beyond satiated (Schunk, 2004) to change a student's behavior. This strategy changes behavior because what was once pleasurable when repeated excessively usually becomes punishing. This change is similar to the effect of the law of diminishing returns such as 1 scoop of ice cream may be delicious and satisfying but by the 20th scoop, a person could feel sick and nauseated. The teacher could have capitalized on the student's love for soccer and created an engaging project and lesson on soccer that may have captured his interest. Additionally, the use of a potential hero or role model to abuse a child is a waste of talent and potential. Her ex could have been used more effectively to motivate the class. Whatever discipline strategy a teacher wants to use, he or she should never plan to harm a student. Positive behavior change and respect for students should be the only goal.

Teacher # 19

A Scenario of a Teacher's Worst Treatment of a Student

I was a summer camp counselor and had a very disruptive, hyperactive, disobedient camper. Every time he was disobedient I would take away his favorite activity for that day and I would sit him so that he could watch the other campers enjoy the activity.

Motive Probe

19.1. Describe the problem and your specific role in it.

I had a disobedient problem-child camper. I was his counselor.

19.2. Why did you do what you did?

I felt like it was the only way to teach him a lesson.

19.3. What emotions or feelings were you experiencing at the time?

I was sad for the kid, but he was so bad and nothing would get through to him.

19.4. Was your behavior justified? If so, why?

Not really, his parents were paying money for him to enjoy summer camp and I took away his favorite activities.

19.5. Do you regret your action(s)?

Activities yes and no; it got me and the other campers through the summer better.

19.6. Do you ever think about this incident? If yes, approximately how often since the occurrence(s)?

Only when I see bad kids that remind me of him.

19.7. If faced with the same or a similar situation, what would you do?

(1) Call the parents earlier and explain. (2) Be sterner in the beginning so hopefully it wouldn't come to this. (3) Get the director involved sooner.

Commentary

Apparently this teacher's tactic crossed over the fine line of reasonable punishment to abuse. This is unfortunate because her ultimate goal was abuse. She could have capitalized on guiding the student toward more self-control by using his favorite activities as incentives. The excessive punishment of forcing the camper to watch other campers enjoying his favorite activity is retribution for the teacher's damaged ego, but it also cheated the camper and his parents out of the camp experience they purchased. She could have avoided this unfortunate incident by redirecting his behavior to more positive, acceptable responses. The punishment, if any, should be limited to forfeiting some or all the activity only, but not being forced to watch.

Teacher # 20

A Scenario of a Teacher's Worst Treatment of a Student

One of my students was consistently late for class. She often disrupted the topic of discussion, would then proceed to talk with total disregard for the teacher (me) while class was in progress. When I asked questions, she would answer with something completely irrelevant to the topic of discussion or try to make a joke of it. Finally one day, I left the door open to let my students come in for class. When I saw her coming, I shut the door in her face just before she walked in.

Motive Probe

20.1. Describe the problem and your specific role in it.

I was tired of a student coming to class late and disrupting things.

20.2. Why did you do what you did?

Out of sheer frustration.

20.3. What emotions or feelings were you experiencing at the time?

Anger and frustration.

20.4. Was your behavior justified? If so, why?

Ethically, as a teacher no, but as an individual with feelings, yes.

20.5. Do you regret your action(s)?

No.

20.6. Do you ever think about this incident? If yes, approximately how often since the occurrence(s)?

(No response.)

20.7. If faced with the same or a similar situation, what would you do?

Have a counselor talk to her.

Commentary

A slammed door in your face sends a very strong message. It says, I am so angry with you, I am hurt and embarrassed, and I want you to feel the same way. Many of us, at some point in time, have wanted to send a similar message by slamming the door in someone's face. I can remember being pursued by an angry co-worker who was ranting and raving at me very publicly. She was following me to my classroom and I locked my door behind me. As she approached, I pulled the shade down slowly in her face. Closing doors in someone's face is a not-so-passive, very-aggressive message that has a latent humiliation factor. To avoid this problem, this teacher could have set up rules of etiquette for the classroom and modeled them. These would include how to enter the classroom when one is late to minimize disruption of the class. They may have to sit close to the door and wait if the teacher is busy instructing. Nowhere does the teacher say that she has ever talked to the girl about her tardiness. There could be a number of reasons for her tardiness. First, she could suggest that the student use an alarm clock; if she does not have one, provide her with one. The student could have a sleep disorder, or perhaps there is a family situation such as violence or alcoholism that keeps her awake at night. Most school districts hold parents accountable for their child's tardiness; notifying the parent may have prevented the slammed-door episode.

Mistake 10: Racial and Cultural Discrimination

Teacher # 21

A Scenario of a Teacher's Worst Treatment of a Student

I was a counselor at a camp for the YMCA. I had a student in my class with special needs. He was in a wheelchair, and had limited motor skills. My training for this type of student at the time was zero. So my day consisted of taking him to the restroom, drying him, wiping him, and including him in as much as possible. My concern was that I had no training on how to handle this situation, and I did not want to be held liable for anything that might happen to him.

Motive Probe

21.1. Describe the problem and your specific role in it.

We were scheduled for a field trip to our camp. There were no wheelchair accommodations at the camp or on the bus.

21.2. Why did you do what you did?

I told him that he wasn't going to go.

21.3. What emotions or feelings were you experiencing at the time?

Frustrated, because I did not want to push him around in a wheelchair. I wanted to devote my time to the other kids. Anger, because of having to change everything just for this one kid.

21.4. Was your behavior justified? If so, why?

No. I was not sensitive to his needs. I did not understand his situation or how he felt.

21.5. Do you regret your action(s)?

Yes.

21.6. Do you ever think about this incident? If yes, approximately how often since the occurrence(s)?

(No response.)

21.7. If faced with the same or a similar situation, what would you do?

More educated now, I would try to include him in everything possible. I would try to understand how limited he was and to see what new experiences and memories I could give him.

Commentary

While progressive parents and school districts embrace a least-restrictive placement policy that seeks the most inclusive learning environment for special-needs students (Woolfolk, 2007), the rest of society is not keeping pace. There is much resistance and resentment toward this policy, especially when the teachers, counselors, or caregivers have no training for working with special-needs children. Resistance and resentment can be replaced with understanding and empathy if people seeking to work in environments that may potentially include special-needs kids were screened for empathy and special education training. Such prescreening could protect special-needs children from any abuse that may be precipitated because of their challenges.

Teacher # 22

A Scenario of a Teacher's Worst Treatment of a Student

H. was a little boy that was a persistent problem for me. He was the stereotypical "at risk" child with major anger problems. There were days when H. and I got along fine and days that we did not. On this particular day, he had been causing trouble for everyone since the bell rang. He was picking on students, disrupting class with inappropriate comments/noises and I had had enough. I called on him to answer a question and he gave me a smart answer and I told him his answer did not matter, because he would never amount to much anyway.

Motive Probe

22.1. Describe the problem and your specific role in it.

I took my frustration out on a student.

22.2. Why did you do what you did?

I lost control of my emotions.

22.3. What emotions or feelings were you experiencing at the time?

Anger, embarrassment, and fear.

22.4. Was your behavior justified? If so, why?

No, no matter what, a teacher should never say those things to a student.

22.5. Do you regret your action(s)?

Yes.

22.6. Do you ever think about this incident? If yes, approximately how often since the occurrence(s)?

Yes, three to four times a year.

22.7. If faced with the same or a similar situation, what would you do?

Tell him that he had a choice: He could either participate appropriately or go to the office and do the work with the vice-principal.

Commentary

Stereotypes and low expectations are common bedfellows. This teacher just used her anger as an excuse to say what she really felt. To avoid making generalizations about at-risk children, teachers should examine the research on resilient children and the ability of those children to rise above their circumstances, particularly when they have supportive adults in their lives. She had a choice; she could remain punitive, knowing the child's circumstances, or she could choose to be a supportive adult fostering his resiliency.

Mistake 11: Humiliation

Teacher # 23

A Scenario of a Teacher's Worst Treatment of a Student

A student was humiliated in front of the whole dance team because she was performing like she was not in the mood, at least that is the way it seemed to me. I shouted at her for doing so and after a few more classes, I found out that she is just very shy.

Motive Probe

23.1. Describe the problem and your specific role in it.

My student was not performing well and I embarrassed her for it.

23.2. Why did you do what you did?

I didn't understand why she performed like that. I didn't know the child well enough.

23.3. What emotions or feelings were you experiencing at the time?

I felt rage and anger because she was performing the dance poorly.

23.4. Was your behavior justified? If so, why?

No, it did not help her to do better; I think I actually made it worse.

23.5. Do you regret your action(s)?

Very much.

23.6. Do you ever think about this incident? If yes, approximately how often since the occurrence(s)?

Yes, about five–eight times in the past 3 years.

23.7. If faced with the same or a similar situation, what would you do?

I would have made a comment to her in a joking manner, something that could have inspired or motivated her.

Commentary

This teacher made an erroneous assumption about a student's mood and performance and did not learn much from her error. When asked what she would do if faced with the same situation, she is still making an assumption about the student's motives and mood although she is framing it as a joke or inspirational message. The magic three-letter word is "Ask." She could have gently questioned the student about the performance, perhaps asking her if everything was alright or if she felt that something was keeping her from performing at her best that day. A great way for teachers to avoid making erroneous assumptions about a student's performance is to refrain from judging the performance until they know the student better and there is enough evidence concerning the student's performance to make an informed judgment.

Teacher # 24

A Scenario of a Teacher's Worst Treatment of a Student

In all honesty, there is not one particular incident that stands out from the others. However, there have been several occasions when I was speaking to students that I was sarcastic or belittling.

Motive Probe

24.1. Describe the problem and your specific role in it.

I belittled a student.

24.2. Why did you do what you did?

I felt frustrated with the student.

24.3. What emotions or feelings were you experiencing at the time?

(No response.)

24.4. Was your behavior justified? If so, why?

(No response.)

24.5. Do you regret your action(s)?

Yes.

24.6. Do you ever think about this incident? If yes, approximately how often since the occurrence(s)?

No.

24.7. If faced with the same or a similar situation, what would you do?

I try to treat my students like I would want my sons to be treated by their teachers.

Commentary

It seems that this teacher's modus operandi for interacting with students is to be belittling or sarcastic most of the time, making it difficult to distinguish any particular incident from another. She is correct; the best way for teachers to avoid verbally abusing students is to make it a personal trait to treat all people, big and small, with dignity and respect. By treating students the way she would like for her children to be treated, she would find a way to help students exercise self-control, eliminating the need to belittle them for their conduct.

Teacher # 25

A Scenario of a Teacher's Worst Treatment of a Student

Students were filling out information forms with their addresses. A student didn't know his address. I asked him how long he had lived there. He said his entire life. I said, "What? Your parents don't want you to find them if you get lost?" The other kids laughed; he was humiliated.

Motive Probe

25.1. Describe the problem and your specific role in it.

There was a student that the other kids picked on, and I did it too.

25.2. Why did you do what you did?

Frustration.

25.3. What emotions or feelings were you experiencing at the time?

Frustration.

25.4. Was your behavior justified? If so, why?

No.

25.5. Do you regret your action(s)?

Yes, from the very instant I said it to this day, 15 years later.

25.6. Do you ever think about this incident? If yes, approximately how often since the occurrence(s)?

Yes, often.

25.7. If faced with the same or a similar situation, what would you do?

I would quietly tell him to leave it blank and look up his address for him.

Commentary

There is a fine line between humor and humiliation, particularly from the perspective of the person who is the butt of the joke. To avoid crossing this line, teachers should craft their humor in such a way that it does not involve personal attributes of their students or their family members. Some people think that wisecracking makes them seem witty. When wisecracking is at the expense of someone else, it may make the person appear witless rather than witty. Sensitivity could have spared this teacher 15 years of regret.

Mistake 12: Inappropriate Classroom Policies

Teacher # 26

A Scenario of a Teacher's Worst Treatment of a Student

In an attempt to train students to use bathroom break time, I singled out a child for requesting to use the restroom during nonbreak time. I did not let her go. I reviewed the class routine and appropriate rules for using the restroom during scheduled breaks and at the end of class. I ended up having to speak with the child's mother and apologizing to Mom and daughter. Each time I see her and our eyes meet, I send an empathetic, unspoken apology to her.

Motive Probe

26.1. Describe the problem and your specific role in it.

I did not let a child go to the restroom.

26.2. Why did you do what you did?

Teaching students a routine and using a schedule break time for restroom use.

26.3. What emotions or feelings were you experiencing at the time?

Frustration.

26.4. Was your behavior justified? If so, why?

Yes, in order to keep the entire class on track, keep the class activity going and class routine of going to the restroom before class, at break, and the end of class.

26.5. Do you regret your action(s)?

Yes, because the child had a medical condition that required her to use restroom more often.

26.6. Do you ever think about this incident? If yes, approximately how often since the occurrence(s)?

Yes, about five times a year since that time. I will never forget this child or the lesson I learned.

26.7. If faced with the same or a similar situation, what would you do?

Check to see if the child had a medical condition prior to saying "NO."

Commentary

This scenario is a classic classroom management problem regarding toileting practices. The teacher's frustration is the result of trying to squeeze the square peg of student bathroom needs into the round hole of classroom management. To avoid the problem in this scenario, teachers must realize that the square peg won't fit because students are complex; they vary in their physiological needs and elimination schedules. This is an area that should not be controlled or denied, but rather monitored and gently managed. They should always let a student go without repercussions or humiliation, but to preserve the integrity of their classroom management policies, they should make every effort to minimize disruption to the class and the school. Allowing students to quietly take the restroom pass and excuse themselves in an emergency will minimize disruption of the lesson.

Mistake 13: Inappropriate Toileting Practices

Teacher # 27

A Scenario of a Teacher's Worst Treatment of a Student

I had a young boy who requested to go to the restroom during class. It was my practice to let children go, if I was not in the middle of a direct teach so they would not miss any instruction. (Of course this was for my convenience.) I asked him to wait until I was done. I forgot after my direct teach to let him go and he ended up having an accident in the classroom!

Motive Probe

27.1. Describe the problem and your specific role in it.

> *I was the teacher and because it was my classroom, I felt it was up to me to give permission to go to the restroom.*

27.2. Why did you do what you did?

> *I only wanted to go over my lesson once without interruption.*

27.3. What emotions or feelings were you experiencing at the time?

> *I was tired.*

27.4. Was your behavior justified? If so, why?

> *No, I should have let him go.*

27.5. Do you regret your action(s)?

> *Yes!*

27.6. Do you ever think about this incident? If yes, approximately how often since the occurrence(s)?

> *Yes, about five–six times a year for 7 years.*

27.7. If faced with the same or a similar situation, what would you do?

> *I would let him or her go to the restroom!*

Commentary

In this scenario, hindsight can be very effective for avoiding this problem. As the teacher said, just let children go to the restroom. Teachers would not say no to an adult that wanted to be excused, so they should not say no to a child.

Mistake 14: Inappropriate Educational Strategies

Teacher # 28

A Scenario of a Teacher's Worst Treatment of a Student

This occurred during my first year of teaching. A student constantly asked questions in my class, and I assumed that she was not paying attention. I got very upset, and called her attention by questioning her choice to disrupt the class environment. From that point on she never spoke, not even to participate. Later in the year, I found that she had ADHD. When I spoke to her about it, she quickly apologized for asking "too many questions." She apologized for having ADHD. I quickly explained to her that she did nothing wrong, and that I was at fault.

Motive Probe

28.1. Describe the problem and your specific role in it.

I caused this student to be afraid to ask questions.

28.2. Why did you do what you did?

I was not aware of the students' medical histories, and did not know how to properly redirect the behavior.

28.3. What emotions or feelings were you experiencing at the time?

I was angry at her constant questioning, but after learning that she was ADHD, I was very ashamed of my initial reaction.

28.4. Was your behavior justified? If so, why?

No, definitely not because this student's ability to communicate was impeded by my lack of knowledge.

28.5. Do you regret your action(s)?

Yes!

28.6. Do you ever think about this incident? If yes, approximately how often since the occurrence(s)?

Yes, for about 5 years.

28.7. If faced with the same or a similar situation, what would you do?

Oh, in education, I am faced with this situation periodically and I now have the tools to better (properly) handle the students.

Commentary

For the teacher in this scenario, the problem is still opaque. Although she admits she is at fault, she cannot clearly see her part in it. When asked what she would do in a similar situation, she says she can now handle students better. To avoid making the same mistake this teacher made, teachers should recognize that help seeking is difficult for most students. If they care enough to ask a question, respect their right to do so as many times as is necessary. Answering questions is a critical part of every teacher's job. Don't be too quick to judge. Find out if the child has special needs such as the one in this scenario. Make special arrangements such as personal tutoring after class if the questions seem to impede the progress of the rest of the class.

Mistake 16: Teacher Insensitivity

Teacher # 29

A Scenario of a Teacher's Worst Treatment of a Student

I had sent a child to another room and he ended up elsewhere. He was lost so he went to the office. I went to the office and got the child. I laid into him and made him cry.

Motive Probe

29.1. Describe the problem and your specific role in it.

I gave the child too much freedom and he could not handle it.

29.2. Why did you do what you did?

I was frustrated.

29.3. What emotions or feelings were you experiencing at the time?

I was angry and embarrassed because this child did not follow instructions.

29.4. Was your behavior justified? If so, why?

No.

29.5. Do you regret your action(s)?

Yes.

29.6. Do you ever think about this incident? If yes, approximately how often since the occurrence(s)?

Yes, about four times per year, since that time.

29.7. If faced with the same or a similar situation, what would you do?

(No response.)

Commentary

In this scenario, the teacher is Anglo and the student is a Hispanic kindergartner. Although an experienced teacher, the teacher may have missed the significance of possible language barriers, particularly at this age. The child apparently did not understand the instructions and, feeling lost, he went someplace safe . . . the office. To avoid such errors, teachers should make themselves aware of language acquisition of children at this age, particularly when English may be their second language. To improve a young child's chances of getting instructions correct, have them repeat them one or more times for accuracy.

Teacher # 30

A Scenario of a Teacher's Worst Treatment of a Student

A male student had just assaulted his girlfriend by punching her in the eye. I escorted the student to my office and yelled at him loudly about how wrong this was and that he was going to be arrested for his actions. I left my office to inquire further into the situation; the student then assaulted a female staff member and ran out the front door. Instinctively, I gave chase and all my other students witnessed the chase.

Motive Probe

30.1. Describe the problem and your specific role in it.

Dealing with the student while upset and not cooling down first.

30.2. Why did you do what you did?

Out of anger and instinct.

30.3. What emotions or feelings were you experiencing at the time?

Anger and frustration.

30.4. Was your behavior justified? If so, why?

No.

30.5. Do you regret your action(s)?

Yes.

30.6. Do you ever think about this incident? If yes, approximately how often since the occurrence(s)?

About five times per year for 1 year.

30.7. If faced with the same or a similar situation, what would you do?

Not chase the student.

Commentary

This teacher is oblivious to the real offense in this scenario. Assault is against the law. The student committed a crime by assaulting two females. This type of offense is beyond the scope of everyday teacher discipline problems and should have been handled by administrators and possibly the local authorities, depending on the severity of the injuries and whether the injured parties wanted to press charges. The teacher was more focused on his own actions, chasing the student and probably not catching him, rather than on what happened to the victims and the proper procedure for handling such a problem. To avoid misguided solutions to very serious problems, teachers should familiarize themselves with the school districts' policy for student offenses. In most districts, offenses are ranked in order of severity with detailed instructions for how they should be handled.

Teacher # 31

A Scenario of a Teacher's Worst Treatment of a Student

I called a student dumb, jokingly, in a conversation in a classroom full of students (ha ha . . . oh you're so dumb . . .) and I realized what I said and the impact it probably had on the student.

Motive Probe

31.1. Describe the problem and your specific role in it.

I jokingly called a student dumb.

31.2. Why did you do what you did?

I was too relaxed in the conversation and was talking like I would to a friend.

31.3. What emotions or feelings were you experiencing at the time?

I felt at ease, laughing, kidding around.

31.4. Was your behavior justified? If so, why?

No.

31.5. Do you regret your action(s)?

Of course.

31.6. Do you ever think about this incident? If yes, approximately how often since the occurrence(s)?

Every few days for 2 months.

31.7. If faced with the same or a similar situation, what would you do?

Watch what I say and remember that I'm talking to a student.

Commentary

It is understandable that teachers are people and in a casual setting, they might make uncomplimentary statements in jest and their friends won't take offense. However, in the classroom, teachers can avoid offending students by being vigilant about professionalism and by remembering that teachers should be friendly, not a friend to their students. An ironclad solution would be to only use kind words when interacting with others, especially your friends, and this kind of behavior will become a default reaction when interacting with students.

Mistake 17: Academic Shortcomings

Teacher # 32

A Scenario of a Teacher's Worst Treatment of a Student

A student in my class was a constant distraction to me and the other students. When asked to stop he was very rude and disrespectful. One long morning, I had asked him to stop talking or sit down eight times in 20 minutes. It was the last straw. Once more I had to stop teaching and wait while he kept talking. Without thinking, I screamed, "Just shut up!" The class was silent as they looked at me in disbelief.

Motive Probe

32.1. Describe the problem and your specific role in it.

I told a student to shut up.

32.2. Why did you do what you did?

I was frustrated and it just came out!

32.3. What emotions or feelings were you experiencing at the time?

Anger and frustration.

32.4. Was your behavior justified? If so, why?

Yes and no. It felt good to say "shut up" because he deserved it, but I should have responded in a more appropriate way.

32.5. Do you regret your action(s)?

No.

32.6. Do you ever think about this incident? If yes, approximately how often since the occurrence(s)?

About two–four times in the past year.

32.7. If faced with the same or a similar situation, what would you do?

I would try not to scream shut up.

Commentary

Reverse psychology has its place in classroom management. To avoid having to constantly say sit down and stop talking, the teacher could give the student what he wants. She could have stopped her lesson and yielded the floor to the student for 5 minutes to allow him to say whatever he needed to say. All eyes would be on him. The class would be quiet and wait until he has finished. Usually, students will find it somewhat unnerving to have undivided attention focused on them. They may talk briefly, but most will decline the rest of the 5 minutes and will quiet down to avoid a redirect of focused attention.

Mistake 20: Teacher Misjudgment

Teacher # 33

A Scenario of a Teacher's Worst Treatment of a Student

I judged a student wrongfully before he ever came to my class. He had an incident with another teacher and this is why they moved him to my class. I had already judged him as a troublemaker and "kept my eye" on him. He had a horseplay incident with another student and I read him the riot act. The next couple of days he got in trouble with illegal drugs and was sent to live with his grandparents.

Motive Probe

33.1. Describe the problem and your specific role in it.

I judged him without knowing him.

33.2. Why did you do what you did?

Ignorance.

33.3. What emotions or feelings were you experiencing at the time?

Angry that he had upset this class that I had, humming right along with his actions and behavior.

33.4. Was your behavior justified? If so, why?

Absolutely not! You should never judge a student before he/she arrives.

33.5. Do you regret your action(s)?

Yes, I could have made a difference.

33.6. Do you ever think about this incident? If yes, approximately how often since the occurrence(s)?

Yes, several times.

33.7. If faced with the same or a similar situation, what would you do?

Not act like that. Be more open and nonjudgmental.

Commentary

The faculty lounge is the source of much gossip about students. Teachers exchange student problems, form opinions, make judgments, develop expectations, and consequently ruin students' chances for a clean slate and new, better behavior. To avoid prejudgment and unfair treatment, teachers can ignore faculty lounge gossip. They should welcome new students with the intent to create a better learning environment for those students and help them succeed, even if they are labeled as troublemakers. Remember, in some cases, the child may be truly innocent of any wrongdoing and indeed, the teacher could be at fault. Such a case would warrant a fresh start for a child, free of bias.

Teacher # 34

A Scenario of a Teacher's Worst Treatment of a Student

It was my second class of 2000 and school house policy was no sleeping, or the appearance of sleeping. One male airman could just not stay awake in class. No matter how many times I had to tell him, he would just fall asleep. One day, I brought in a digital camera and when he fell asleep, I took some digital pictures, then downloaded them and displayed them in front of the whole class. The class was laughing hysterically, but he still did not awaken. At this point I was concerned so I scheduled him for an appointment at the Air Force medical center. It turns out he had sleep apnea.

Motive Probe

34.1. Describe the problem and your specific role in it.

An airman was sleeping in class. My job was to keep him awake.

34.2. Why did you do what you did?

I wanted to make an example of him.

34.3. What emotions or feelings were you experiencing at the time?

At first I was angry, then I was concerned because students must complete 13 semester hours of college credit in 6 weeks. They cannot afford to miss a minute.

34.4. Was your behavior justified? If so, why?

No, I should have taken a different approach. Send him to the doctor first!

34.5. Do you regret your action(s)?

Yes.

34.6. Do you ever think about this incident? If yes, approximately how often since the occurrence(s)?

Five years.

34.7. If faced with the same or a similar situation, what would you do?

I am still faced with this situation daily, but I stick to strict school policy of pulling an AF form 341 for the student. This will cause the student to receive remedial military training on the weekends.

Commentary

This teacher is guilty of assumption, a common "crime" where a teacher accepts something as true without corroborating evidence. He assumed the student airman was slacking because sleeping is incompatible with paying attention and learning. It would behoove all teachers to gather information before making an assumption. Insightful teachers suspect a problem when certain behaviors persist. He could have suggested that the airman see a medical doctor as his first attempt to deal with the problem. The public shaming appeared to be retribution for his belief that the airman was disrespecting him by sleeping; he retaliated by making a public display of the sleeping. The public shaming could have been avoided if the teacher had scheduled a private conference with the airman to gather information.

Teacher # 35

A Scenario of a Teacher's Worst Treatment of a Student

A student was stealing from his classmates. I asked the entire class who had taken a specific item that particular day; I had an idea who it was because that same student had taken a watch from his grandmother. (This was another incident.)

Motive Probe

35.1. Describe the problem and your specific role in it.

   I had everyone take everything out of their desks and I had everyone open their backpacks for a search.

35.2. Why did you do what you did?

   I was determined to find out who was stealing. There had been more than one occasion.

35.3. What emotions or feelings were you experiencing at the time?

   I was furious, at first, because I tried to approach the situation in a positive way. I had asked everyone to return the item and no questions would be asked.

35.4. Was your behavior justified? If so, why?

   Searching the backpacks, I found the culprit and embarrassed him for not coming forth. He was now in more trouble.

35.5. Do you regret your action(s)?

   Yes, I shouldn't have embarrassed him.

35.6. Do you ever think about this incident? If yes, approximately how often since the occurrence(s)?

   Yes, for one year.

35.7. If faced with the same or a similar situation, what would you do?

   I'm not sure, maybe call the vice-principal and have her speak to him.

Commentary

I think the golden rule applies in situations like this. The student was clearly wrong, and should have consequences. However, I heard someone say that when we are wronged, we want justice and we want the person to pay, but when we are wrong and guilty, we want mercy and understanding. If this teacher was ever found guilty of some wrongdoing, I'm sure she would appreciate compassion and an opportunity to save face. To avoid embarrassing students, teachers should discipline with dignity by making their reprimands as private as possible. Once she knew who stole the item, she could have waited for an opportune time to talk to the student and to discuss the consequences. What the student was stealing may also be important. If a child steals food because they are hungry, reprimands and consequences may be inappropriate.

Teacher # 36

A Scenario of a Teacher's Worst Treatment of a Student

I threw a bucket and accidentally hit a student. I was trying to get a toy out of a tree.

Motive Probe

36.1. Describe the problem and your specific role in it.

I threw the bucket in order to get a ball from the tree.

36.2. Why did you do what you did?

See above.

36.3. What emotions or feelings were you experiencing at the time?

The student was crying and I felt badly for him.

36.4. Was your behavior justified? If so, why?

No.

36.5. Do you regret your action(s)?

Yes.

36.6. Do you ever think about this incident? If yes, approximately how often since the occurrence(s)?

(No response.)

36.7. If faced with the same or a similar situation, what would you do?

I would not throw a bucket in the tree to get a toy. I will leave the toy in the tree.

Commentary

The impulsive act of throwing a bucket into a tree, with children around, surely suggests a lack of good judgment and a basic knowledge of physics such as what goes up, must come down. Situations like this can be avoided if the teacher exercises good judgment and puts safety first when solving problems. If using a ladder or some other safe method of retrieval was not possible, the teacher could have explained to the student that the toy was irretrievable and next time to try to find a clear area to play in when playing with toys that could get stuck in the tree.

Mistake 21: Teacher Bias or Expectations

Teacher # 37

A Scenario of a Teacher's Worst Treatment of a Student

I was short with a student because of his parent's lack of responsibility and his learned helplessness. I had little patience with him when he messed up or complained of little things. My frustration was more with his mom than with him, but I took it out on him.

Motive Probe

37.1. Describe the problem and your specific role in it.

I was short with a student because of my lack of patience for a situation.

37.2. Why did you do what you did?

I was frustrated with the mom because she allowed him to manipulate her and she taught him to use his dyslexia as a crutch.

37.3. What emotions or feelings were you experiencing at the time?

Frustrated, angry, and annoyed.

37.4. Was your behavior justified? If so, why?

To some extent, because this student never tried and gave up immediately on "challenging" tasks. He cried any time I challenged him and would go home and paint pictures in his mother's mind of a monster, because I challenged him instead of babying him.

37.5. Do you regret your action(s)?

To some extent, yes. I should have had more patience with him because his actions are learned behaviors from his mom.

37.6. Do you ever think about this incident? If yes, approximately how often since the occurrence(s)?

Yes, three or four times since it happened 2 months ago.

37.7. If faced with the same or a similar situation, what would you do?

Step away and take deep breaths.

Commentary

This teacher's frustration is a manifestation of a deeper problem, namely, that some teachers are inadequately trained to deal with the complexities of inclusion. Many of the teachers that I have taught in previous years have complained about their feelings of inadequacy when having to work with special-needs children. This teacher's lack of sensitivity to the child's challenge suggests that she was ill prepared to work with dyslexic children and blamed the child and the mother, to avoid accepting that she, the teacher, may be the source of the problem. Inclusion is probably here to stay. Teachers can avoid feelings of inadequacy by getting additional training for working with special-needs children and by seeking the help of an experienced teacher.

Mistake 22: Unethical Behavior

Teacher # 38

A Scenario of a Teacher's Worst Treatment of a Student

The student was continuously acting out in class. He would do anything to get the attention of his peers, including making fun of and mocking me in front of the entire class. I was in my third month of teaching, and I was already fed up. One day, after he mocked me in front of the class, I gave him the middle finger. He noticed, and announced that I had done it. No one else saw it, so I convinced him that he must have been seeing things.

Motive Probe

38.1. Describe the problem and your specific role in it.

I gave a student the middle finger.

38.2. Why did you do what you did?

I was fed up.

38.3. What emotions or feelings were you experiencing at the time?

Extreme frustration.

38.4. Was your behavior justified? If so, why?

No.

38.5. Do you regret your action(s)?

Yes.

38.6. Do you ever think about this incident? If yes, approximately how often since the occurrence(s)?

Yes, about eight times per year for 4 years.

38.7. If faced with the same or a similar situation, what would you do?

I have much better classroom management skills now and I would have put a stop to his behavior before it escalated. However, if it continued, and I was in the exact same situation, I would not do this again.

Commentary

This teacher's reaction to frustration is a character issue. To avoid situations like this, teachers should refrain from any type of vulgar or profane behavior and it will not become a default reaction. To maintain credibility with students, teachers should not lie to their students. In this case, the teacher realized that there may be serious consequences for her behavior and opted to lie to the student. Integrity and avoidance of inappropriate behavior are important components of professional teacher behavior.

Mistake 23: False Accusations

Teacher # 39

A Scenario of a Teacher's Worst Treatment of a Student

It was not a student; it was my grandson that I mistreated. He was always doing something bad and lying about it. This time he was innocent. My nephew said he broke the VCR. I was tired of hearing him whine that he wanted to see a movie. I said if you hadn't broken the VCR, you could watch it. I didn't, he said. So I spanked him for lying.

Motive Probe

39.1. Describe the problem and your specific role in it.

The VCR was broken and I spanked him.

39.2. Why did you do what you did?

I was tired that day.

39.3. What emotions or feelings were you experiencing at the time?

Anger.

39.4. Was your behavior justified? If so, why?

No.

39.5. Do you regret your action(s)?

Yes.

39.6. Do you ever think about this incident? If yes, approximately how often since the occurrence(s)?

No.

39.7. If faced with the same or a similar situation, what would you do?

Count to 10 and walk away.

Commentary

Tattletales or children who voluntarily report on the activities of others are a particular dilemma for teachers. Who should the teacher believe? Certainly the tattletale is not always correct and could be lying. An underlying problem in this scenario is the grandmother's perception that the grandson is always doing something bad and lying about it. That description of the child may have some merit, but it is too absolute to be true. The use of always doing something bad and lying suggests a negative perception of the grandson that probably clouds the grandmother's judgment or she is using this negative perception to excuse her actions. Teachers can avoid a similar problem by discouraging tattletales, treating each situation as a new case and listening to both sides of the story. If the accused denies wrongdoing and the teacher did not see it, she must drop the matter because a lack of proof or evidence could lead to false accusation and harm to the innocent.

Teacher # 40

A Scenario of a Teacher's Worst Treatment of a Student

We were at the mall (my mother, myself, and my two children) and we were driving around the parking lot trying to decide what to eat for lunch. We all decided on Luby's except my 10-year-old son who was being disagreeable because he wanted Applebee's. Finally my mother drove off and we headed to Applebee's, which was further down the road. As we turned into the parking lot, a truck ran into my mother's Jeep. I then looked at my son and said, "It's all your fault."

Motive Probe

40.1. Describe the problem and your specific role in it.

I blamed my son for my mother's accident.

40.2. Why did you do what you did?

I blamed him because he was the one who wanted to go to Applebee's.

40.3. What emotions or feelings were you experiencing at the time?

Frustration and anger.

40.4. Was your behavior justified? If so, why?

No, that was the wrong thing to say to a child and I never should have said anything like that to him.

40.5. Do you regret your action(s)?

Yes.

40.6. Do you ever think about this incident? If yes, approximately how often since the occurrence(s)?

About twenty times a year since 2003.

40.7. If faced with the same or a similar situation, what would you do?

I would not say it is anybody's fault, it just happened.

Commentary

In this scenario, it is difficult to see who is the most immature, the adult or the child. The mother lacked the courage of her wishes and gave in to the child. She was resentful and blamed him for her decision to go to his choice of restaurants. She used the accident to express her resentment. To avoid scenarios like this, adults should not give in to childish demands no matter how disagreeable the child becomes. If they do, they are begging to be manipulated in the future and to subsequently feel exploited. They should not pout and sulk and show resentment; they should be decisive and stick to their choice. Ideally, adults can solicit children's input with the understanding that the child will not make the final decision. A very democratic approach may be to take turns picking a restaurant and each member of the group agrees to abide by the choice of the decision maker.

Teacher # 41

A Scenario of a Teacher's Worst Treatment of a Student

My class was standing in the hall waiting for an assembly to end and for the students to exit. I reminded them multiple times to follow the hallway procedures and stand quietly. A student whistled very loudly. When I turned around, it appeared that a student nearby had been whistling. I went up one side of him and down the other. I was going to have him sit in the office for the whole assembly. I said let's go and started walking to the office. Never once did I stop and ask him a question or try to listen to what he had to say. As we rounded the corner toward the office, he told me that he did not do it.

Motive Probe

41.1. Describe the problem and your specific role in it.

I jumped to a wrong conclusion.

41.2. Why did you do what you did?

I had just finished saying to be quiet.

41.3. What emotions or feelings were you experiencing at the time?

I felt overwhelmed and frustrated. It was the Friday of the first week of school. I was tired and needed a break.

41.4. Was your behavior justified? If so, why?

No, I just should have remained calm.

41.5. Do you regret your action(s)?

Yes.

41.6. Do you ever think about this incident? If yes, approximately how often since the occurrence(s)?

(No response.)

41.7. If faced with the same or a similar situation, what would you do?

Find out the offender before I speak.

Commentary

Teachers can avoid a rush to misjudgment by asking the student if he or she committed the offense in question. However, if the teacher did not see who committed the offense and no one confesses, it's best to drop the matter to avoid punishing an innocent person.

Mistake 24: Inappropriate Reactions

Teacher # 42

A Scenario of a Teacher's Worst Treatment of a Student

I punished my class for something that I didn't have 100% proof that they committed. One student voiced her disagreement subversively to the other students within my range of hearing. My emotions went from stressed to angry to yelling out the phrase, "No ma'am! You will not do that in my classroom," which instantly took the air out of the cooperative learning atmosphere that I had been creating all year. The looks on the other students' faces were fearful, shocked, and submissive. I immediately told the student to meet me outside, where the verbal tirade, not discussion, continued. When I discussed this with the child's guardian, I received a well-deserved verbal lashing and apologized profusely. Every time I have to deal with student discipline now, the experience usually comes to mind, and I think before I act.

Motive Probe

42.1. Describe the problem and your specific role in it.

I gave a consequence for the entire class, one student led a revolt, and I openly persecuted her.

42.2. Why did you do what you did?

At the time, to maintain class control, to prevent a mutiny.

42.3. What emotions or feelings were you experiencing at the time?

Anger, betrayal, resentment, and regret.

42.4. Was your behavior justified? If so, why?

No.

42.5. Do you regret your action(s)?

Yes.

42.6. Do you ever think about this incident? If yes, approximately how often since the occurrence(s)?

About three to five times in the past year.

42.7. If faced with the same or a similar situation, what would you do?

I would remain calm and not display my emotions in that manner. I would have the discussion after class and in private.

Commentary

The power of a few words is demonstrated in the reaction of the students, in this scenario, to their teacher's caustic outburst. The class identified with the student that was wrongfully reprimanded, wrongfully reprimanded because the teacher was treating the class unfairly and the student gave voice to the teacher's error. Teachers can avoid dismantling the trust they have built with their students by being straightforward and owning mistakes, making apologies, and always righting their wrong actions immediately. To do this successfully, it is best to leave ego out of the discipline equation.

Teacher # 43

A Scenario of a Teacher's Worst Treatment of a Student

I cursed at a student.

Motive Probe

43.1. Describe the problem and your specific role in it.

He was deliberately disrupting the class, engaging in private conversations and had not done any work.

43.2. Why did you do what you did?

(No response.)

43.3. What emotions or feelings were you experiencing at the time?

Frustration and anger.

43.4. Was your behavior justified? If so, why?

Yes, sometimes you have to use shock to get a student's attention.

43.5. Do you regret your action(s)?

No, I was successful. His behavior changed. He passed the class.

43.6. Do you ever think about this incident? If yes, approximately how often since the occurrence(s)?

None.

43.7. If faced with the same or a similar situation, what would you do?

Depends on the student.

Commentary

Cursing a student is a vulgar way of expressing an interpersonal emotion of fury that says you make me very, very angry. It is meant to abuse and show irreverence for the person. It harbors the implied threat of further out-of-control action. It's also an invitation for students to further misbehave by cursing the teacher in return. It's troubling that the teacher thinks cursing is an acceptable practice because he was satisfied with the resulting behavioral change in the student. I was taught that the use of profanity or four-letter words suggested a limited vocabulary. I think that premise holds true for teachers; using profanity as a discipline method suggests a limited repertoire of discipline strategies. To avoid resorting to profanity, teachers must challenge themselves to expand their knowledge of ways to motivate students to work and cease disrupting the class without such an angry display of emotion.

Mistake 25: Sexual Harassment

Teacher # 44

A Scenario of a Teacher's Worst Treatment of a Student

I was working with girls in a residential treatment unit who had previously been abused and neglected by their families or legal guardians. One girl was upset and I put my arms around her to comfort her and she got even more upset.

Motive Probe

44.1. Describe the problem and your specific role in it.

The problem was there was a child/student that was upset and I tried giving comfort with a hug.

44.2. Why did you do what you did?

I was comfortable with hugs, touches, etc., and I assumed that the other individual was too.

44.3. What emotions or feelings were you experiencing at the time?

I felt angry with myself for being too touchy feely with a population that had been abused physically and sexually.

44.4. Was your behavior justified? If so, why?

No.

44.5. Do you regret your action(s)?

Yes.

44.6. Do you ever think about this incident? If yes, approximately how often since the occurrence(s)?

No.

44.7. If faced with the same or a similar situation, what would you do?

I would wait for a child/student to ask me for a hug rather than giving one without asking.

Commentary

The teacher may have had good intentions, but she could have avoided this situation by making it a practice to first ask anyone that she is not close to for permission to give them a hug. Most teachers avoid making any unnecessary physical contact with student, to avoid giving others the wrong impression, possibly embarrassing the child and possibly endangering their teaching careers. "Hands off" is an appropriate mantra for teachers.

Underlying Causes and Reasons
That Some Teachers Mistreat Students

An analysis of the 44 teacher responses of why they did what they did revealed commonalities in the content of their responses that give ear to a collective voice of frustration that is very obvious. Most of the teachers reported that they did what they did because they were angry and/or frustrated. In their efforts to discipline and control their students, some teachers do and say things that traumatize students, creating acute anxiety or stress . . . in effect, they cause what I refer to as academic trauma. I define academic trauma as a construct or concept that represents the effect of a student's reaction to aversive academic experiences such as extreme or harsh discipline, negative teacher–pupil interactions, unfair treatment, poor instruction, physical or psychological injury, or any other occurrence that may manifest as a significant emotional event. These aversive experiences typically involve victimization by a teacher or an administrator. Academic trauma may have long-term consequences that can have detrimental effects from childhood on into adulthood. Victims of academic trauma may be psychologically scarred, meaning, they never seem to forget what happened to them when they were young students. Academic trauma appears to be a legacy of early educational practices rooted in Puritan and Colonial tradition, the antiquated, abusive discipline strategies and ineffective practices that were characteristic of the early twentieth century.

Further analysis of the motive probes provided an enlightening revelation; namely, that the teachers' offensive acts were most often an outcome of "emotional snapping." I believe this "snapping" is one of the main reasons that teachers did what they did in their worst treatment of a student. I think the genesis of emotional snapping lies in the teachers' perceptions of themselves and what Woolfolk (2007) refers to as their teacher efficacy or their perception of their ability, particularly in the context of dealing with student misbehavior.

After further examination of their responses, I conclude that the participating teachers were very troubled when their students exhibited strong opposition, particularly any of the behaviors that I'll call the 5 D's of discipline problems; disrespect, defiance, disruption, disdain, and disorder. Fueled by ingrained beliefs of ultimate teacher power and authority, many teachers become frustrated when they are unable to penetrate the wall of opposition that is often perceived by the teacher when a student or students engage in any of the 5 D's of misbehavior. The apparent wall of opposition often strains the teacher's emotional resources. The resistance or student misbehavior generates an unbearable level of frustration and the teacher "snaps" under the pressure. Unfortunately, as a result of their anger, many teachers step out of character and impulsively seek relief from their emotional snap through vengeful, offensive acts.

In Figure 7.1, I have created a detailed, social interaction model that depicts the dynamics of teachers' confessions of their worst treatment of

Figure 7.1 A Social Interaction Model of Teachers' Worst Treatment of Students That May Result in Academic Trauma

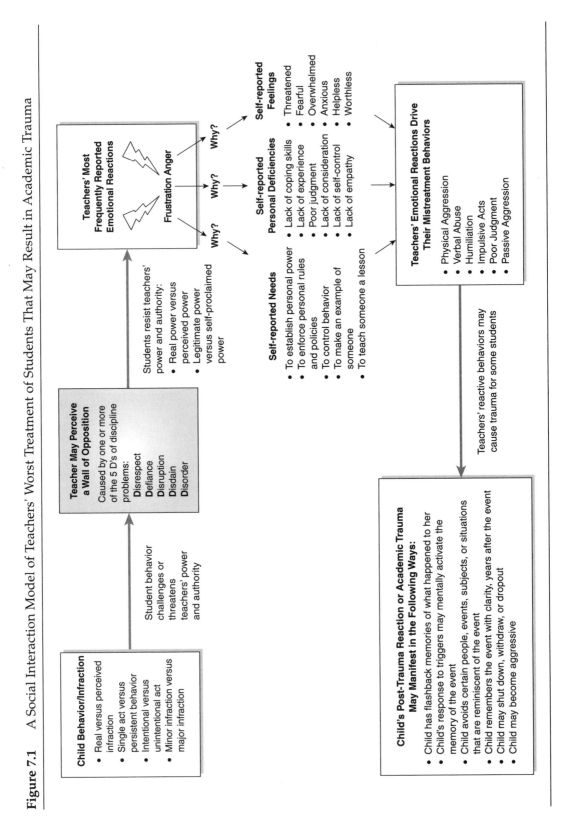

students and the possible long-term effects of such treatment that often causes academic trauma. A graphic depiction of the dynamics between frustrated teachers and misbehaving students offers a comprehensive, enlightening approach to understanding this interaction.

The Triggers or Emotional Catalysts for Aberrant Teacher Behavior

The purpose of this section is to try to understand the why of teacher mistreatment of a student. It is imperative to recognize the underlying causes of the 5 D's of discipline problems, as depicted in Figure 7.1.

- Disrespect
- Defiance
- Disruption
- Disdain
- Disorder

All of these categories represent some violation of accepted classroom mores such as students should respect teachers by doing what the teacher tells them to do without resistance or backtalk. If the student is satisfying her personal needs by talking, or not working, she is being disruptive. If a student shows blatant disregard for teacher wisdom and authority, the student is being disdainful. A student that is playing, yelling, or not following the rules is being disorderly. The intensity and nature of the teacher's response to the 5 D's of discipline may reflect the teacher's perceived needs, deficiencies, and feelings. When any of the 5 D's are apparent in student misbehavior, the teacher often feels opposed; when that misbehavior is persistent, it becomes a perceived wall of opposition that the teacher feels she cannot break through and as a result, she becomes very frustrated and frustration leads to an anger that can range from moderate to pathological. This range of emotional reaction is again dependent on the teacher's needs, deficiencies, and feelings, such as those that manifest in the survey responses. Additional analysis of the teacher's responses revealed needs to establish the legitimacy of their power, to enforce rules and policies that they have established, to control the outcomes of classroom events and situations, to make an example of students that misbehave to discourage the misbehavior of others, and to teach a student a lesson and show them who's boss.

The environment of the typical classroom crackles with opportunity for sparks to fly between teachers and students. Teacher mistreatment of students can be unprovoked, but quite often it is precipitated by some action or infraction committed by a child. This is not to say that the child is at fault, because the action or infraction may only be the teacher's perception, masquerading as something real. The infraction may be a single incident or it may be some persistent behavior that crosses the teachers' tolerance threshold. There are many dimensions of students' perceived or real misbehavior; it may be intentional or unintentional, a major incident or minor incident; legal or illegal activity. Regardless, it is how the students' behavior affects the teacher and that teacher's response that is important. Teachers' response to students' real or imagined misbehavior is equally varied. When a teacher responds by mistreating a child, the trigger for this behavior is usually that the teacher feels the child's misbehavior is a threat to her power and authority. Inevitably, the bubbling cauldron of emotion that teachers refer to as "snapping," erupts into various forms of offensive, undesirable behaviors such as physical aggression, verbal abuse, humiliation, impulsive acts, and passive aggression that may cause academic trauma in some students.

The punitive legacy of antiquated, abusive discipline strategies and ineffective practices that were characteristic of the early-twentieth-century "Hickory Stick Era" in education (McFee, 1918) has endowed many teachers with a flawed sense of omnipotence in classroom settings. This flawed perception may cause teachers to view students as subordinate to all teachers. Consequently, teachers view misbehavior as a form of insubordination that should not be tolerated. It is also an accepted societal convention that children should respect authority and their elders. The teacher's interpretation of the misbehavior sets the tone of the teacher's reaction to the behavior.

Most teachers really want to be good teachers, but their deficiencies in various professional capacities inhibit their development and may cause problems. In the worst treatment survey responses, teachers candidly admitted their shortcomings. When explaining the cause of their mistreatment of students, many readily attributed their behavior to a lack of experience, a lack of coping skills, poor judgment, impulsivity, lack of consideration and empathy for others. The teacher survey responses provided much evidence of a lack of anger-management skills, and a lack of knowledge of child development and typical behaviors that can be expected at each stage of development.

All of the participating teachers seemed to carry some form of emotional baggage, some more than others. Feelings of being anxious, fearful, overwhelmed, helpless, worthless, vengeful, and threatened, were fuel for their frustration and anger.

Some of this baggage includes the beliefs and perceptions that many teachers have formed on their own or assimilated from other people. For example, some teachers feel they have to follow through on threats to save face and protect their credibility. Some teachers classify themselves as being from the "old school" or from a different culture of so-called genteel ways and often feel offended by the perceived brashness of the younger generation. There are teachers that have firm beliefs about the inherent "badness" of children, some believing that children spend a lot of their time thinking of creative ways to challenge authority and incite controversy. This thinking is rooted in a legacy of past beliefs that children are inherently evil and must have the "devil" beat out of them. A mismatch of position and qualifications and subsequent feelings of inadequacy, challenges teachers' self-efficacy beliefs (Bandura, 1969) or their confidence about their capabilities. As a consequence, they may feel inadequate or incompetent, feelings that foster feelings of defensiveness or resentment. Teachers' biased beliefs and perceptions about students that are ethnically and economically different and teachers' limited exposure to such children may manifest as culture clash and incite discriminatory behavior. Unfortunately, some preservice teachers view teaching as a "soft" profession. They come into the profession unaware and unprepared for the "hard" side of teaching such as student misconduct, drug use, assault, insubordination, and so on. Such beliefs are often the basis of negative classroom interactions and possible academic trauma for students.

There are a number of psychosocial factors underlying the causes of aberrant teacher behavior. Some of them are listed below, accompanied by recommendations for avoiding the negative outcomes of these factors.

Sometimes teachers experience a discrepancy between their actual self and their ideal self. Such a perception fosters feelings of inadequacy, discontent, dissatisfaction, and displaced anger. To avoid this perception, they could develop a more realistic perspective of their strengths and weaknesses and make a concerted effort to close the gap. Substance abuse is a reality for millions of people; teachers are no exception. Teachers under the influence of alcohol or drugs are very likely to be irritable, reactive, and short on patience. Fortunately, there are rehabilitation facilities, professional counseling and support groups to help them manage their addiction. A family history of substance abuse has its own set of problems. People from such families are referred to as adult children of alcoholics. They have what their support groups refer to as a laundry list of problems that can be directly attributed to the dysfunction of the addicts in their family, parents in particular. To minimize the negative outcome of this family situation, teachers can avail themselves of the positive support groups that help them to recognize and minimize the effects of their childhood, by stressing that childhood is over and they must find positive ways of coping with life and move on.

Sadly, teachers who have had an oppressive or abusive teacher in the past may identify with the oppressor because they know what hurts or what has a negative effect because it was done to them. They may see the oppressor as having the power and that is what they want, the power and control that they did not have as a child. Those teachers who have experienced being a powerless child dealing with aversive academic experiences can put their past situation into perspective through guided imagery. Using this technique, they mentally place themselves in a protective bubble to mentally revisit the past scenario of their mistreatment, to be reminded that it was not a desirable situation, but they lived through it, and to assure that they would never want to emulate the offending teachers' behavior.

Unfortunately, allergies, physiological imbalances such as menopause, PMS, bipolar disorder and other mental illnesses can fuel out-of-control teacher behavior. Fortunately, negative outcomes can be avoided with appropriate medical help, counseling, and behavioral management of various disorders. Some teachers have an excessive need for control; they feel they can't trust others to do things right. They are not comfortable if they are not sure that they can control the outcome. These need issues may be the result of childhood trust issues; professional intervention may be needed to help the teacher learn to trust their world and minimize irrational acts of need for control.

Teachers who experienced a rigid upbringing may develop a very dominant, authoritarian teaching style that demands absolute obedience to authority. An analysis of their teaching style may create awarenesses that will encourage them to alter their style and to embrace a more positive authoritative style of teaching and relating to students.

Many people, not just teachers, fear being taken advantage of, insubordination, or any other perceived threat to their authority. To avoid the negative outcomes of this fear, teachers should not expect unquestioned obedience; they will learn acceptance and be more willing to let someone get away with something, particularly if it is insignificant.

Long ago, teaching was viewed as a noble, elite profession and consequently, some teachers developed a sense of privilege—a feeling that they were like royalty and students were peons, there to do the teachers' bidding. Such an omnipotent perception of themselves fosters feelings of entitlement that allows teachers to say or do anything to students because they are believed to be in a lower position. To avoid the outcomes of this perception, such teachers need a wake-up call, the illusion is over, teacher-centered education is out and student-centered education is in. It's a new day; the ivory tower is crumbling to make way for duplexes where teachers and students work together.

In a small number of cases, there may be some pathology where a teacher enjoys inflicting hurt or pain. To avoid the outcome of possible pathology, teachers should always question their motives when they feel inclined to hurt or punish students, particularly if it is cruel, unusual, or excessive punishment.

Some teachers lack knowledge of acceptable ways of interacting with students and the ability to recognize their deficit as unacceptable. To avoid the negative outcomes of their lack of knowledge, they should observe master teachers to become more aware of how to relate to students and how to cease and desist their own unacceptable behavior. They also should participate in professional development workshops on improving teacher–student interactions. Some teachers lack the empathy or compassion necessary to relate to and understand their students. They can avoid the outcomes of their deficit by making an effort to put themselves in their student's place; understanding how their students feel may help them to be more effective teachers.

Hidden Hazards: Negative Outcomes of Student Mistreatment

Unfortunately, some children are less resilient than others. Children who are less resilient and experience gross mistreatment are more likely to experience academic trauma, a strong reaction to aversive academic experiences. Children who are very resilient and experience minimal mistreatment are less likely to experience academic trauma. Children with various levels of resiliency fall somewhere along the above continuum. Factors such as personality, age, economic status, psychological makeup, and family background, influence a child's predisposition for experiencing academic trauma. Some students experience psychological scarring, or psychological wounds so deep they leave emotional scars to evidence their presence. Outcomes or effects on the student who experiences academic trauma may be classified into six categories; academic, behavioral, cognitive, psychosocial, personality, and self-concept. The following are nonexclusive listings of various negative outcomes and emotional scars, by category, that children affected by academic trauma may experience:

Academic Outcomes

- They may become hypervigilant in academic settings that pose a perceived threat.
- Some become nervous and uncomfortable or insecure in academic settings.
- They may have difficulty concentrating on academic tasks.
- Some may be unwilling to ask questions or to seek help from instructors.
- They may experience academic and developmental lags in school where poor teachers were in charge and students missed important required knowledge.

Behavioral Outcomes

- They may avoid people, places, or events that are reminiscent of the event, or withdraw or have an irrational reaction to a similar event.
- Some may elect not to participate in academic tasks that could result in similar maltreatment experienced in the initial episode . . . which may cause the person to appear uncooperative or nonparticipatory.
- They may become conditioned to hate school or subjects associated with bad experiences in school. Teachers should be the social glue in the classroom, bonding students with the teacher and with each other. In situations, where teachers misuse their position of authority, it's impossible for bonding to occur.
- Some may become dysfunctional, punitive teachers when they grow up and join the teaching profession. Teachers often teach as they were taught.
- They may turn to substance abuse to deal with their problems.
- They may lower their level of academic performance because they are unwilling to work hard for the offending student.

Cognitive, Thinking, or Perceptual Outcomes

- Many nurture unhealthy memories for many years without intervention.
- Their perceptions of their abilities may be affected.
- Some may fail to see school as a safe haven of learning and fun.
- They may generalize the traumatic experience to other situations.
- They may promise themselves that they will not let their children experience what they had to go through.

Affective Outcomes or Feelings

- They may experience feelings of fear, shame, depression, sadness, anxiety, frustration, grief, or other socially handicapping emotional disorders.
- Some may continue to experience intrusive flashbacks or recollections that may cause them to relive the event or experience over and over again.
- Some develop an intense dislike for teachers, school, or others in educational settings.
- They may experience feelings of vulnerability and a lack of trust in academic settings.
- Some may have feelings of inadequacy or apathy.
- They may internalize feelings of shame and have no viable outlet.
- A few may get sucked up into the pathology of the event and think it's ok, that they deserved whatever happened to them.
- Some become reactive and revenge seeking toward teachers.

Psychosocial Outcomes

- Their performance may be affected in the workplace as an adult, such as not being able to give presentations because of fear of making a mistake.
- A few may identify with their oppressor and do what was done to them.
- They may be afraid to ask questions or seek help.
- Some may be reluctant to participate in school activities.
- Many become risk-averse in academic settings.
- They may develop a negative self-concept. We define ourselves partly by what is communicated to us by others; some people fixate on the negative comments.
- In some cases, they may cause the traumatic experience to become a self-fulfilling prophecy or they could strive to prove the teacher was wrong about them.
- They may avoid academic settings years after the event, which may contribute to a lack of parent involvement in their children's education.
- Some of them may experience diminished self-esteem or self-confidence.
- They may feel disempowered and through criticism, experience learned helplessness, where they have difficulty learning to be autonomous.
- Regrettably, some are moved to aggression or thoughts of aggression, mimicking what was done to them.

How to Avoid Making the 25 Biggest Mistakes

The following strategies and policies are suggested ways to avoid making the twenty-five biggest mistakes teachers make that are featured in this book:

Mistake 1: Inappropriate Discipline Strategies. Stress positive discipline and self-control. Use proven strategies like assertive discipline and behavior modification. Avoid discipline tactics that require inflicting pain or emotional abuse.

Mistake 2: Physical Aggression. Have a personal hands-off policy when interacting with students. Always use restraint and avoid physical contact with students, particularly aggressive contact. Choose and use your words wisely to resolve conflict.

Mistake 3: Purposeful Alienation. Refrain from comments or actions that isolate students or turn their peers against them. Befriend the alienated child and protect him or her from the alienation attempts of others.

Mistake 4: Public Ridicule. Know that soft, private reprimands and public praise are much more effective than ridicule. Disparaging remarks made in a public forum are not motivators. Give freely of meaningful, well-deserved praise.

Mistake 5: Favoritism. Treat all students the same, no matter how much you like one over the others. Be fair, be consistent . . . no exceptions. Love the unlovable or difficult child.

Mistake 6: Physiological Discrimination. Never comment on a student's physical features. Preserve students' dignity at all times. Cheerfully make accommodations for students with physical challenges when necessary.

Mistake 7: Personal Attacks. Avoid making negative comments about a student's person, keep comments factual and focused on academics and classroom behavior. Make no disparaging references to a student's family or personal life. Make positive comments frequently.

Mistake 8: Inappropriate Teacher–Student Relations. Have professional boundaries that you never cross and respect student's personal boundaries. Don't make students your confidants and share personal problems and stories with them. Your relationships with your students should be professional and above reproach. Be friendly, not a friend.

Mistake 9: Deliberate Mistreatment. Never allow yourself to plot a cruel or intentionally harmful act against a student. Child abuse is illegal. Take advantage of every opportunity to treat students well.

Mistake 10: Racial and Cultural Discrimination. Embrace cultural differences and encourage your class to do the same. Help students to focus on each other's commonalities rather than differences. Love and respect mean the same, regardless of the language.

Mistake 11: Humiliation. Never make disparaging remarks that diminish the self. Treat students' fragile egos and precious psyches as you would fine china. Elevate, don't humiliate your students.

Mistake 12: Inappropriate Classroom Policies. Establish policies that promote the well-being and academic achievement of all students.

Mistake 13: Inappropriate Toileting Practices. Never deny students permission to use the restroom or employ ridiculous contingencies such as carrying a toilet seat pass or holding up one or two fingers to indicate what they have to do in the restroom. Don't assume that you can tell if someone really has to go or if they just want to play. Take the risk that they might play if they pretend that they have to go; it's much better than causing someone to have an unforgettable accident.

Mistake 14: Inappropriate Educational Strategies. Strive to create meaningful instruction that is engaging, that fosters retention and facilitates transfer of knowledge. Collect effective strategies to increase your repertoire of teaching skills.

Mistake 15: Inappropriate Assessment. Use grades for feedback only. Don't use grades as punishment. Be a fair grader; grades should mirror the success of your teaching.

Mistake 16: Teacher Insensitivity. Be aware of words and deeds that assault a student's ego and self-esteem. Harsh words, once spoken, are difficult to recall. Be sensitive to the needs and tender feelings of children. Treat them the way you would want someone to treat your child.

Mistake 17: Academic Shortcomings. Assess your strengths and weaknesses as a teacher. Take additional courses or participate in professional development opportunities to minimize your weaknesses. Always give your students the benefits of your strengths.

Mistake 18: Poor Administration. Strengthen your organization skills. Keep track of student records and papers. Return papers in a timely manner and keep your classroom functioning like a well-oiled machine.

Mistake 19: Reputation. A reputation should read like an epitaph, do and say what you would want others to say about you after you are gone. Do the right things; people are watching. Earn the reputation of being a caring effective teacher.

Mistake 20: Teacher Misjudgment. Entertain the idea that no matter how right you think you are, you can be wrong. Get all of the facts before you make a judgment. If you don't have the facts, don't make a judgment. Assume innocence until proven guilty.

Mistake 21: Teacher Bias or Expectations. Have high expectations for all students; it will become a prophecy. Seek help with getting rid of personal bias or prejudice; it has no place in the repertoire of a caring teacher.

Mistake 22: Unethical Behavior. Educate yourself on what is considered unethical. Follow all laws of society and observe school policy. Be professional at all times; put the needs of your students first.

Mistake 23: False Accusations. Don't lie to, on, or about students. When you point a finger at someone falsely, three fingers point back at you. Model the behavior that you expect from your students; tell the truth.

Mistake 24: Inappropriate Reactions. Good teaching requires focus and attention. To act impulsively is usually an inappropriate reaction. Teachers should try to gather as much information as possible and try to understand the situation before acting on it.

Mistake 25: Sexual Harassment. Make yourself aware of current sexual harassment regulations. You and the school can be liable for inappropriate behavior. To be on the safe side, keep your hands off students, don't entertain any inappropriate thoughts, stay out of student's personal space, watch your mouth, don't ask inappropriate questions, minimize or avoid alone time with students. Make every effort to see them in appropriate places, preferably in the presence of other adults. Leave no doubt about your professionalism by always acting appropriately.

Further Thoughts on Avoiding Mistakes

When teachers make mistakes in spite of their efforts to avoid them, their actions may cause academic trauma in their students that can have long-term effects. Some form of intervention may be necessary to counter the effects on the students.

Traditional education systems are not designed to offer students a voice and a means to address concerns regarding their education and their participation in the educational process. In fact, traditional classrooms are very behaviorist and teacher-centered, a concept that has hindered effective education of students for decades. Constructivism, an approach to educating students that advocates helping students to create meaning and to make sense of their world (Schunk, 2004), is gaining in popularity. A constructivist approach, such as helping students make sense of what has happened to them, may minimize the effects of the academic trauma that some students may have experienced due to teacher mistakes. Not all children experience academic trauma, but for those that do, the following strategies based on Sprague (1995) offer help to children that have been exposed to extreme stress or trauma to minimize the effects of that trauma.

1. Help students to put the event into perspective, knowing that bad things may happen to good students, but that the majority of teachers are hardworking and caring. They should understand that sometimes teachers make mistakes and most of them are sorry for the bad things that they do.

2. Listening to children and validating their experiences are critical factors in intervention.

3. Offer a variety of ongoing opportunities for children to express their feelings such as small support groups, art therapy, bibliotherapy, role play, one-on-one conversation with a caring empathic adult.

Writing and talking about aversive academic experiences is an important step toward helping to heal the wounds of academic trauma. Retelling the event may have a cathartic or purge effect that will help students to move on with their lives. For those students who may have internalized the behavior, it may help them to make connections between the aversive academic experiences in their past and any present-day symptoms and behaviors. Having an adult help to interpret and evaluate the problem and its effects may validate a student who had internalized the problem and felt like it was his or her fault.

Expect to help students who are having trouble, but encourage them to try to help themselves first, to avoid dependency and learned helplessness. Wood, Bruner, and Ross (1976) advocate scaffolding or assisting students with tasks that they may have difficulty completing independently. Have high expectations for all of your students. Believe they are capable and convince them that they are capable. Have students keep a journal; it helps to know what they're thinking, feeling, wanting, and experiencing. Respond to their entries frequently; it is an opportunity to console, encourage, motivate, and build rapport.

Use written, physical, and verbal cues, to make students aware of the behavior that you expect. For example

1. Post reminders to help students stay focused and on task.

2. Write your penalty system on the chalkboard. For example
   • Offense #1 Warning to quiet down
   • Offense #2 Loss of privilege
   • Offense #3 Loss of recess or something

3. Use a peace sign made with your fingers to signal quiet time.

4. Never leave students unsupervised; have a system in place for emergencies, such as a student messenger or preferably an adult to substitute for you.

5. Avoid personal liability; know the laws and insurance rules that affect what you can and cannot do.

6. Develop a good professional relationship with administrators. Prepare well for evaluation instead of worrying.

7. Find ways that you can help improve yourself and your school.

8. Use a variety of strategies to encourage family involvement.

9. Have parents take turns bringing packaged snacks every day if allowable, or come in to talk about their occupations and so on.

10. Keep in contact with parents through e-mail, send parents helpful links on parenting or homework tips.

11. Learn to gauge the time necessary to complete a lesson or task.

12. Start on schedule, allow for interruptions, stay on task, allow adequate time, maximize student engagement, and always try to end the lesson on time.

13. Clearly communicate expectations often.
   - Expect them to learn "all" of the material; this may be difficult but aspire to it.
   - Expect them to seek help.
   - Expect them to complete assignments.
   - Expect them to proof assignments.
   - Expect their best work.
   - Expect them to turn in all assignments.
   - Expect them to be there every day.
   - Expect them to participate.
   - Expect them to be courteous.
   - Expect them to be self-regulatory.
   - Expect good behavior.

14. Model the positive, productive behavior that you expect from your students. For example, make sure you're self-regulated so that you can model the behavior for your students (Orange, 2002).

15. Be accommodating; try to say yes to students' requests, whenever possible.

16. Keep an open mind about including students with disabilities; it's the law.

17. Be open to teaching students of various cultures; teach your students to respect and celebrate each others' differences

For additional ideas, see *44 Smart Strategies for Avoiding Classroom Mistakes* (Orange, 2004).

Epilogue

After examining and analyzing hundreds of students' scenarios that depict their worst experience with a teacher, I have concluded that students may experience varying levels of academic trauma, depending on what was done to them and on their predisposition to react to such mistreatment. Many of the student scenarios appear to meet the criteria for posttraumatic stress reaction. Students as old as 56 remember traumatic events that happened to them in first grade. Wetting their pants in the presence of the class is a common event that is often recalled. Many of the students reported flashbacks where they feel like they are reliving the event. Some report triggers such as the smell of juicy fruit gum or chalk, plaid pants, and long red fingernails that evoke a memory of the event. Many will avoid certain subjects or activities because they connect them with the event. The long-term negative effects of academic trauma underscore the importance of the need for good, healthy student–teacher interaction. Teachers must shed the legacy of punitive, teacher-centered educational practices of the past and unshackle their hearts and minds to embrace a more caring, student-centered plan for the future . . . a plan that will restore the psychological balance in the classroom and end academic trauma.

References

American Association of University Women. (1992). *How schools short change girls.* Washington, DC: Author.

American Heritage Dictionary of the English Language (3rd ed.). (1992). Houghton Mifflin. Electronic version licensed from InfoSoft International, Inc. All rights reserved.

Anderson, L. M. (1989). Learners and learning. In M. Reynolds (Ed.), *Knowledge base for beginning teachers* (pp. 85–100). New York: Pergamon.

Bandura, A. (1986). *Social foundations of thought and action: A social cognitive theory.* Englewood Cliffs, NJ: Prentice Hall.

Banks, J., & Banks, C. A. M. (1993). *Multicultural education: Issues and perspectives* (2nd ed.). Boston: Allyn & Bacon.

Belenky, M. F., Clinchy, B. M., Goldberger, N. R., & Tarule, J. M. (1986). *Women's ways of knowing: The development of self, voice, & mind.* New York: Basic Books.

Black, C. (1991). *It will never happen to me.* New York: Ballantine.

Block, J. H. (1980). Promoting excellence through mastery learning. *Theory Into Practice, 19*(1), 66–74.

Bradshaw, J. (1988). *Healing the shame that binds you.* Dearfield Beach, FL: Health Communications.

Brophy, J. (1982). Research on teacher effects: Uses and abuses. *Elementary School Journal, 89*(1), 3–21.

Brophy, J., & Evertson, C. M. (1981). *Student characteristics and teaching.* New York: Longman.

Campbell, L., Campbell, B., & Dickinson, D. (1996). *Teaching and learning through multiple intelligences* (p. 282). Needham Heights, MA: Allyn & Bacon.

Canfield, J. (1990). Improving student's self-esteem. *Educational Leadership, 48*(1), 48–50.

Canfield, J., & Wells., H. C. (1976). *100 ways to enhance self-concept in the classroom: A handbook for teachers and parents.* Englewood Cliffs, NJ: Prentice Hall.

Canter, L., & Canter, M. (1992). *Assertive discipline: Positive behavior management for today's classroom.* Santa Monica, CA: Lee Canter & Associates.

Charles, C. M. (1983). *A handbook of excellence in teaching: Elementary classroom management.* New York: Longman.

Clifford, M. M. (1990). Students need challenge, not easy success. *Educational Leadership, 48*(1), 22–26.

Collier, V. P. (1992). The Canadian bilingual immersion debate: A synthesis of research findings. *Studies in Second Language Acquisition, 14,* 87–97.

Concise Columbia Encyclopedia. (1995). New York: Columbia University Press.

Crumpler, L. E. (1993). Sexual harassment in schools. *NASB Employee Relations Quarterly, 1*(4), 5.

Cuban, L. (1984). *How teachers taught: Constancy and change in American classrooms 1890–1980.* New York: Longman.

Cushner, K., McCelland, A., & Safford, P. (1992). *Human diversity in education: An integrative approach.* St. Louis, MO: McGraw-Hill.

DeCecco, J., & Richards, A. (1974). *Growing pains: Uses of school conflicts.* New York: Aberdeen.

deCharms, R. (1976). *Enhancing motivation.* New York: Irvington.

Delgado-Gaitan, C. (1990). *Literacy for empowerment: The role of parents in children's education.* New York: Falmer.

Delpit, L. (1988). The silenced dialogue: Power and pedagogy in educating other people's children. *Harvard Educational Review, 58*(3), 280–298.

DeMott, R. M. (1982). Visual Impairments. In N. Haring (Ed.), *Exceptional children and youth* (pp. 271–295). Columbus, OH: Merrill.

Dinkmeyer, D., & Losoncy, L. E. (1980). *The encouragement book: Becoming a positive person.* Englewood Cliffs, NJ: Prentice Hall.

Dreikurs, R. B., Grunwald, B. B., & Pepper, F. C. (1982). *Maintaining sanity in the classroom: Classroom management techniques* (2nd ed.). New York: Harper & Row.

Education of All Handicapped Children Act, Public Law 94–142. (1975). *Individuals with Disabilities Education Act (IDEA).* Last amended 1990 (P.L. 101–476).

Eisenberg, N., & Harris, J. D. (1984). Social competence: A developmental perspective. *The School Psychology Review, 13*(3), 267–277.

Elkind, D. (1989). Developmentally appropriate education for 4-year-olds. *Theory Into Practice, 28*(1), 47–52.

Epanchin, B. C., Townsend, B., & Stoddard, K. (1994). *Constructive classroom management: Strategies for creating positive learning environments.* Pacific Grove, CA: Brooks/Cole.

Erikson, E. (1963). *Childhood and society* (2nd ed.). New York: Norton.

Flanders, N. A., & Morine, G. (1973). The assessment of proper control and suitable learning environment. In N. L. Gage (Ed.), *Mandated evaluation of educators: A conference on California's Stull Act.* Stanford: California Center for Research and Development in Teaching.

Froyen, L. A. (1993). *Classroom management: The reflective teacher-leader* (2nd ed.). New York: Macmillan.

Gagne, R. (1977). *Conditions of learning* (3rd ed.). New York: Holt, Rinehart & Winston.

Galloway, C. (1977). Nonverbal. *Theory Into Practice, 16*(3), 129–133.

Garcia, E. E. (1995). Educating Mexican American students: Past treatment and recent developments in theory, research, policy, and practice. In J. A. Banks & C. A. M. Banks (Eds.), *Handbook of research on multicultural education* (pp. 372–381). New York: Macmillan.

Gardner, H. (1993). *Multiple intelligences: The theory in practice.* New York: Basic Books.

Gearheart, B. R., Weishahn, M. W., & Gearheart, C. W. (1992). *The exceptional child in the regular classroom* (5th ed.). Upper Saddle River, NJ: Merrill/Prentice Hall.

Gelman, D. (1983, November 7). A great emptiness. *Newsweek, 102*(1), 120–126.

Gersten, R. (1996). Literacy instruction for minority students: The transition years. *The Elementary School Journal, 96*, 227–244.

Gibbs, J. (1988). *Young, black, and male in America: An endangered species.* Dover, MA: Auburn House.

Glaser, R., & Silver, E. (1994). *Assessment, testing and instruction.* Pittsburgh, PA: Learning Research and Development Center.

Good, T. L., & Brophy, J. E. (1991). *Looking in classrooms* (5th ed.). New York: HarperCollins.

Good, T. L., & Brophy, J. E. (1997). *Looking in classrooms* (7th ed.). New York: Longman.

Gottfredson, G. D. (1984). *How schools and families can reduce youth crime.* Baltimore, MD: Center for Social Organization of Schools, Johns Hopkins University.

Gronlund, N. E. (1995). *How to write and use instructional objectives.* Upper Saddle River, NJ: Merrill/Prentice Hall.

Gronlund, N. E. (2000). *How to write and use instructional objectives* (6th ed.). Upper Saddle River, NJ: Merrill/Prentice Hall.

Harvard University. (1988). Student questions in K–12 classrooms. *Harvard Education Letter, (1)*, 7.

Heath, S. (1983). *Ways with words: Language, life, and work in communities and classrooms.* Cambridge, MA: Cambridge University Press.

Henson, D. T., & Eller, B. F. (1999). *Educational psychology for effective teaching*. Belmont, CA: Wadsworth.

Huston, T. C. (1993). Handling sexual harassment complaints. *NASB Employee Relations Quarterly, 1(2)*, 6.

Irving, O., & Martin, J. (1982). Withitness: The confusing variable. *American Educational Research Journal, 19*, 313–319.

Johnson, D. W., Johnson, R., Dudley, B., Ward, M., & Magnuson, D. (1995). The impact of peer mediation training on the management of school and home conflicts. *American Educational Research Journal, 32(4)*, 829–844.

Kauffman, J. M. (1989). *Characteristics of behavioral disorders of children and youth* (4th ed.). Columbia, OH: Merrill.

Kerman, S., & Martin, M. (1980). *Teacher expectations and student achievement: Teacher handbook*. Bloomington, IN: Phi Delta Kappa.

Kindsvatter, R., Wilen, W., & Ishler, M. (1988). *Dynamics of effective teaching*. New York: Longman.

Lancon, J. A., Haines, D. E., & Parent, A. D. (1998). Anatomy of the shaken baby syndrome. *Anatomical Record (New Anatomy), 253*, 13–18.

Levin, J., & Nolan, J. R. (1996). *Principles of classroom management: A professional decision-making model*. Boston: Allyn & Bacon.

Lindholm, K. J., & Fairchild, H. H. (1990). Evaluation of an elementary school bilingual immersion program. In A. M. Padilla, H. H. Fairchild, & C. M. Valdez (Eds.), *Bilingual education: Issues and strategies* (pp. 91–105). Newbury Park, CA: Sage.

MacDonald, R. E. (1991). *A handbook of basic skills and strategies for beginning teachers*. New York: Longman.

Macias, R. (1986). *Teacher preparation for bilingual education*. Report of the Compendium of Papers on the Topic of Bilingual Education of the Committee on Education and Labor House of Representatives, 99th Congress, 2D Session. Washington, DC: U.S. Government Printing Office, 1986, pp. 43–44.

Maple, S. A., & Stage, F. K. (1991). Influences on the choice of math/science major by gender and ethnicity. *American Educational Research Journal, 28(1)*, 37–60.

Maslow, A. H. (1970). *Motivation and personality*. New York: Harper & Row.

Mason, D. A., & Good, T. L. (1993). Effects of two-group and whole-class teaching on regrouped elementary students' mathematics achievement. *American Educational Research Journal, 30*, 328–360.

McConnell, S. R., & Odom, S. L. (1986). Sociometrics: Peer referenced measures and the assessment of social competence. In P. S. Strain, M. J. Gralnick, & H. M. Walker (Eds.), *Children's social behavior: Development, assessment, and modification* (pp. 215–284). Orlando, FL: Academic Press.

McFee, I. N. (1918). *The teacher, the school, and the community*. New York: American.

Messick, S. (1984). The nature of cognitive styles: Problems and promise in educational practice. *Educational Psychologist, 19*, 59–74.

Moll, L. C., & Diaz, S. (1985). Ethnographic pedagogy: Promoting effective bilingual instruction. In E. E. Garcia & R. V. Padilla (Eds.), *Advances in bilingual education research* (pp. 127–149). Tucson: University of Arizona Press.

O'Connor, M. (1998). The power of feedback: Improving standards by identifying children's need via assessment. *Times Educational Supplement, 4258*, 22.

O'Leary, K. D., Kaufman, K. F., Kass, R. E., & Drabman, R. E. (1970). The effects of loud and soft reprimands on the behavior of disruptive students. *Exceptional Children, 37*, 145–155.

O'Leary, K. D., & O'Leary, S. G. (1972). *Classroom management: The successful use of behavior modification* (p. 152). New York: Pergammon.

Orange, C. (1997). Gifted students and perfectionism. *Roeper Review, 20(1)*, 39–41.

Orange, C. (1999, Fall). Using peer models to teach self-regulation. *The Journal of Experimental Education, 68(1)*, 21–39.

Orange, C. (2002). *Quick reference guide to educational innovations*. Thousand Oaks, CA: Sage.

Orange, C. (2005). *44 smart strategies for avoiding classroom mistakes*. Thousand Oaks, CA: Sage.

Ormrod, J. E. (1998). *Educational psychology: Developing learners* (2nd ed.). Englewood Cliffs, NJ: Prentice Hall.

Piaget, J. (1952). *The language and thought of the child*. London: Routledge & Kegan Paul.

Piaget, J. (1965). *The moral judgment of the child*. New York: Free Press.

Renzulli, J. S., & Reis, S. M. (1991). The schoolwide enrichment model: A comprehensive plan for the development of creative productivity. In N. Colangelo & G. Davis (Eds.), *Handbook of gifted education* (pp. 111–141). Boston: Allyn & Bacon.

Reutter, E. (1975). *The courts and student conduct*. Topeka, KS: National Organization on Legal Problems of Education.

Rogers, C. R. (1969). *Freedom to learn*. Columbus, OH: Merrill.

Rosenthal, R., & Jacobson, L. (1968). *Pygmalion in the classroom*. New York: Holt, Rinehart & Winston.

Rotter, J. (1954). *Social learning and clinical psychology*. Englewood Cliffs, NJ: Prentice Hall.

Rowe, M. B. (1987). Wait-time: Slowing down may be a way of speeding up. *American Educator, 11*, 38–43.

RWJ Medical School. Appropriate treatment in medicine. Available: http://www.umdnj.edu/rwjcweb/docs/apptrtmed.html (Accessed 1/03/07).

Sabers, D. S., Cushing, K. S., & Berliner, D. C. (1991). Differences among teachers in a task characterized by simultaneity, multidimensionality, and immediacy. *American Educational Research Journal, 28*(1), 63–88.

Schunk, D. H. (2004). *Learning theories: An educational perspective* (4th ed.). Upper Saddle River, NJ: Pearson Merrill/Prentice Hall.

Shore, S. (1999, April 27). Littleton buries teacher, 3 teens. *San Antonio Express-News*, p. 6A.

Skinner, B. F. (1950). Are theories of learning necessary? *Psychological Review, 57*(4), 193–216.

Skinner, B. F. (1953). Science and human behavior. New York: Macmillan.

Skinner, B. F. (1987). *Upon further reflection*. Englewood Cliffs, NJ: Prentice Hall.

Slavin, R. E. (1990). Achievement effects of ability grouping in secondary schools: A best-evidence synthesis. *Review of Educational Research, 6*(3), 471–500.

Slavin, R. E. (1994). *Educational psychology: Theory and practice* (4th ed.). Needham Heights, MA: Allyn & Bacon.

Smith, T. (1995). *Findings from the condition of education 1994: America's teachers ten years after the "A Nation at Risk."* (NCES Publication No. 95–766). Washington, DC: U.S. Department of Education.

Smith, T. M., Young, B. A., Bae, Y., Choy, S. P., & Alsalam, N. (1997). *The condition of education 1997*. (NCES Publication 97–388). Washington, DC: U.S. Department of Education.

Snow, R. E., Como, L., & Jackson, D., III (1996). Individual differences in affective and conative functions. In D. Berliner & R. Calfee (Eds.), *Handbook of educational psychology* (pp. 243–310). New York: Macmillan.

Sprague, M. (1995). *Helping children cope with stress and trauma*. California: Child Development Programs Advisory Committee Issue Brief 1995.

Sprinthall, N., Sprinthall, R., & Oja, S. (1994). *Educational psychology: A developmental approach* (6th ed.). St. Louis, MO: McGraw-Hill.

Stiggins, R. J. (1994). *Student-centered classroom assessment*. Upper Saddle River, NJ: Merrill/Prentice Hall.

Thompson, M., & Cohen L. (2005). When the bullied must adjust. *Education Digest: Essential Readings Condensed for Quick Review, 70*(6), 16–19.

Tirri, K. (2001, April). *What can we learn from teacher's moral mistakes?* Paper presented at the Annual Meeting of the American Educational Research Association. Seattle, WA.

Torrance, E. P. (1972). Predictive validity of the Torrance tests of creative thinking. *Journal of Creative Behavior, 6*, 236–232.

Torrey, J. W. (1983). Black children's knowledge of standard English. *American Educational Research Journal, 20*(4), 627–643.

U.S. Department of Education. (1991). *Youth indicators*. Washington, DC: Author.

Vygotsky, L. S. (1993). *The collected works of L. S. Vygotsky: Vol.* 2 (J. Knox & C. Stevens, Trans.). New York: Plenum.

Warriner, J., & Griffith, F. (1977). *Warriner's English grammar and composition: Fourth course.* New York: Harcourt Brace Jovanovich.

Weiner, B. (1979). A theory of motivation for some classroom experiences. *Journal of Educational Psychology, 71,* 3–25.

Weinstein, C. S. (1996). *Secondary classroom management: Lessons from research and practice.* New York: McGraw-Hill.

Wenze, G. T. &. Wenze, N. (2004). Helping left-handed children adapt to school expectations. *Childhood Education* [Online] 81. Available: www.questia.com/PM.qst?a=o&se= gglsc&d= 5007580142&er=deny (Accessed 1/03/2007).

Wertsch, J. V. (1991). *Voices of the mind: A sociocultural approach to mediated action.* Cambridge, MA: Harvard University Press.

Wigfield, A., & Eccles, J. S. (1989). Test anxiety in elementary and secondary school students. *Educational Psychologist, 24*(2), 159–183.

Wood, D., Bruner, J., & Ross, G. (1976). The role of tutoring in problem-solving. *Journal of Child Psychology and Allied Disciplines, 17*(2), 89–100.

Woolfolk, A. E. (1998). *Educational psychology* (7th ed.). Boston: Allyn & Bacon.

Woolfolk, A., & Brooks, D. (1983). Nonverbal communication in teaching. *Review of Research in Education, 10,* 103–150.

Woolfolk, A., & Hoy. (1990). Prospective teachers' sense of efficacy and beliefs about control. *Journal of Educational Psychology, 82,* 81–91.

Index

CORWIN PRESS

The Corwin Press logo—a raven striding across an open book—represents the union of courage and learning. Corwin Press is committed to improving education for all learners by publishing books and other professional development resources for those serving the field of PreK–12 education. By providing practical, hands-on materials, Corwin Press continues to carry out the promise of its motto: **"Helping Educators Do Their Work Better."**